# A Handbook
# for Scholars

# A
# HANDBOOK
# FOR
# SCHOLARS

### REVISED EDITION

Mary-Claire van Leunen

New York   Oxford
**OXFORD UNIVERSITY PRESS**
1992

Oxford University Press

Oxford  New York  Toronto
Delhi  Bombay  Calcutta  Madras  Karachi
Petaling Jaya  Singapore  Hong Kong  Tokyo
Nairobi  Dar es Salaam  Cape Town
Melbourne  Auckland

and associated companies in
Berlin  Ibadan

First published in the United States in 1978 by Alfred A. Knopf, Inc.,
New York, and simultaneously in Canada by Random House of Canada,
Toronto. Distributed by Random House, Inc., New York.

First issued in revised cloth and paperback editions by
Oxford University Press, 1992
Published by arrangement with Alfred A. Knopf, Inc.

Oxford is a registered trademark of Oxford University Press

Library of Congress Cataloging-in-Publication Data
van Leunen, Mary-Claire.
A handbook for scholars / Mary-Claire van Leunen. — Rev. ed.
p. cm.  Includes bibliographical references and index.
ISBN 0-19-506953-6. — ISBN 0-19-506954-4 (pbk.)
1. Authorship—Handbooks, manuals, etc. I. Title.
PN146.V36  1922
808'.027—dc20  91-19230

4 6 8 10 9 7 5 3
Printed in the United States of America

*To Mark; to Joan; to Margaret*

# Contents

# A Handbook
# for Scholars

# Introduction

Scholarly writing is formal, precise, and allusive. It has to be. It does not have to be wooden, finicking, and cabalistic. The idea of this book is to help you achieve the first set of characteristics without sinking into the second.

Let us not deceive ourselves. "There is no God but Allah" is a more gripping sentence than

> Mohammed (also Mahomet, Muhammad; 570?–632) asserted a doctrine of unqualified monotheism (suras 8, 22, 33–37, 89, 91, Koran).

By its very nature, scholarly prose lacks the rhetorical virtues of reckless passion. Custom and propriety hem the scholar in on every side. Her obligation to her material and her obligation to her sources restrain her. She may not gloss over imperfections, smooth out irregularities, turn a blind eye to objections, no matter what good effects these temptations might offer in the way of clarity and simplicity.

On the other hand, the built-in limitations of scholarly prose are no excuse for bad writing. Bad scholarly prose results, as all bad prose does, from laziness and hurry and muddle. Good scholarly prose is probably even harder to produce than other kinds of good prose. All that means is that the scholar must work even harder at it.

This book will not tell you everything you need to know about scholarly writing. At most points scholarly writing is no different from any other kind of writing. The scholar should aim at clarity and force and grace, but so should every writer. There are any number of books to help you with those aims. This book is about the mechanical problems that are specific to scholarly writing. I have tried to avoid overlap with general manuals of style except in the sections on quotation and on scholarly peculiarities. For help with punctuation, spelling, grammar, diction, style, organization, logic, and rhetoric, look elsewhere. For help with citations, quotations, footnotes, references, and reference lists, you have come to the right place.

In order to focus on the points I wished to make, with no distractions or irrelevancies, I made up many of the illustrative examples in this book whole cloth. Others I wove together with threads of fact and fantasy. Don't rush to your library for *Frontiers in Psychometrics, The House of Plantin,* or *The Journal of Classical Philology;* they are inventions. Don't puzzle over the texts on chemistry, sociology, and mathematics; they may mean nothing. I have tried to avoid plain silliness, but pastiche is a difficult art. I can only hope that real psychologists and historians, philologists and chemists, sociologists and mathematicians will enjoy any howlers and understand I mean no disrespect by them.

Two points of diction: Throughout this book, for my own convenience, I have used "citation" as the name for the mention you make in your text of a source you are indebted to and "reference" as the name for the bibliographic item that appears in the list at the end of your text. The distinction does not exist in the language as a whole, and there is no reason for anyone else to observe it.

A decade or so ago, when I was working on the introduction to the previous edition of this book, I wrote:

> My expository style relies heavily on the exemplary singular, and the construction "everybody . . . his" therefore comes up frequently. This "his" is generic, not gendered. "His or her" becomes clumsy with repetition and suggests that "his" alone elsewhere is masculine, which is isn't. "Her" alone draws attention to itself and distracts from the topic at hand. "Their" solves the problem neatly but substitutes another. "Ter" is bolder than I am ready for. "One's" defeats the purpose of the construction, which is meant to be vivid and particular. "Its" is too harsh a joke. Rather than play hob with the language, we feminists might adopt the position of pitying men for being forced to share their pronouns around.

Since then, I've come to realize that that was twaddle. What did I think an ungendered human being would be like? Divine? Linda Hunt? These days I try to say "their" when I'm talking out loud. (Mother to sons and daughters: "Everybody eat their cereal." No sillier than mother to sons and daughters: "Everybody pick up his socks.") And for this pass of this book I've used "her" for all the extended examples. Most of the people in my examples are confused. Some of them are dreadfully earnest, a few are sly, a few thoroughly thick-headed. All of them used to be men; now all of them are women. Third time through, maybe I'll balance them out fifty-fifty.

Now and then, some nice person tells me she would love to use my book but the journals she submits to use a different reference style. I suggest the style I do because its simplicity makes it easy for a novice to manipulate and interpret. But even the most baroque and arcane style can with guile and determination be subverted to serve the same purposes as this simple one. If you must conform to a convoluted style, don't lose sight of the objectives: laying out the evidence; acknowledging indebtedness; welcoming the outsider.

# THE TEXT

The four sections that follow take up the major mechanical issues scholars encounter in writing their texts: citation, quotation, content footnotes, and a miscellany of small matters.

Problems with citation result from the scholar's unique responsibility to her sources. Essayists may pass on anybody's ideas as their own; penny-a-liners plagiarize with abandon; journalists go to jail rather than reveal the names of their informants. Not so the scholar. For her the open acknowledgment of where she got her stuff is at least a duty, and possibly a joy. You can observe the shift in each generation of undergraduates. At first they say "I think" and follow it with a mishmash of received ideas. But in a few weeks they've learned the ropes, and then you hear "Hegel thinks" and "Freud thinks" and "Aristotle thinks." We smile, but such habits are the stuff of scholarship.

Scholars and novelists share the need to quote extensively, but in different ways. I have ignored the creation of dialog and stuck to the matter of quoting from a source. In the first draft of this book, I tried to skirt the issue by sending readers to the standard guides, but I found them wanting. The conventions for quotation are outrageously complex, and someone had to spell them out.

The section on scholarly peculiarities takes up a group of questions related only by some relevance to scholarly writing. This section demonstrates the soapbox phenomenon: Given any slim excuse, 99.624 percent of all persons will sound off; given no excuse at all, 99.608 percent of them will do so. I hope that you will have even a tenth of the pleasure in reading the section that I had in writing it.

But what about content footnotes? How do they come to be characteristics of scholarly prose? The rest of the world gets along without them very nicely, and they have seduced many a young scholar into writing that is so highly parenthetical as to be incoherent. I believe they date from the time when scholarship consisted mainly of biblical exegesis, with a little patristics and canon law thrown in. Scholars dealt with set and sacred texts, and they dealt with them reverently, pushing their own ideas off into the margins. Today, although the scholarly purview extends from cash flow to cough syrup, from color blindness to comic books, and although few scholarly fields require the reverent explication of texts, the habit of content footnotes lingers. Why? I think it's that soapbox phenomenon again. The footnote permits the scholar to say another word, just one other word, just one word more, before she has to stop.

To avoid confusion, I should mention that this book is arranged seductively, not chronologically. In real life, you do your research and collect your references first, then compile your reference list, and then write your text. There may be a good deal of backing and forthing along the way, but that's the over-all order. Here I've begun with the text because it's the goal the whole process is intended to reach and because it's the most interesting part. You don't need to feel guilty about considering your reference list a chore; only a bibliographic maniac could care more about a list of sources than about her own ideas and her own words.

# Citation

Scholarly writing is distinguished from all other kinds by its punctilious acknowledgment of sources. This acknowledgment is not an empty form.

For the reader, citation opens the door to further information and to independent judgment. She can find more about your topic, fill in the background, catch up on what she's missed. She can also judge for herself the use you've put your sources to. Have you left a mitigating clause out of a quotation? Have you ignored the gerrymander of a data base? Have you misinterpreted a nuance? Have you misread a line? Have you failed to notice a qualification?

For the writer, these are frightening possibilities. Contrary to vulgar belief, the world of scholarship is no place for the timid. By disclosing freely and fully the origins of your thought, you may be putting a sword into your enemies' hands. If you can welcome that risk, it must be because your acuteness, your thoroughness, your scrupulosity have already, so to speak, beat the sword into a plowshare. Citation keeps you honest.

The documentary function of citation need not be carried to extremes. Young scholars have a tendency to overcite. "The variorum edition [6,19,38] cannot be used [2,12] to verify [8,28,31] this conjecture [2,8,28]." It comes out like a stutter. Still, this is a better fault than citing too little.

Citation relieves you of expository burdens in your writing. You needn't recover every piece of old territory that lies behind you before going on to the new. In theory, if your citations are honest, and your sources' citations are honest, and so on back, an assiduous reader should be able to trace every notion in your writing to its beginnings. If you abuse this evocative function of citation, your writing will become cryptic. If you keep it within sensible limits, citation can strengthen and simplify your expository line.

Citation can also strengthen your rhetoric. When you must stand alone in an opinion, so be it. But when you have allies, call them to your side by citing them. Again, you must not abuse the seconding function of citation. All too much scholarly disagreement degenerates to the level of "My advisor's bigger than your advisor." But within limits, citation can lend force to your arguments.

There is one last reason for every scholar to cite her sources. The greatest reward scholarship has to offer is the respect of one's peers. Citation is the courtesy of scholars. In the simplest way, the attribution says thank you to the source. Even a negative citation asserts that the source requires consideration. Every scholar remembers the pleasure of first finding herself cited in a stranger's work, and even the most blasé among the elders relish praise in the form of apt acknowledgments. The scholar who hopes to receive such praise will award it gladly.

For a student writing papers, it's hard to achieve the right frame of mind for citation. Your reader is no hazy construct of hopes and expectations; she's your teacher, a single, solid human being whom you know and who probably knows many of your sources at least as well as you do. In all student writing, there's an element of let's-pretend that you need in order to prepare yourself for the future. Pretend, then, that your instructor is the reader you will write for in your later life, the reader who will look to you for guidance. Write your citations for that reader.

## The New Style of Citation

The chief reform this book recommends is the elimination of bibliographic information in footnotes. Content footnotes still exist, but the bibliographic ones disappear. Old style:

> ▷ Grandin's work on Lawrence[7] develops the themes of caste and untouchability.

---

7. Jonathan Grandin. "Lawrence among the Philistines." *English Letters* XI(4):203–226, 1974.

At the back of the old-style text the bibliographic information appeared again in an unnumbered reference list. In the new style, the number is bracketed on the line instead of superscripted, and it points to a numbered item on the reference list. New style:

> Grandin's work on Lawrence [12] develops the themes of caste and untouchability.

No bibliographic information appears at the bottom of the page. The corresponding entry in the reference list appears only once, no matter how many times the source is cited in the text:

> 12] Jonathan Grandin.
> Lawrence among the Philistines.
> *English Letters* XI(4):203–226, 1974.

## Meaningful Citations

Doing away with bibliographic footnotes saves space, makes a handsomer page, and avoids interrupting the reader's attention. These are automatic benefits. A much greater benefit is possible, but it will not come automatically. Abolishing bibliographic footnotes can help the scholar overcome some of the stylistic difficulties that footnotes encourage, but the process requires work.

Take a typical old-style citation:

> ▷ It has been argued[10] that the transformation of France into a cohesive state was accomplished by the Jacobins.

There's little value in merely making it new style:

> ▷ It has been argued [4] that the transformation of France into a cohesive state was accomplished by the Jacobins.

---

Bad examples are marked with an arrowhead (▷). I will repeat this notice at the first bad example in each section for the benefit of the reader who skips around. "Bad" often means bad in the context of the discussion, not absolutely evil.

It's still as vague as ever. The writer who mechanically goes through her work transforming superscripted numbers into bracketed ones has missed the point. The new style is not a tidying device. It is meant to nudge the scholar toward making her writing more concrete and vivid. Without the excuse of a footnote below, the deficiencies of the sentence are glaring.

You have to add to the bracketed number enough information so that your reader can tell what you're talking about. Mentioning the author's name is a good start:

> Butterfield [4] argues that the transformation of France into a cohesive state was accomplished by the Jacobins.

*[handwritten margin note: after author's name]*

But, again, this is not a mechanical process. The sentence as it now reads may be a rich, full, evocative citation in a paper on the Napoleonic period, where Butterfield is a household word; it may be utterly opaque in a paper on the modern French state or the origins of dictatorship or the effects of revolutionary democracy. Depending on the topic of the paper you are writing and the audience you hope to reach, any of the following citations might be appropriate:

Herbert Butterfield [4] argues . . .

Herbert Butterfield [4], former regius professor at Cambridge University and an authority on modern European history, argues . . .

A modern historian, Herbert Butterfield [4], argues . . .

Butterfield argues in his little book on Napoleon [4] . . .

There is no easy formula. Take another example, starting with the old style:

> One student of the subject[44] identifies forms by syntax rather than morphology.

Changing this mechanically to the new style is clearly insufficient:

> One student of the subject [28] identifies forms by syntax rather than morphology.

Nor is it necessarily enough to write:

> F. R. Palmer [28] identifies . . .

There are any number of ways to expand the sentence and any number of contexts in which it needs to be expanded. What are you getting at?

*[handwritten margin note: and of source]*

> F. R. Palmer, writing in the distinguished Miami Linguistic Series [28], quite sensibly called "better" a verb in the spoken sentence "You better go."

*[handwritten margin note: and of idea]*

> F. R. Palmer, one of Firth's more prominent epigones, outdoes even his mentor in extending the concept of predication beyond all recognition [28].

Much information and emotion was hidden behind those old-style superscripts; let it out into the open.

In general, you will find that you can improve your text by avoiding not only footnote references but the empty allusions that footnote references encouraged. The scholar has extraordinary opportunities for being compact and concise. She can rely on her audience to fill in reams of information at a mere hint. She can say "Halliday's versions of Scott" or "Watson on annuities" or "Lyman's life of Perry" or "Strassen's algorithm" and with the single phrase call up in her reader's mind whole articles and books and bodies of work, all the information in them, complicated lines of reasoning, attitudes and biases and strengths and failings.

With the opportunity for conciseness comes also an unparalleled opportunity for being obscure. The reader can take a hint and run with it, but she does need at least the hint. "It has been said" and "a scholar of the period asserts" are not enough. The scholarly writer who is too lazy or too snobbish or too insecure to spell out what she means can produce sentence after sentence, paragraph on paragraph of hot air. Then young scholars mistake the habit for "professionalism" or "playing the game" and carry it further still, as the review-of-the-literature section of almost every dissertation is at pains to demonstrate. "A specialist in the field" follows "according to some of the early researchers" and that follows "the argument has been made" with never so much as the name of a single human being in sight.

We all encounter scores of bad examples daily. Here are a few at random, with suggestions on how to improve them.

▷ The robust application[9] of Lipton's theorem unfortunately proved ineffective.[10]

Dobkin and Snyder [3] tried applying Lipton's theorem to each member of the lower-order matrices. They themselves later repudiated the results as absurd [4].

▷ Another interpretation[15] attributes a duality of purpose to Plato's characterization.

J. Horning points out in his monograph on the *Phaedrus* that Plato has it both ways. He is both playful and rationalist in making Socrates pour cold water on his own words [9].

▷ A superior exposition can be found elsewhere.[22]

Hermione Mummson, who is a painter rather than a physiologist, produced a better outline of study in her book *The Human Frame* [18], which is unfortunately out of print.

 In other words, scholarly writing, like all kinds of writing, improves as it becomes more concrete and less ethereal, more tangible and less abstract.

## Citations Without References

If you can embed in your text all the information about a source that your reader needs, then you don't have to give her a bracketed number pointing to your reference list. For most sources citations without references would be unwieldy:

▷ R. M. Canter's *Game Breeding in Elizabethan England* (Routledge & Kegan Paul, 1958) describes the attempt of a Yorkshire cartel to introduce turkey-shooting to the British Isles (pages 441–452).

But there are a very few central sources for which short but thorough citations are possible. The Bible, Shakespeare, and the Greek and Latin classics have been worked over by generations of scholars, and we fall heir to the fruits of their passion for numbering and counting.

> John 6:41–58 so elaborates the image that even today we can feel the horror of it.

> Another of his infrequent descriptions of infancy is in *The Two Gentlemen of Verona* I(2):55.

> I am reminded of Catullus, who also loved and hated (*Carmina*, 85).

Citations without references work only when you can be both complete and brief.

## Brackets Alone

Now, having examined in such detail the case for meaningful citations, let us consider the opposite. When do you want merely to point? When do you want to drop in a bracketed number and let it go at that?

Your citation is just a courtesy, a bob of the head toward the original discoverer of a result you are using:

> Since the lower bounds approach zero [17], we can feel confident in setting your constant equal to zero as well.

You are citing too many sources to mention each one gracefully (or, as my mathematical friends say, the case of *n* citations where *n* is large):

> Hugh Peters was probably the son of Thomas Dyckwoode, alias Peter or Peters [6,15,28,29,34].

You're trying to carry forward a narrative line without too much intrusion of scholarship:

> Swiftly the men reloaded their guns and remounted their positions. "Bait their bluidy ayes oot," said Old Fain [3]. His companions licked their chops and fired.

You're giving so complete a summary that your reader never need look at the source. This comes up when you need the summary to round out your own exposition. It comes up when the source is difficult to get hold of or written in a foreign language. It also comes up when the source is so badly written that you summarize it to be sure your reader gets it straight.

> There are three ways of forming phenanthrene—by passing the vapors of benzene and toluene, stilbene, dibenzyl, ortho-ditolyl, or coumarone through a red-hot tube; by distilling morphine with zinc dust; and (along with anthracene) by the action of sodium on ortho-brombenzyl bromide [22].

Notice in all these examples the wholehearted use of the brackets alone. What you want to avoid is half measures. Do not write:

▷ Many authorities [6,15,28,29,34] agree that Hugh Peters was probably the son of Thomas Dyckwoode, alias Peter or Peters.

Do not write:

▷ According to a research paper on the subject [22] there are three ways of forming phenanthrene.

If you have something to say about a source, spit it out; otherwise, let the bracketed numbers alone do the work. Betwixt and between lies flaccid writing.

No rule of thumb exists for when a meaningful citation is better than brackets alone and vice versa. In making your decision you have to consider your material, you have to consider your source, and you have to consider your reader. What will help her understand what you mean? What will convince her to agree with you? What will interest her and give her pleasure?

## Handling Bracketed Numbers

### Placement

Tuck your bracketed numbers neatly inside the phrases they annotate:

▷ But it proved impossible to find a centrosome in some resting cells, like muscle cells, [6] and Maeton and Standish concluded that the organ might be formed anew at each cell division. [9]

*punctuation placement*

But it proved impossible to find a centrosome in some resting cells, like muscle cells [6], and Maeton and Standish concluded that the organ might be formed anew at each cell division [9].

On the larger question of what to annotate, saying a word or two about the source insures against misinterpretation. Any of these is perfectly acceptable:

Timothy Mann uses the word "plunder" in his *Annals of the Long Parliament* in talking about the Thirty Years' War [3].

Timothy Mann uses the word "plunder" in his *Annals of the Long Parliament* [3] in talking . . .

Timothy Mann uses the word "plunder" [3] in . . .
Timothy Mann [3] uses . . .

Using brackets alone can be trickier. You must be cautious about the possibility of accidental misattribution.

The annotation of the north mound manuscript [31] was obviously faulty.

The annotation of the north mound manuscript was obviously faulty [31].

Neither of these is necessarily wrong, but there's a world of difference between them. Spelling out what you mean can save you from embarrassment:

Zeeman's annotation of the north mound manuscript was obviously faulty [31].

or

Zeeman [31] found some obvious faults in the annotation of the north mound manuscript.

## Frequency

Try to avoid scattering your pages with bracketed numbers like buckshot. Use a bracketed number at the first mention of a source or at the first mention after a long gap; use a bracketed number to point your reader to a specific page or passage when you must. But assume that she is of at least average intelligence, that she has a modest attention span, and that she is reading through your work in order, at least within each section, not skipping hither and thither. Young, inexperienced scholars tend to cite too much and too often. They are at their worst in comparative studies:

> ▷ Another tragic type is the faithful friend of the hero, like Horatio in *Hamlet* [18]; more often he is an outspoken critic of the tragic action, like Kent in *King Lear* [19] or Enobarbus in *Antony and Cleopatra* [17]. Horatio's role is supportive and reinforcing [18]. Kent and Enobarbus are more abrasive [19,17]. Hamlet and Lear each comment in their own way on the relationship [18,19].

Taking the word "another" as a clue about where this discussion falls in the exposition, we can guess that all of these bracketed numbers are unnecessary. Hypercitation is a funny and touching fault, and certainly a better one than failing to give credit where credit is due.

## Page Numbers

Don't mingle page numbers in with citation numbers. Young scholars typically make this error because they don't understand how to handle multiple references to the same source:

> ▷ Einstein said that the physics should "represent a reality in time and space, free from spooky actions at a distance" [17, page 223]. Pauli railed against tormenting oneself about "the problem of whether something one cannot know anything about exists all the same" [17, page 158].

Pinpointing information belongs in the reference list, not in the text. The right thing to do is construct a compound reference in your reference list:

Amron Bevels, editor.
*Questions in the Philosophy of Science.*
Wiley, 1979.
  [17] Page 158.
  [18] Page 223.

The text then contains only pointers to references, not an uneasy mixture:

Einstein said that the physics should "represent a reality in time and space, free from spooky actions at a distance" [18]. Pauli railed against tormenting oneself about "the problem of whether something one cannot know anything about exists all the same" [17].

## Clustering Brackets

Group bracketed numbers whenever you can do so without causing confusion.

▷ Similar claims are made with a similar lack of conviction by Sparrowthwaite [29], Fanphman [5], and Hoolinan [18].

Similar claims are made with a similar lack of conviction by Sparrowthwaite, Fanphman, and Hoolinan [29,5,18].

Note that no spaces follow the commas that separate clustered numbers in brackets. You may break a cluster at the end of a line:

Abadi on the semiotics of the contemporary coffeehouse in Europe and California has no rivals for wit [2,4, 10].

It is a further refinement to cite your sources as they appear on your reference list (usually in alphabetical order) so that the bracketed numbers appear in numerical order:

Similar claims are made with a similar lack of conviction by Fanphman, Hoolinan, and Sparrowthwaite [5,18,29].

But it's hardly worth wasting your time on if they don't come out that way.

## Brackets Are Not Words

A bracketed number is just a pointer, not a word. Never, ever, use a bracketed number as if it were the name of an author or a work.

▷ [5] and [63] have turned their attention to less weighty matters of late.

▷ The elevated language of [19], the poetic sensibility of [7], the insight and vision of [22], the rapture of [36]—how thrilling a combination!

The temptation to use a bracketed number as a word is greatest when you have nothing to say about the source:

▷ As we can see in [18], developments in lexicology and lexicography require a comprehensive inventory of machine-readable texts.

When you have nothing to say, say nothing:

Developments in lexicology and lexicography require a comprehensive inventory of machine-readable texts [18].

When you have very little to say, talk about what the bracketed number refers to, not about the number itself:

▷ Jones, Smith, and Wesson [7,8,9] have proved several related results. Theorem 1 of [7], as well as its generalization in Lemma 13 of [9], can be derived from our Corollary 8 by taking the quadratic Imre coefficients to be zero.

Jones, Smith, and Wesson [7,8,9] have proved several related results. Theorem 1 of reference [7], as well as its generalization in Lemma 13 of reference [9], can be derived from our Corollary 8 by taking the quadratic Imre coefficients to be zero.

## No Brackets

When you're buying a typewriter or a word processor, look for crisp, well-drawn brackets in a convenient location. Many students have no choice; they get their machines as gifts from unscholarly relatives or inherit ancient cast-iron castoffs. If you have no brackets, you may on student papers use parentheses instead:

> On 22 May he took command of the British forces
> occupying Germany (14).

On manuscripts to be set in type, draw the brackets in by hand:

> On 22 May he took command of the British forces
> occupying Germany [14].

Do not attempt to construct brackets out of other symbols on your keyboard:

▷ On 22 May he took command of the British forces
occupying Germany /_14_7.

They look dreadful.


## Citation Words

### "See"

There is seldom any reason to tell your reader to "see" a source.

▷ See J. Thornton Green [27] for an explanation of several systems for transliterating Russian.

J. Thornton Green [27] explains several systems for transliterating Russian.

Any time you can eliminate words without changing the sense or the force of a sentence, do so. "See" must of course never take a bracketed number as its object:

▷ B. P. Brown (see [1]) comments on Franklin's magpie mind.

B. P. Brown [1] comments on Franklin's magpie mind.

"*Vide*" is even worse than "see," being pompous as well as wordy. "Q.v." is worse yet.

## "Cf."

This abbreviation stands for the Latin *confer,* compare. It does not mean "see." If you're going to use it at all, reserve it for times when your source disagrees with you or arrives at your position by an entirely different line of reasoning. Even if you are an exceptionally fierce and cantankerous person, such occasions are rare; when they do occur, "cf." is seldom the best way to introduce them.

Here is a technically correct "cf.":

▷ Then $x_{i,j} \equiv \{\Lambda_{i,j} \mid 1 \leq {}_i \leq {}_j \leq 3^n\}$, which is a contradiction. Cf. Zalcstein and Meyer [41] for a constructive proof.

In other words, the author has completed the proof of a theorem by contradiction, and Zalcstein and Meyer have another proof of the same theorem by construction, an entirely different method. The "cf." is correct, but wordy. The author would do better to write simply:

Zalcstein and Meyer [41] give a constructive proof.

Here, again, is a technically correct use of the expression:

▷ Blessed Oliver made a good defense, but the jury convicted him of treason on absurd evidence (cf. Stratton [19]).

In other words, Stratton disagrees. Correct, but bloodless. Which version would you rather read, that one or this?

Blessed Oliver made a good defense, but the jury convicted him of treason on absurd evidence. (Stratton, on the other hand, thinks that Blessed Oliver was guilty and the jury was quite fair, if a little enthusiastic, in having him hanged, drawn, and quartered [19].)

If you eliminate the wordy "cf." and the "cf." that is too mild, none will be left.

## "Reference"

"Reference" is not yet accepted as a verb in most polite circles. At the least you should correct it to "refer to":

▷ Reference Volka and James [31] for the origin of "bogus."

Refer to Volka and James [31] for the origin of "bogus."

But then "refer to" has all the flaws of "see" and should itself be eliminated from most sentences.

Volka and James [31] describe the origin of "bogus."

## "Ed. Cit.," "Loc. Cit.," "Op. Cit.," "Idem," "Ibid."

It would be a waste of time to explain the fine points of these expressions because they should have no place in your writing. Even in the past, they were never common in text, although footnotes were riddled with them. In the new style of citation, they are extinct—and good riddance. Never should you catch yourself writing something like this:

▷ Grady, op. cit., suggests that the storax might serve as the Oriental counterpart to the linden.

If it's been some time since you gave a pointer to the Grady item on the reference list, repeat it:

Grady [8] suggests . . .

Otherwise, forget it:

Grady suggests that the storax might serve as the Oriental counterpart to the linden.

In the section on your reference list, we'll talk about how to handle multiple references to different pages in the same book.

# Tense in Citations

Is it "Schneider [42] says" or "Schneider [42] said"? Either. Just remember to stick by the tense you started out with, at least in the immediate vicinity.

> ▷ Y. Aharoni [2] gave other examples of the same motif on stamps of the period, which he dates by metallurgical development.
>
> Y. Aharoni [2] gives other examples of the same motif on stamps of the period, which he dates by metallurgical development.

or

> Y. Aharoni [2] gave other examples of the same motif on stamps of the period, which he dated by metallurgical development.

# Citing Authors

### Naming Names

The first time you mention an author, call her by a name your audience can recognize. In an article on Tudor historiography, "Hexter" is sufficient for a first citation; in an article on historiography in general, "J. H. Hexter" is a better choice. If you're not sure, use for the first citation the full name the author uses to sign articles.

Be sure to respect her preference. You may know from private knowledge that behind the initials of "M. H. Peters" lies Mandrake Hannibal, but it's no business of yours to tell the world. Familiarity is equally out of place. "G. Kitson Clark" is the way to style the author you are citing even if he asks you to call him "Kitsy" over lunch.

With joint authors, the combination of last names is usually sufficient identification. "Hall and Lindzey" is in fact easier for a personality theorist to recognize than "Calvin S. Hall and Gardner Lindzey."

Once past the first mention, family name is sufficient unless you have the misfortune to be using two or more authors with the same family name.

Do I need to say that male and female authors are treated alike? Apparently, since I have seen an article in which C. Vann Woodward was consistently called "Woodward" and C. V. Wedgwood was consistently called "Cecily Wedgwood" or "Miss Wedgwood." A pox on false gentility.


## Personal Titles *

The rule of thumb is that personal titles don't belong in scholarly citation. Why this should be so is hard to say. The feeling may be something like: The reason for citing X's work is not that she holds position Y; rather, the reason for her holding position Y is that her work is cited. Whatever its origin, this bias is so strong that citing "Professor So-and-so" or "Dr. So-and-so" is likely to be meant and taken as sarcasm. If you must mention credentials, bring them in after the name:

▷ Professor Harlan Cooke starts from a different angle [5].

Harlan Cooke, a professor of pathology at the University of Texas Middle School, starts from a different angle [5].

This feeling extends beyond academic titles and degrees to all titles. Only in writing about an institution should you call your sources by the titles they hold within that institution. Naval historians properly call their sources by their Navy rank, "Admiral So-and-so," "Lieutenant So-and-so." A student of church polity properly calls her sources by their ecclesiastical rank, "Father So-and-so, S.J.," "Archbishop So-and-so." But in using these sources for some other field, once again you dodge around their titles.

▷ Invaluable observations on dormancy and hibernation have now come to light in the diaries of Captain Edward M. Hayes, USN [16].

Invaluable observations on dormancy and hibernation have now come to light in the diaries of Edward M. Hayes, an officer in the United States Navy who was stationed in the Antarctic for eighteen months in 1935–36 [16].

Once past the first mention, family name is sufficient: Cooke, not Professor Cooke; Hayes, not Captain Hayes.

Nobles and royals are a special headache. We of humble birth are dim about sorting out their titles. How "John Emerich Edward Dalberg, Baron Acton of Aldenham" comes to be "Lord Acton" is mysterious to us. Why not "Dalberg" or "Aldenham" or "Sir John"? If you're citing such sources in their political and historical roles, you have your own knowledge, the practice of your colleagues, and the standard reference works to go by (Cokayne, Burke, and Debrett for England, the *Almanach de Gotha* for the Continent). But what in the world does the poor geometrician do who finds herself citing a paper on oblate spheroids by "Adolf George Meitmann, Schlechtgraf von Schwarzburg"? I take the disgruntled egalitarian view that nobles should never sign themselves that way to start with. (I respect authors' preference about their names but not their titles.) The gentle, conscientious geometrician who wishes to do so may telephone the nearest German department to find out how one styles Schlechtgrafen in the third-person singular. The geometrician who shares my plebeian ill-temper will call the fellow "Meitmann" and have done with it. To accommodate the reader who knows more than I do, I'd spell out the full version on my reference list; alphabetize it under "Meitmann," since that was what I called him; and put a cross-reference at "Schwarzburg" and perhaps at "Adolf" on a long list.

These strictures may be relaxed a little in talking about historical sources. To the scholar immersed in her period, calling Samuel Johnson "Dr. Johnson" comes naturally. Thomas More can come out "More," "Sir Thomas," or "St. Thomas," depending on how you think of him. But be cautious. Calling Abigail Adams "Mrs. John Adams" is anachronistic; that version of the title wasn't yet in use. And calling William Morris "Topsy" is likely to strike any reader over the age of eight as cloying.

## "Et al."

Particularly in the sciences, collaborative research produces papers with monstrous long strings of joint authors. In citing a joint work, name up to three authors.  For four authors or more, give the first author's name followed by the expression "et al." It stands for the Latin *et alii*, or *et aliae*, meaning "and others." Notice that the "al."

has a period after it and the "et" does not—it's treacherously easy when you're writing quickly to do both the same way. Use the expression only with the first author's name, not with the first and second or the first, second, and third.

▷ Schultz, Eisenstat, Sherman, Lewis, Chandra, and Schreiber [23].

▷ Schultz, Eisenstat, Sherman, et al. [23].

▷ Schultz, Eisenstat, et al. [23].

Schultz et al. [23].

Two papers of joint authorship with the same first author will come out looking the same:

▷ Levin, Schroeder, Birrell, Satterthwaite, and Lampson [6] and Levin, Chiu, Hanna, Kalsow, and Sclafani [5].

▷ Levin et al. [6] and Levin et al. [5].

▷ Levin et al. [5,6].

Usually it's best to write in one language at a time and to search for native equivalents of foreign expressions. But for indicating joint authorship "et al." is preferable to "and others," which can too easily be taken to mean that other authors have written other papers on the topic at hand.

"& al." is just not the way it's done. Write it without either underlining or italics. Pronounce it, when you must say it aloud, "et all" as in "Did you et some of Aunt Sukie's cake?" "Nope, I et all."

## Spelling Authors' Names

From what I understand, spelling ability correlates with nothing — not with intelligence, not with verbal ability, not with age (after childhood), not with eye color, left-handedness, cyclothymia, blood type, structure boundedness, authoritarian impulses, sex, race, religion, national origin, or any other measure the testers can develop. Some people spell well, some people don't, and that's all there is to it. If by the time you're twelve or thirteen you don't spell well, you probably never will, and you should plan your life accordingly. I know what I'm talking about—I have already had to look up how to spell two words in this paragraph.

Spelling other people's names correctly is the most difficult task the poor speller can undertake. Undertake it she must, for the sake of her readers and her sources. The reader who goes to a card catalog for "Cheryl Smith" is a long way away from "Sherril Smithe." And as for Smithe herself, she's likely to hold it against you forever. The old newspaper joke about names is quite accurate. Print a piece that calls Simon T. Watchmere a bounder, a crook, and a drunkard, and he'll telephone to tell you there's no "t" in "Wachmere." People are irrational about their names; they know perfectly well that names are harder to spell than anything else, they may even spell other people's names incorrectly, but they expect you to get theirs right. Again, I am ashamed to say, I know what I'm talking about.

If you spell well, I envy you. If you spell poorly, here are some tricks to try: Take your bibliographic notes in block capitals. Go back and check the spelling of the names again, while you still have the source in front of you. Circle each verified spelling and write "stet" beside it. If you use a computer, enter the spelling once, preferably with the source in front of you, and from then on never type them afresh, always copy them. Check the spelling in your manuscript against the spelling in your notes—preferably aloud, enunciating each letter. Enlist if you can the help of a friend to check over the names once again. If you work with an editor, be frank about your difficulties. Knock on wood, keep your fingers crossed, and the best of luck to you.

## Concord

Is it "Ullman and Aho [62] say" or "Ullman and Aho [62] says"? Either. The former stresses the authors, the latter stresses the work. Don't change horses midstream:

> ▷ Perls, Hefferline, and Goodman [35] has a tendency to ig-nore problems of resistance, and they are sometimes equally unrealistic in their belief that the therapist can withstand all temptation to manipulate.

Perls, Hefferline, and Goodman [35] have a tendency . . . and they are sometimes equally unrealistic in their
belief . . .

or

Perls, Hefferline, and Goodman [35] has a tendency . . . and
it is sometimes equally unrealistic in its belief . . .

## Citation with Possessives

Form any singular possessive by adding apostrophe-"s" regardless
of the root word.

Peterson; Peterson's book.

Manderewski; Manderewski's book.

Minsky; Minsky's book.

▷ Charles; Charles' book.

Charles; Charles's book.

▷ Patrice; Patrice' book.

Patrice; Patrice's book.

▷ Labox; Labox' book.

Labox; Labox's book.

("Charles's" may be pronounced if you like with only one final *z*
sound and "Patrice's" and "Labox's" with only one final *s* sound
apiece by an interesting phenomenon called haplology.)

Form the possessive of an *s*-plural by adding an apostrophe. (This
won't come up often.)

Sidney and Beatrice Webb; the Webbs; the Webbs' book.

Indicate joint possession by adding apostrophe-*s* to the last name
in the series. Indicate multiple possession by adding apostrophe-*s* to
each name in the series:

Mummson and Wilshire's books—the books they have written together.

Marriman's and Leander's books—some books by Marriman, some by Leander.

The double genitive is a correct construction required by English idiom that timid authors wrongly shy away from. Test the construction with a pronoun if you're in doubt.

▷ A book of B. Ayers; a book of her.

A book of B. Ayers's; a book of hers.

## Citing Characters

Attributing to an author the words of her fictional characters is sloppy scholarship, and rather hard on the author. Shakespeare is not retailing the advice on borrowing and lending he puts in Polonius's mouth; Dickens is not endorsing the solecisms he gives his lowlife characters to speak; quite the contrary. Always be sure there's no confusion in your reader's mind.

▷ "All journalists are dirty dogs," wrote Place [9].

"All journalists are dirty dogs," said Matty Small in Place's *Antics* [9], and we have reason to believe Place shared the sentiment.

Although you may sometimes see it, putting quotes around the names of fictional characters is neither necessary nor desirable.

▷ Ford Madox Ford's "Christopher Tietjens" may be the last hero in the history of the novel.

Ford Madox Ford's Christopher Tietjens may be the last hero in the history of the novel.

# Citing Works

## Books and Non-books

In citing a work by title, you need to decide whether it's a book or a non-book. Since you usually do your research and compile your references before writing your text (I hope), I have put the long discussion of books versus non-books in the section on references (pages 168–169). Briefly, a book is a book or a journal; a fat thing bound by itself; or the equivalent in some other medium of a fat thing bound by itself. A non-book is an article or a story or a poem or a pamphlet; a thin thing or a thing that's part of something else; or the equivalent in some other medium of a thin thing or a thing that's part of something else. The long discussion goes into these distinctions in great detail. Be sure to be consistent; don't punctuate a borderline work as a book in your text and as a non-book in your reference list.

## Book Titles in Text

*→ Not in APA style*

Use uppers-and-lowers capitalization (capitalize the first word, the first word after a colon, and all other words except articles, unstressed conjunctions, and unstressed prepositions). Use italics; or underline straight through, spaces as well as words.

> Kaman has an essay on the theater in Godfrey Halliwell's *The Arts Today* and a contribution in the memorial volume *Berlin Symphony: Portrait of a Great Orchestra* [6,14].

or

> Kaman has an essay on the theater in Godfrey Halliwell's <u>The Arts Today</u> and a contribution in the memorial volume <u>Berlin Symphony: Portrait of a Great Orchestra</u> [6,14].

In your reference list, these titles will appear as:

> *The Arts Today.*
>
> *Berlin Symphony: Portrait of a Great Orchestra.*

or

> The Arts Today.
>
> Berlin Symphony: Portrait of a Great Orchestra.

or

<u>The Arts Today.</u>

<u>Berlin Symphony: Portrait of a Great Orchestra.</u>

or

<u>The Arts Today.</u>

<u>Berlin Symphony: Portrait of a Great Orchestra.</u>

In a short, simple reference list, you can omit the italics or under-lines, but not in your text.

If you're working in a medium where neither italics nor underlin-ing is available to you (in old-fashioned electronic mail to your fellow scholars, for instance), treat books like non-books in text; put quotes around the titles:

Kaman has an essay on the theater in Godfrey Halliwell's "The Arts Today" and a contribution in the memorial vol-ume "Berlin Symphony: Portrait of a Great Orchestra" [6,14].

If you have occasion to do a reference list in such a medium, leave the quotes off book titles there:

The Arts Today.

Berlin Symphony: Portrait of a Great Orchestra.

## Non-book Titles in Text

Use uppers-and-lowers capitalization (capitalize the first word, the first word after a colon, and all other words except articles, un-stressed conjunctions, and unstressed prepositions). Use quotation marks around the title:

He reaches the height of his powers in "A Drunk Man Looks at the Thistle" [17].

In your reference list, non-book titles will appear with sentence punctuation (capitalize the first word, the first word after a colon, and no other words except proper nouns and proper adjectives) and without quotation marks:

A drunk man looks at the thistle.

The layout of the reference list permits this pleasing representation, but in text both the quotation marks and the uppers-and-lowers punctuation are necessary.

If there's no way around it, use single quotes inside double quotes:

Horn's "Threads in the Makeup of the Verb 'to Be'" [26] puts the case most convincingly.

Usually, however, a little cleverness can get you out of the situation:

Horn's piece on the makeup of the verb "to be" [26] puts the case most convincingly.

## Short Titles in Text

Often in your text you'll want to see a short title for a work:

Roseman's "Heating and Cooling in Igneous Rocks" [55] calculates the time elapsed from the outbreak of the magma to its cooling in terms of hours, not days.

Short titles never appear in your reference list:

The effects of heating and cooling in igneous rocks of the Hassar region: A preliminary investigation.

Some works, especially journals, have initialisms you'll want to use in your text. They need neither underlines nor quotes.

Seymour's blast at the phonics-mongers in JEEM [36] was greeted by a vast silence.

But initialisms, like short titles, should never appear in your reference list:

> *The Journal of Elementary Educational Methods.*

## Peeling Off Initial Articles

To make your prose flow smoothly you may want to peel off the initial article from a title you mention in your text. (Only in your text—titles on your reference list are never altered.) "The" can almost always be peeled off from the beginning of a title; "a" or "an" can be peeled off unless the title sounds like nonsense without it. Peeling off is optional with possessives:

> Prochaska's *The Functions of the Nervous System;* Funey's "An Inquiry into Metanephrosis."

or

> Prochaska's *Functions of the Nervous System;* Funey's "Inquiry into Metanephrosis."

To avoid doubling up on articles, use peeling off whenever you can:

▷ The revised "The Habitat of the Badger"; the well-known *A Man of the People.*

The revised "Habitat of the Badger"; the well-known *Man of the People.*

The article you peel off is the one within the title, not the one from the surrounding sentence:

▷ "A" late "Housewife's Lament"; *The* famed *Attack of the Hussars.*

A late "Housewife's Lament"; the famed *Attack of the Hussars.*

When you can't peel off an initial article, consider using a construction that dodges the need to double up on articles:

The original "A Physician Speaks."

or

The original version of "A Physician Speaks."

When you use as an adjective a title that begins with an article, the title loses its article:

▷ for the "The Dunciad" controversy; in an *An Inevitable Consequence* review

▷ for "The Dunciad" controversy; in *An Inevitable Consequence* review

for the "Dunciad" controversy; in an *Inevitable Consequence* review

## Pasting on Initial Articles

A pasted-on article belongs to the surrounding sentence, not to the title. This group of examples concerns a volume called *Larousse Gastronomique:*

▷ Try *The Larousse Gastronomique.*

▷ Try [T]*he Larousse Gastronomique.*

▷ Try [*The*] *Larousse Gastronomique.*

▷ Try The *Larousse Gastronomique.*

Try the *Larousse Gastronomique.*

Paste articles onto titles only in your text, never in your reference list.

## Interpolation into Titles

Resist the urge to add bracketed information to titles. It's usually newspaper titles that give people this itch; because they're published for local audiences, their titles often lack identifications that outsiders need. But a word or two solves the problem more gracefully than interpolating:

▷ *The [Milford, Connecticut] Day.*
*The Day,* published in Milford, Connecticut.

And it's especially important to avoid interpolation on your reference list, where it would spoil the alphabetical order:

▷ *The [Springton, Lincolnshire] Sun.*
*The Sun* (Springton, Lincolnshire).

## Citing Yourself

### Citing Other Papers of Yours

Always say a word or two rather than using brackets alone when you're citing your own work:

▷ Further examination of the epistle [2,3,5,6,8] shows that it could not have been written during the earlier part of the Roman captivity.

This looks unexceptionable till your reader checks the reference list and finds that you have written all five of the papers you are citing. If all of the papers are by you alone, say:

My research on the epistle [2,3,5,6,8] shows . . .

If you have a co-author on one or more of the papers, acknowledge her as well:

The research Banton and I have done on the epistle [2,3,5,6,8] shows . . .

If you have more than one co-author, you may sweep their individual identities under the rug:

The research my colleagues and I have done on the epistle [2,3,5,6,8] shows . . .

## Cross-reference

Mention of another portion of the paper you are currently writing requires no bracketed number pointing to the reference list:

▷ I attempt to demonstrate [9] that Pernambuco is a special case.

The reader who looks up reference [9] and finds that it points to chapter 6 of the very paper she is reading will be disconcerted. Try something along these lines:

I attempt to demonstrate later that . . .

In chapter 6, I attempt to demonstrate that . . .

A computer system that keeps track of cross-references for you automatically is a worthwhile investment; when you swap chapter 6 with chapter 9, the cross-reference gets updated automatically; if you eliminate chapter 6 altogether, you get warned about dangling cross-references.

Consistency is a virtue in cross-reference. It doesn't matter whether you write "chapter 6" or "chapter six" or "Chapter 6" or "Chapter Six," as long as you stick to one method through the course of any one paper.

"Above" and "below" are among the most common ways of doing cross-reference. Some people object to them because a statement cited as "above" may lie physically lower on the previous page than the cross-reference does on the current page; this objection strikes me as silly. "Below" may mean "immediately following," but "above" is often overkill for "immediately preceding"; ask yourself whether "this" or "these" wouldn't serve as well.

Remember that "above" as an adjective falls in the appositive (following) rather than the attributive (preceding) position: "the lemma above," not "the above lemma." I never heard anyone try to say "the below lemma," but that's wrong too. "Above-mentioned" is a vile locution; "the stanza mentioned above" takes up no more space than "the above-mentioned stanza" and spares your reader's eardrums.

"Supra" and "infra" are obsolete ways of doing cross-reference

and should be changed to "above" and "below." Consign
"aforesaid" and "aforementioned" to the dustbin, where they belong.

Another common way to do cross-reference is with tenses, a past
or a perfect tense for what came before, a future tense for what will
follow. Do not ball yourself up with complicated tense structures:

▷ Having had in Section 3 and having in the current section the
advantage of dealing with questions that have lent themselves to an art-historical perspective, we turn toward the
end of this section and then shall turn increasingly in future
sections to problems that have required recourse to physical
evidence.

If you find yourself enmeshed in one of these, stop, take a deep
breath, and start over:

The questions in Section 3 and so far in this section have lent
themselves to an art-historical perspective. But from now on,
many of the problems we turn to will require recourse to
physical evidence.

Now for a warning: Be on your guard against abundant cross-
reference.

One kind of excessive cross-reference, the compulsive summary,
can simply be eliminated. There are the scholars who close each
section of their work with summaries of what has gone before and
what will come after:

▷ This chapter has dealt with the over-all structure of the German Stock Exchange. In the next chapter the workings of the
Berlin Börse, the principal market, will be examined in detail.

There are the scholars who open each section with a set of summaries:

▷ Having laid out the general make-up of the German Stock
Exchange in the previous chapter, we turn our attention in

this chapter to a detailed description of the principal market of that Exchange, the Berlin Börse.

And then there are the scholars who do both. After a while, the reader begins to feel that she's engaged in some terrifically hazardous but slow-motion enterprise, like something in a bad dream. Not all summaries should be eliminated, just the ones that come like clockwork.

Sometimes you may find yourself using a great number of cross-references that you cannot merely cut. These usually indicate a fundamental error in your organization. If you need to say over and over, "Section 7 will cover this," "The details are in section 7," "Section 7 explains this more fully," maybe you should change section 7 to section 2. Organization is the most elusive of all qualities in writing. We recognize badly organized material when other people produce it, but spotting our own failures is more difficult. Heavy cross-reference is one of the few hints you'll ever have to guide you; heed its warning.

## What to Call Yourself

Some characteristic faults of scholarly writing result from authors' attempts never to call themselves anything at all. They seem to confuse objectivity with disembodiment. This misconception leads to the dangling participle:

▷ Comparing Sir Philip Sidney with his younger brother Robert, who in 1618 was created earl of Leicester, Philip seems to have been the more gifted.

It leads to excesses of the passive voice:

▷ It is then observed that the absorbed exudate can be found to be mainly excreted by the kidneys, and by the use of standard techniques much nitrogen can be established to be present in the urine during this period.

It leads to the presumptuous "we" in a paper by a single author:

▷ We have assumed that the set has cardinality at most $n$.

It leads to the coy (and sometimes misleading) designation "the author":

> ▷ Thus Thackeray comes like a breath of fresh air into the musty, draperied apartments of established wealth. The author must confess to some sympathy for the victims of the invasion.

It leads to the overuse of "one," making one's writing, if one were but aware of it, sound as if one's lines were written by Noël Coward. It frequently leads all round Robin Hood's barn:

> ▷ It is thus the considered position of the present author in relation to her previous work [9] as well as to that of others [3,17] that certain too hasty and perhaps too general assertions may in the past have been made by the aforementioned.

Welcoming "I, me, my, mine" to the scholarly vocabulary can at a single stroke improve thousands of sentences. Compare the last example with the following version, revised almost beyond recognition.

> I now think that in my essay on imitative signs [9] I overstated the case for onomatopoeia, as Bainton and Morrow do also [3,17].

The same technique works with the Thackeray example:

> Thus Thackeray comes like a breath of fresh air into the musty, draperied apartments of established wealth. I must confess to some sympathy for the victims of the invasion.

But the first-person singular is no panacea. The examples about Sir Philip Sidney and the kidney disorder cannot be fixed up by splicing in a few pronouns. What they need is a firmer narrative stance:

> Sir Philip Sidney seems to have been more gifted than his younger brother Robert, who in 1618 was created earl of Leicester.

Then the kidneys excrete the exudate they absorbed, and the urine contains much nitrogen.

The point about narration shows up best in revising the $n$-cardinality example:

▷ We have assumed that the set has cardinality at most $n$.

The reader who comes across this sentence in the midst of a difficult mathematical exposition is justified in thinking "We who? You and who else? I never made any such assumption." So you try again:

▷ I have assumed that the set has cardinality at most $n$.

This is a definite improvement over dragging your reader along with you by the heels, but it's not enough. What you need to do is lay out the story:

The proof works only if the set has cardinality of at most $n$.

If novelists wrote like scholars, *Great Expectations* would begin:

▷ The family name of the current author's father being Pirrip, and the Christian name of the former Philip, our infant tongue could make of both names nothing longer or more explicit than Pip. So one called oneself Pip, and Pip was adopted to be called by.

When you're part of your story, bring yourself in directly, not in a submerged and twisted way.

*A Tale of Two Cities* in scholarly style would begin:

▷ The statement can be made with regard to the times that they were the best; that they were the worst seems to this author an assertion of equal weight.

When you have nothing to do with your story, leave yourself out.

## "We"

Each of the several varieties of "we" requires separate consideration.

The "we" that means "we the authors of a joint paper" is never objectionable. Just don't shove yourselves in where the story of your paper can be told more directly without you.

The "we" that means "I" is always objectionable except in monarchs, popes, and the front columns of *The New Yorker*.

The "we" that means "you and I, reader" is the tricky one. As long as your reader's going along with you, it's fine. But you can't suck her in against her will. "We see," "we observe," and "we notice" are therefore dangerous. The reader who doesn't see, doesn't observe, doesn't notice resents the pretense that she does. This "we" is just another version of the rhetorical error often found in "obviously" and "of course." Anything you label obvious had better be very obvious indeed, or your reader may think you're high-hatting her.

The "we" that means "everyone" or "all the world" is unobjectionable when what you assert is really common knowledge. "We do not know" is therefore always safe, while "we know" again runs the risk of cutting the reader to whom your statement comes as news.

## "Myself"

"Myself" is an intensive or a reflexive:

> I myself have no doubts about the accuracy of Griggs's account [12].

> I found myself in the classic position of the pure theoretician with a rough-hewn, inelegant, but eminently practical solution before her.

It is not a softened form of "I" or "me":

> ▷ Travis, Ichikawa, and myself [17,18] turned to Littré's dictionary.

> Travis, Ichikawa, and I [17,18] turned to Littré's dictionary.

▷ Olson was able to identify the spore-print for myself.

Olson was able to identify the spore-print for me.

Until you get used to it, the first-person singular may strike your ear as harsh and assertive; don't try to duck around it with "myself."

# Citations to Avoid

### Citation Versus Acknowledgment

There are two ways to learn about a source you've never actually had your hands on. You can read about it or you can be told about it. The first way requires a citation; the second requires an acknowledgment.

Say that you've never worked your way through Puicon on torts, but you're struck by an apt observation another author attributes to her. You may make use of the observation without recourse to the original:

> But joint perpetrators are severally liable without the right to contribution from each other [19].

Your reference is to Puicon, but through the secondary source:

19] E. K. Puicon.
*The Law of Torts.*
Cited in L. Wallichensky, *The Victorian Courtroom*
page 179. Indiana University Press, 1961.

If Wallichensky has misinterpreted or misrepresented, the fault is hers, not yours. And you have withstood the harried scholar's chief temptation, citing unseen sources.

Now suppose, once again, that you learn about the Puicon secondhand, but this time over coffee or in a seminar. You may still make use of her, but you have no secondary source to cite:

▷ But joint perpetrators are severally liable without the right to contribution from each other [19].

What would your reference read?

▷  19] E. K. Puicon.
    *The Law of Torts.*
    Cited in a private communication by Arthur Hadley.

No, what you must do instead is bring both Puicon and Hadley into
the light:

> But according to Puicon on torts, joint perpetrators are sev-
> erally liable without the right to contribution from each oth-
> er. (Arthur Hadley was kind enough to point this out to me.)

or

> But joint perpetrators are severally liable without the right to
> contribution from each other.*

---

* My colleague Arthur Hadley tells me that E. K. Puicon enunciates this
  principle in her classic work on torts.

Of course, you can save yourself all this grief by going and looking up Puicon yourself. (You might still want to thank Hadley.)

## Analogy

A telling analogy is one of the best teaching devices known. Do by
all means help your reader to see your point by drawing comparisons from general knowledge, from natural science, from world
literature. These comparisons should require no citations:

▷  The hydrogen, helium, and oxygen atoms respond to this
   pressure in turn, like the three little pigs responding to pressure from the big bad wolf [9].

That bracketed number disperses much of the charm of the
analogy—to say nothing of how odd a treasury of fairy tales looks
on the reference list for a physics paper. The whole point of the
comparison is to make your material more accessible and vivid by
relating it to something your reader already knows; if she knows it,
she doesn't need a citation. If she doesn't know it, the comparison
probably isn't very helpful:

▷ The hydrogen, helium, and oxygen atoms respond to this pressure in turn, much as Trinkhilda, Stefan, and wee Dormhart responded to pressure from Baldograd the giant seamonster in Welke's translation of the Finnish epic [41].

## Citing Axioms

Do not cite authority for the fundamental assumptions of your discipline or for common knowledge. The chemist who gives a citation for the existence of tin, the historian who gives a citation for the fact of Lincoln's presidency, the grammarian who gives a citation for the conjugation of "to be"—they give a shaky impression.

# Citations in Draft

Although by the time you begin to write you should have a fair idea about the contents of your reference list, there may be changes along the way. Numbering and renumbering and re-renumbering is no fun, to say nothing of the fertile ground it provides for error. The best system for handling citations in draft is to assign each item on your reference list a non-numeric code, to leave the brackets in your text empty, and to enter the code in the margin. (Putting the code in the margin rather than in the brackets keeps you from missing brackets when you go back to enter the numbers on your final draft.)

```
          on special techniques for teaching
   Rex    math under open admissions [ , ]. There
   SS&A   is much more information about the
```

A computer system that keeps track of the correspondence between the citation in your text and the reference in your reference list is a boon.

*Or just use APA!!*

# Quotation

## A Plea Against Quotation

Most young scholars overquote. Their motives are unimpeachable. Scrupulously honest by nature and by training, they want no credit for words not strictly and solely their own. As a result, they violate a basic rule of composition: Quote only the quotable. Quote for color; quote for evidence. Otherwise, don't quote.

When you are writing well, your sentences should join each other like rows of knitting, each sentence pulling up what went before it, each sentence supporting what comes after. (That's how I think knitting works.) Quotation introduces an alien pattern—someone else's diction, someone else's voice, someone else's links before and afterward. Even necessary quotations are difficult to knit smoothly into your structure. Overquotation will result in something more like a bird's nest than like fine handiwork.

It's easy to see how overquotation occurs. Picture the upright student who is looking at C. A. Beard's *The American Party Battle*. She finds the following sentence:

> A very large number of Democrats voted the Republican ticket outright.

This is exactly the point she herself was interested in, and Beard is sufficient authority for it, so she writes:

> According to Beard [3], a very large number of Democrats voted the Republican ticket outright.

Now her conscience begins to trouble her. She has used Beard's exact words without quotation marks. Is this perfidy? She begins to tamper with the sentence:

▷ According to Beard [3], an exceedingly large amount of Democratic voting power was applied to the whole of the GOP slate.

The wording is now distinct from Beard's. It is also repulsive. She tries to improve it:

▷ According to Beard [3], many Democrats voted . . . many Democrats placed their votes . . . a large number of members of the Democratic . . . votes from persons of the Democratic . . .

She despairs. Beard put the idea about as well a it can be put, she decides, so she writes:

▷ According to Beard [3], a "very large number of Democrats voted the Republican ticket outright."

The trouble with this quotation is that it's a red herring for the reader, who has a right to expect that quotation will be reserved for color or evidence. She examines the quotation quizzically. Certainly it can't be color that the author was aiming at; Beard's words are as bland as bathwater. So she concludes that the writer must be quoting for evidence.

Evidence of what? Since the statement seems otherwise unexceptionable, the author must disagree with it. (All this goes through the reader's mind in a fraction of a second.) Perhaps, the reader conjectures, Beard asserts this Democratic switchover on insufficient ground. Perhaps the author is quarreling with "large" and thinks the number of Democrats voting Republican was modest. Perhaps "outright" is the key word, and the author thinks that there was actually much soul-searching among Democratic voters. The reader's curiosity is aroused—and dashed to the ground. There was no

---

Bad examples are marked with an arrowhead (▷).

reason for the quotation marks. She flicks aside her irritation and reads on.

This episode is over almost as soon as it has begun. No reader really articulates these hypotheses as she goes along; no reader pauses long enough. But the expectations are real, the disappointment, however slight, is real, and the reader's confidence in the writer is now a little shaken.

Pity the reader. (That's as good a rule for writing as you will find—pity the poor reader.) And have mercy on your fellow authors. It's hard enough to write something worth reading. No one should be under the perpetual requirement to make her every word worth repeating.

## Quotation to Avoid Plagiarism

Most of us who went to American grade schools can remember long hours of copying articles out of encyclopedias. "The abode of the penguin is a hard and difficult one." It was called doing research. Then in college we found that it was also called plagiarism. This disjuncture is so common and so upsetting that plagiarism has become a bugbear. Of course you mustn't steal other people's words and present them as your own. But neither must you quote what's not quotable. Quote what is vivid or memorable or questionable, strange or witty. Paraphrase the rest.

If your paraphrase agrees with the original in a key word or group of words, you are right to examine it closely. Heaven knows, there are few sentences written that can't stand improvement. Try taking a fresh piece of paper and writing the same idea without looking at the original. (There would be less overquotation if people took notes in their own words instead of defacing books with yellow highlighters.) Still no luck? Try jotting a cryptic note " ↑ Dems v. all Repub," letting a day pass, and then rewriting the sentence from your note.

I see that like most instructors I have an exaggerated idea of how much time a student can give to my pet topic—you may not have a day. Take a day if you can; take ten minutes if that's all you have.

If after all this there is still some agreement between what you have written and the original, and if the original is really in no way striking, let your version go without quotation marks. The language is our common property. That two people should express the same simple idea similarly is not such a surprise.

### Tag Phrases

Writers inherit not only words but phrases and sentences from the past. No one, I hope, would feel she had to put quotation marks around a word she learned from someone else. But there is a class of phrases and sentences called tags that are felt as operating on one level like quotations and on another level like part of the common language.

Putting quotation marks around tag phrases is pedantry; the reader already knows the words are not the author's own:

▷ To apply "a little learning" dangerously, let us attempt to fit a curve to these data.

▷ Turning, then, to "*arma virumque*," there is the question of Owen's military service.

▷ DeTreville's description is perhaps "gild[ing] the lily."

Her use of quotes reveals the first author as a pedant, but a mere garden-variety pedant. The second author is more notable for her conceit. Does she really fear that we believe her capable of lapsing into Latin, let alone the Latin of Virgil?

But the third author is my favorite. She seems to be trying for Pedant of the Year award with her quotation marks and brackets. But what Shakespeare actually wrote was "to gild refined gold, to paint the lily." I hasten to add that Pedant #3 should have written:

DeTreville's description is perhaps gilding the lily.

Not:

▷ DeTreville's description is perhaps painting the lily.

And certainly not:

▷ DeTreville's description is perhaps "paint[ing] the lily."

Correcting tags is the most arrant pedantry of all. Quotation marks around full-sentenced tags are inoffensive but confining. When the tag is identical to the quotation, use quotes or not, as you like:

> A strict application of Barrett's guidelines would produce classrooms of tiny Fascists. "The letter killeth, but the spirit giveth life."

or

> A strict application of Barrett's guidelines would produce classrooms of tiny Fascists. The letter killeth, but the spirit giveth life.

When the tag departs from the quotation, leave the quotes off and bend to the common wisdom:

> ▷ So the proof works after all. "I am escaped with the skin of my teeth."
>
> So the proof works after all. I have escaped by the skin of my teeth.

For a quotation that you feel is almost a tag but not quite, use no quotation marks and a loose attribution like "in the words of $X$" or "as $X$ says":

> But, as Oscar Wilde put it, you cannot be too careful in the choice of your enemies.

No bracketed number, of course.

There was a time when a warning would have been needed against larding scholarly writing with endless biblical and classical tags, but today the practice has pretty well died out. Most scholars now use tags lightly and cleverly when they use them at all—go and do thou likewise.

### Quotation on the Rack

If you quote, quote whole. If you paraphrase, paraphrase. Don't combine the two. Don't tear quotations apart and leave them to suffer all crippled and broken.

▷ Albert Schweitzer [27] stressed the "one truth" that, according to him, "something spiritual" lies beneath "all that happens in world history."

Either quote:

Albert Schweitzer [27] wrote, "One truth stands firm. All that happens in world history rests on something spiritual."

Or paraphrase:

It was Albert Schweitzer's view [27] that some spiritual essence underlies world history.

## Imaginary Quotation

You can say hello without saying the word "hello." Ditto for say yes, say no, say boo, say good-bye, say when. These expressions can introduce a pleasantly colloquial note into scholarly writing if you don't ruin their flavor by mistaking them for quotations.

▷ Edward's favorite sport was saying "No" to his ministers.
   Edward's favorite sport was saying no to his ministers.

The author does not intend to indicate that Edward repeatedly spoke the word "no"; "say no" here means balk or thwart or deny or disappoint. Use the quotation marks only when you mean that the exact word was said.

Edward looked at his minister coldly. "No," he said. "No, I think not."

## Quotation to Fill Up Space

Any serious young scholar will be scandalized at the idea, but there are students who quote because they don't know what to say. A friend of mine calls it Tarzaning, swinging from quoted vine to quoted vine with little but thin air between.

To some extent, the practice may result from taking assignments with deadly literalness. The instructor who assigns a twenty-page paper usually does not mean longer than nineteen pages and shorter than twenty-one; the length is a hint about what sort of response she expects, not a requirement. Obviously I can't speak for all teachers everywhere, but many would rather have three pages of your own writing undiluted than twenty sodden with quotations.

For those who are no longer students, padding with quotations has no excuse. One of the pleasures of adulthood is saying nothing when you have nothing to say.

## A Plea for Quotation

I know of only one place where scholars consistently underquote, and that is in subjecting texts to close analysis. There are situations in which you can't quote the material you're analyzing because it's simply too long. But readers rightly loathe the author who fails to reproduce a verse or two, a sentence, a stanza, or a short paragraph for which she's offering a reading.

> ▷ The balance of fricatives and dentals, the susurrative alliteration achieved in part by anaphora, and the robust march of the open assonants make this quatrain a small jewel of English sound color.

Without the quatrain, the sentence is a small jewel of vagueness. The higher the ratio of analysis to original, the more pressing the obligation to quote.

Mathematicians building on previous work seldom think of needing to quote, but failure to restate a crucial result, whether exactly or in a paraphrase, can cause the same sort of fury in the reader.

It is true that most scholarly writing reaches only a tiny audience. There are papers that no more than a handful of readers will examine closely. The temptation to write private communications for those few readers is understandable. "It's hardly necessary to quote from the *Hermotimus*," thinks the scholar. "Anyone who reads a paper of mine must know her Lucian backwards and forwards." So she leaves a line unquoted and misses a chance for welcoming the unforeseen reader—the bright ninth-grader in Moline, the retired librarian in Manitoba.

Failure to quote is not the shameful crime that failure to cite is.
The reader can dig out for herself what you should have given her.
But you've turned a cold shoulder to newcomers, you've con-
tributed another stone to the edifice of scholarly snobbishness, and
you may have cheated yourself of an additional reader or two.

## Quote Whole

When you are quoting a text for analysis, quote it in reasonable
pieces. Don't cut it to ribbons.

> ▷ "Their son having fallen sick," begins the story parallel to 1
> Kings 14, "the old man sent his wife," unnamed, as
> Jeroboam's wife was, "with ten loaves," the same number as
> in Kings, "biscuits," a more familiar term than the King
> James "cracknels," "and a cruse"—here the clinching argu-
> ment, for the word was obsolete in the United States by 1866
> [36]—of honey."

This is like a Sears, Roebuck catalog without the pictures. Your
poor reader cannot be expected to piece a quotation together from
little bits and snippets. Give it to her whole, even if you have to
repeat to make your point:

> "Their son having fallen sick, the old man sent his wife with
> ten loaves, biscuits, and a cruse of honey." Right from the
> beginning, the story is parallel to 1 Kings 14. The wife is
> unnamed, as Jeroboam's wife was. She takes ten loaves, the
> same number as in Kings; biscuits, a more familiar term than
> the King James "cracknels," and a cruse of honey. "Cruse" is
> the clincher, for the word was obsolete in the United States
> by 1866 [36].

# Epigraphs

The epigraph is among the most delightful of scholarly habits. Do-
nald Knuth's work on fundamental algorithms would be just as
important if he hadn't begun with a quotation from Betty Crocker,

but not so enjoyable. Part of the fun of an epigraph is turning a source to an unexpected use. Use a quotation from Isaiah, not for an article on biblical criticism, but for one on the Industrial Revolution:

> Neither shall there be any work for Egypt which the head or tail, branch or rush, may do.

Use a quotation from Mauriac's Monsieur Puybaraud, not for an article on French literature, but for one on educational reform:

> Get as many diplomas as you can, my boy. You don't need them now, but one never knows.

There's nothing wrong with using expected sources for your epigraphs—Engels for the first one, say, and Dewey for the second. But most scholarly writing needs all the leavening it can get, and unlikely epigraphs help.

People who get their epigraphs from books of quotations rather than from their own reading are like people who cheat at solitaire. I do not understand what game they're playing, but it's obviously not the same one I am.

## Quotation and Citation

All quotations except tags need a word or two about the source as well as a bracketed reference number if you haven't mentioned the source already. This requirement needn't lead to a dull progression of "he said," "she said," "he wrote," "she wrote." Just be sure your reader knows where the quotation comes from without having to flip back to your reference list.

Putting a bracketed number at the end of a quotation sometimes looks odd, although it is correct; putting it by the attribution is often more graceful.

> Melbourne then got off another shot. "Things have come to a pretty pass when religion is allowed to invade the sphere of private life" [7].

or

Melbourne [7] then got off another shot. "Things have come to a pretty pass when religion is allowed to invade the sphere of private life."

An epigraph, whether from an expected or an unexpected source, requires only a brief attribution—no bibliographic information and no bracketed numbers:

▷ There should be no false shame about accepting odds, but there frequently is.
> —F. V. Morley.
> *My One Contribution to Chess.*
> George W. Stewart, New York, 1946.

▷ There should be no false shame about accepting odds, but there frequently is.
> —F. V. Morley [26].

There should be no false shame about accepting odds, but there frequently is.
> —F. V. Morley.

Even if the article for which this is an epigraph is about Frank Morley and contains thirty other references to *My One Contribution,* the epigraph is cited only with his name. And if the article is about probability and statistics, all the more reason to cite the epigraph by the author's name alone; don't clutter up your reference list with extraneous material.

Tags require no citations at all.

## Inlaid versus Displayed Quotations

An inlaid quotation is set into your text. "Cauliflower is nothing but cabbage with a college education." That's an inlaid quotation (from Mark Twain). A displayed quotation is set off from your text.

If once a man indulges himself in murder, very soon he comes to think little of robbing; and from robbing he comes next to drinking and sabbath-breaking, and from that to incivility and procrastination.

That's a displayed quotation (from Thomas De Quincey). How do you decide which to use?

Inlays are unobtrusive; they save paper; they save time for the typist or the compositor; and they are a little harder to read than displayed quotations. Displays are showy; they use up paper; they take extra time for the typist or the compositor; and they are a little easier to read than inlaid quotations. So, as a rule of thumb, display long quotations (over fifty words, over two sentences, over two lines of verse) and inlay short ones. Display hard quotations regardless of their length; hard quotations are heavy in symbols, heavy in non-Roman letters, or heavy in small details. In this book, for instance, many of the displayed examples focus on minute details; it would be unreasonable to ask a reader to sort out without the aid of displays differences that often amount to no more than a comma.

> Shaw's first version of Drinkwater's opening line went: "Yr naht best plaized t'baw hint'rhupted in yr bi o gawdnin baw th'lawk o mai, gavnuh." The standard edition reads: "Youre not best pleased to be hinterrapted in yr bit o gawdnin baw the lawk o me, gavner." So he did make concessions.

Shaw's first version of Drinkwater's opening line went:

Yr naht best plaized t'baw hint'rhupted in yr bi o gawdnin baw th'lawk o mai, gavnuh.

The standard edition reads:

Youre not best pleased to be hinterrapted in yr bit o gawdnin baw the lawk o me, gavner.

So he did make concessions.

The only rigid rule about display format is that your display indentation must be different from your paragraph indentation—visibly different, preferably about four typed characters or two ems. Otherwise, let your eye and your common sense guide you. Display indentation may be larger or smaller than paragraph indentation.

You may leave a little extra space above and below a display. You may space a display more closely than your text; you may also use a smaller (but still readable) type size for display than for text. You may indent at the right margin as well as the left, or you may use the right margin of your text. Pick a style and stick to it for the length of any one paper.

Epigraphs are always displayed, and they should be displayed in a format that's different from the one you choose for the rest of a piece. You might use a display indentation of three spaces in your text and one of twenty spaces for your epigraphs. You might center your epigraphs or (in printing but not in typing) set them flush right, things you would never do for ordinary displays. The attribution for an epigraph is usually set to the right and below:

> A great empire and little minds go ill together.
>
> —Edmund Burke

The dash before the attribution is optional but useful.

Tags are always inlaid, never displayed.

Either inlay a quotation or display it—don't do half one and half the other.

> ▷ His audience knew what to expect. "I suppose," he read,
>    that the high-water mark of my youth in Columbus, Ohio,
>    was the night the bed fell on my father.
>
> Already there was laughter.

This is a split quotation (one with the attribution in the middle), and all split quotations must be inlaid:

> His audience knew what to expect. "I suppose," he read, "that the high-water mark of my youth in Columbus, Ohio, was the night the bed fell on my father." Already there was laughter.

You may not split a quotation so long or so complicated that it requires display.

# Punctuating Quotations

In the United States, the mark of primary quotation is a small, high double scratch (") and the mark of quotation within quotation is a small, high single scratch ('); elsewhere the conventions are reversed. Don't worry about punctuating quotations within quotations within quotations; worry about avoiding them. Quotes come in pairs, one at the start of the quotation and one at the end; in checking over your work, be sure that all quotes are indeed paired off. A computer system that does quote-balancing can come in handy. In some typefaces there's a difference between open-quotes and close-quotes, which makes checking the pairs easier; peer even more closely when open-quotes and close-quotes look the same.

Inlaid quotations (except for tags) always require quotation marks:

▷ Kierkegaard had no high opinion of academics: One way is to suffer; the other is to become a professor of the fact that another suffered.

Kierkegaard had no high opinion of academics: "One way is to suffer; the other is to become a professor of the fact that another suffered."

With displayed quotations, the display itself usually takes the place of quotes:

Kierkegaard had no high opinion of academics:
One way is to suffer; the other is to become a professor of the fact that another suffered.

The exceptions are rare, but suppose that in one piece you were displaying both equations and quotations. Using two different display formats is madness; your pages will look terrible, and your readers will never figure out what's going on. So you might want to use quotes around the displayed quotations.

If you have occasion to put quotes around an entire display, place the open-quote one character to the left of the display (that's what's called "setting to clear"):

▷ Stamper's advice [76] bears repeating:
  "The statistician who looks for a bell curve anywhere in
  nature above the atomic level has failed to grasp the essential nature of his tools."

Stamper's advice [76] bears repeating:
  "The statistician who looks for a bell curve anywhere in
  nature above the atomic level has failed to grasp the essential nature of his tools."

This is such a tiny detail that you may have trouble even seeing it—
in the bad example, the open-quote is set above the *n* at the beginning of the second line; in the good example, it's set off by itself.
Setting to clear is one of the marks of professional copy. It comes up
again in numbering the items in a displayed list:

▷ Latrobe [41] suggests the following division:
  1. Inherent powers are enjoyed by the possessors of natural right.
  2. Derivative powers are received from another. They may
  come from authority or interest.

Latrobe [41] suggests the following division:
  1. Inherent powers are enjoyed by the possessors of natural right.
  2. Derivative powers are received from another. They may
  come from authority or interest.

Partial clearing is helpful in quoting dialog:

▷ Consider the famous exchange:
  Medvedenko: Why is it that I always see you wearing
  black?
  Masha: I am in mourning for my life. I am unhappy.

▷ Consider the famous exchange:
  Medvedenko: Why is it that I always see you wearing
              black?
  Masha:      I am in mourning for my life. I am unhap-
              py.

Consider the famous exchange:
    Medvedenko: Why is it that I always see you wearing
      black?
    Masha: I am in mourning for my life. I am unhappy.

## Final Punctuation

Life would be easy if all quotations were full sentences and stood on
their own:

> For the origin of the argument we must go back to Tertullian
> [27]. "It is certain because it is impossible." No later for-
> mulation was ever so forceful or attractive.

> The master of the art was Finley Peter Dunne [8].
>     Th' dead ar-re always pop'lar. I knowed a society wanst to
>     vote a monyment to a man an' refuse to help his fam'ly, all
>     in wan night.
> For forty years Dunne set the standard of dialect transcrip-
> tion.

But, as luck would have it, most quotations fall within your own
sentences, and punctuating them becomes a trouble.

When you intend to put a quotation within a sentence of your
own, start by chopping off from the end of the quotation any mark
of punctuation except a question mark, an exclamation mark, or a
period of abbreviation. There are only nine possibilities. The item
you intend to quote can end with one of the marks of punctuation
that you let alone:

> What cat's averse to fish?

> Glorious style of weakness!

> All his emotions were bound up in Standers, Inc.

It can end with one of the five marks you chop off (a sentence
period, a comma, a semicolon, a colon, or a dash):

  ▷  But leave us still our old nobility.

     But leave us still our old nobility

▷ Make my thy lyre,
  Make my thy lyre
▷ Remember that the most beautiful things in the world are the
  most useless;
  Remember that the most beautiful things in the world are the
  most useless
▷ Trust thou thy Love:
  Trust thou thy Love
▷ Shovel them under and let me work—
  Shovel them under and let me work

Or it can have no final punctuation, in which case you let it alone:

This translation became the standard for literary German

This is as good a time as any to look at quotation marks within
quotations because you need to know what to do if your quotation
itself ends with a quotation. If your quotation is going to be displayed with no surrounding quotation marks, let internal double
quotes alone:

Call the world if you please "The Vale of Soul-making."

If the whole quotation is going to be enclosed in quotes, demote
internal double quotes to single quotes:

Call the world if you please 'The Vale of Soul-making.'

Whether the close-quote at the end is now single or double, look
one character to the left of it. If the character to the left is a sentence
period or a comma, toss it out; any other character you leave alone.
   Now you're ready to lower the quotation gently into your own
sentence, with quotation marks around it if it's inlaid, usually with
no quotation marks if it's displayed. For instance, suppose your
sentence is:

Shelley's _____ is an echo of a line from Walter Savage
Landor [19].

Then you surround the quotation with quotation marks and drop it in:

> Shelley's "Make me thy lyre" is an echo of a line from Walter Savage Landor [19].

Or again:

> The question _____ summed up his attitude toward women.

> The question "What cat's averse to fish?" summed up his attitude toward women.

Or:

> Tossing off an elevated sentiment like _____ with a shrug was all a part of his pose.

> Tossing off an elevated sentiment like "Call the world if you please 'The Vale of Soul-making'" with a shrug was all a part of his pose.

Listing every possibility would be a bore; you get the point. If, however, a comma or a sentence period comes right after the close-quote, you must not let it stand:

> We readily hear the alliteration in _____, but we need to listen again for the assonance.

▷ We readily hear the alliteration in "Trust thou thy Love", but we need to listen again for the assonance.

> Ruskin wrote, _____.

▷ Ruskin wrote, "Remember that the most beautiful things in the world are the most useless".

"What's wrong with those?" I can hear an angry reader asking. "They're logical, aren't they? And consistent?" Yes, they are, and the convention of pushing the comma and the period into the quotation is illogical and inconsistent. But before you decide to adopt another system, think about a lifetime of niggling controversy with typists and printers. There are better things to fight about. Go ahead; push the comma and the period under the quotation marks; it's only a convention.

We readily hear the alliteration in "Trust thou thy Love," but we need to listen again for the assonance.

Ruskin wrote, "Remember that the most beautiful things in the world are the most useless."

If the mark you've pushed under finds no other mark, you've finished. If another mark is there, you have one more step to go. A period that finds any other mark disappears. Here, for instance, the period moves under and finds a question mark:

He wrote, ————.

▷ He wrote, "What cat's averse to fish?".

▷ He wrote, "What cat's averse to fish?."

He wrote, "What cat's averse to fish?"

Here it moves under and finds a period of abbreviation:

The only epitaph he wanted was ————.

▷ The only epitaph he wanted was "All his emotions were bound up in Standers, Inc.".

▷ The only epitaph he wanted was "All his emotions were bound up in Standers, Inc.."

The only epitaph he wanted was "All his emotions were bound up in Standers, Inc."

A comma that finds a period of abbreviation stays:

The only epitaph he wanted was ————, and he got it.

▷ The only epitaph he wanted was "All his emotions were bound up in Standers, Inc.", and he got it.

The only epitaph he wanted was "All his emotions were bound up in Standers, Inc.," and he got it.

A comma that finds a question mark or an exclamation mark should go; letting it stay looks old-fashioned:

He wrote, ————, and he meant it literally.

▷ He wrote, "Glorious style of weakness!", and he meant it literally.

▷ He wrote, "Glorious style of weakness!," and he meant it literally.

or

 He wrote, "Glorious style of weakness!" and he meant it literally.

## Final Punctuation Summary

At first, the whole routine for the final punctuation of quotation may seem like a nightmare to you, but after a while it will become almost second nature. Then all you'll need is a summary for the tricky cases that come up seldom:

1. Chop off from the end of your quotation any mark of punctuation except a question mark, an exclamation mark, or a period of abbreviation.
2. If there is a quotation within your quotation:
   2a. Demote double quotes to single quotes unless you plan to display the whole quotation without quotation marks.
   2b. If the quotation within your quotation falls at the end of your quotation and ends with sentence-period-quote, delete the sentence period; if it ends with comma-quote, delete the comma.
3. Now drop the quotation into your own sentence. Use quotation marks around it if it's inlaid; usually you don't need quotation marks around it if it's displayed.
4. If a comma or a sentence period comes right after the close-quote, push it under the close-quote into the quotation.
   4a. A pushed-under period that meets another mark of punctuation inside the quotation disappears.
   4b. A pushed-under comma that meets a period of abbreviation inside the quotation stays; one that meets a question mark or an exclamation mark should go.

You can even, if you like charts, generate a chart of all the possibilities. Pretend that the last word of the quotation is either

"Hawaii" or, to get in the period of abbreviation, "C.I.I." (for Chartered Insurance Institute). Let # stand for a space. Then there are nine ways the quotation can end:

| | | |
|---|---|---|
| ii? | ii. | ii: |
| ii! | ii, | ii— |
| I.I. | ii; | ii# |

Quotation within and at the end of your quotation adds another six possible endings:

| | |
|---|---|
| ii." | ii!" |
| ii," | I.I." |
| ii?" | ii" |

Now for the surrounding sentence. Pretend that the first word after the quotation is "ooze." That gives eight possibilities:

| | |
|---|---|
| #oo | : oo |
| ? Oo | —oo |
| ! Oo | . Oo |
| ; oo | , oo |

With the options for the pushed-under commas, that makes 124 possible combinations. The thing is laid out in all its glory below. If you don't like charts, don't even look at it, because it's a dilly.*

| | #oo | ? Oo | ! Oo | ; oo |
|---|---|---|---|---|
| ii? | ii?" oo | ii?"? Oo | ii?"! Oo | ii?"; oo |
| ii! | ii!" oo | ii!"? Oo | ii!"! Oo | ii!"; oo |
| I.I. | I.I." oo | I.I."? Oo | I.I."! Oo | I.I."; oo |
| ii. | ii" oo | ii"? Oo | ii"! Oo | ii"; oo |
| ii, | ii" oo | ii"? Oo | ii"! Oo | ii"; oo |
| ii; | ii" oo | ii"? Oo | ii"! Oo | ii"; oo |
| ii: | ii" oo | ii"? Oo | ii"! Oo | ii"; oo |

*The remainder of the chart appears on the following page.

| | | | | |
|---|---|---|---|---|
| ii— | ii" oo | ii"? Oo | ii"! Oo | ii"; oo |
| ii# | ii" oo | ii"? Oo | ii"! Oo | ii"; oo |
| ii." | ii'" oo | ii'"? Oo | ii'"! Oo | ii'"; oo |
| ii," | ii'" oo | ii'"? Oo | ii'"! Oo | ii'"; oo |
| ii?" | ii?'" oo | ii?'"? Oo | ii?'"! Oo | ii?'"; oo |
| ii!" | ii!'" oo | ii!'"? Oo | ii!'"! Oo | ii!'"; oo |
| I.I." | I.I.'" oo | I.I.'"? Oo | I.I.'"! Oo | I.I.'"; oo |
| ii" | ii'" oo | ii'"? Oo | ii'"! Oo | ii'"; oo |

| : oo | —oo | . Oo | , oo |
|---|---|---|---|

| | | | | |
|---|---|---|---|---|
| ii? | ii?": oo | ii?"—oo | ii?" Oo | ii?" oo / ii?," oo |
| ii! | ii!": oo | ii!"—oo | ii!" Oo | ii!" oo / ii!," oo |
| I.I. | I.I.": oo | I.I."—oo | I.I." Oo | I.I.," oo |
| ii. | ii": oo | ii"—oo | ii." Oo | ii," oo |
| ii, | ii": oo | ii"—oo | ii." Oo | ii," oo |
| ii; | ii": oo | ii"—oo | ii." Oo | ii," oo |
| ii: | ii": oo | ii"—oo | ii." Oo | ii," oo |
| ii— | ii": oo | ii"—oo | ii." Oo | ii," oo |
| ii# | ii": oo | ii"—oo | ii." Oo | ii," oo |
| ii." | ii'": oo | ii'"—oo | ii.'" Oo | ii,'" oo |
| ii," | ii'": oo | ii'"—oo | ii.'" Oo | ii,'" oo |
| ii?" | ii?'": oo | ii?'"—oo | ii?'" Oo | ii?'" oo / ii?,'" oo |
| ii!" | ii!'": oo | ii!'"—oo | ii!'" Oo | ii!'" oo / ii!,'" oo |
| I.I." | I.I.'": oo | I.I.'"—oo | I.I.'" Oo | I.I.,'" oo |
| ii" | ii'": oo | ii'"—oo | ii.'" Oo | ii,'" oo |

## Dicey Situations

If you follow the steps illustrated in the chart, you will never make a technical error in punctuating the ends of your quotations. But you can produce technically correct hash. Questions within questions, for instance, are difficult for a reader to make sense of, no matter how accurately you punctuate them. Especially in scholarly prose, where most questions are rhetorical, try another construction.

▷ Is it then necessary to return to Morrison [8] merely in order to ask, "Where are the Merovingian remains today?"?

It seems unnecessary to return to Morrison [8] merely in order to ask, "Where are the Merovingian remains today?"

or

▷ Is it then necessary to return to Morrison [8] merely in order to ask where the Merovingian remains are today?

Some of the combinations are highly unlikely. For exclamation within exclamation, I can conjure up:

Blast your "Ouch!"!

But what would question within exclamation be like?

Blast your "Who?"!

It's difficult to think of any piece of scholarly writing in which such sentences might occur.

The conventions about final punctuation can lead to confusion:

▷ To produce an x you must type "y."

This is technically correct punctuation but lousy writing; the reader can't tell whether she should type one character or two. If she's supposed to type two characters, you'd better rewrite the sentence:

To produce an x you must type "y."—that's a "y" and a period.

If she's supposed to type one, violate the convention:

To produce an x you must type "y".

But violate it only to improve communication, not from infatuation with regularity and logic.

In theory, the rules about final punctuation apply to quotations of all lengths. In reality, quotations of more than one sentence should be worked around to the end of the surrounding sentence. This example is technically correct but ill advised:

▷ I have puzzled over Johnson's "Subordination tends greatly to human happiness. Were we all upon an equality, we should have no other enjoyment than mere animal pleasure" in the light of what we know about his social habits.

Displays of whatever length should be worked around to the end of a surrounding sentence that ends with a period, not the middle of a sentence and not the end of a sentence that ends with a question mark or an exclamation mark. These examples are technically correct, but irksome to look at:

▷ London [22] addressed his subject in no uncertain terms:

> A scab is a two-legged animal with a corkscrew soul, a waterlogged brain, a combination backbone of jelly and glue

and went on to compare strike-breakers unfavorably to Benedict Arnold and Judas Iscariot.

▷ Why should we be interested in a philosopher who writes:

> The result is not to make the majority adopt the belief with a low degree of conviction, but to make some hold the belief with a high degree of conviction while others reject it, also with a high degree of conviction?

Rewrite:

London [22] addressed his subject in no uncertain terms:

> A scab is a two-legged animal with a corkscrew soul, a waterlogged brain, a combination backbone of jelly and glue.

He then went on to compare strike-breakers unfavorably to Benedict Arnold and Judas Iscariot.

Why should we be interested in a philosopher who writes like this?

> The result is not to make the majority adopt the belief with a low degree of conviction, but to make some hold the belief with a high degree of conviction while others reject it, also with a high degree of conviction.

Long or complicated equations should be displayed, not inlaid, the display should stand alone or come at the end of a declarative sentence, and the end of the display should serve as final punctuation—no sentence periods, no question marks, no exclamation marks.

## Quotes Versus Parens

Parentheses do not follow the rules for quotation marks. When a period or a comma falls logically outside a close-paren, put it outside:

▷ Sadism, the desire to force one's will on others and to cause unhappiness while doing so, is the basis of authoritarianism in any field (including language.)

Sadism, the desire to force one's will on others and to cause unhappiness while doing so, is the basis of authoritarianism in any field (including language).

## Quote–Cap

A quotation construed as a sentence, no matter how short, begins with a capital letter:

According to Jones [9], Freud said something along the line of "Nuts!" and went on his way.

A quotation construed as a fragment, no matter how long, begins with a lower-case letter (unless the fragment begins the sentence it lies within):

During the interview, the subject said "waving the wiwwy pretty once" for "wearing the really pretty ones."

"Wearing the really pretty ones" came out "waving the wiwwy pretty once."

A quotation mortised into a subordinate clause with an introductory word like "when" or "whether" is a fragment, not a full sentence. Among the introductory words that can cancel out a full sentence, "that" is the most common.

▷ Vanbrugh [26] said that "The want of a thing is perplexing enough, but the possession of it is intolerable."

Vanbrugh [26] said that "the want of a thing is perplexing enough, but the possession of it is intolerable."

or

Vanbrugh [26] said, "The want of a thing is perplexing enough, but the possession of it is intolerable."

▷ Though "Slumber is more sweet than toil," he was famous for the long hours he worked.

Though "slumber is more sweet than toil," he was famous for the long hours he worked.

or

Though he wrote, "Slumber is more sweet than toil," he was famous for the long hours he worked.

The first word of the first part of a split full-sentence quotation is capitalized; the first word of the second part is not (unless it's a proper noun or a proper adjective).

▷ "God is decreeing to begin some new and great period in His Church," he wrote, "Even to the reforming of the Reformation itself."

"God is decreeing to begin some new and great period in His Church," he wrote, "even to the reforming of the Reformation itself."

## The Comma-Quote Convention

Just to make life more difficult, there is a convention that requires a comma to separate any transitive verb analogous to "say" from a whole-sentence quotation that is its direct object.

Lamb [64] said, "Boys are capital fellows in their own way, among their mates; but they are unwholesome companions for grown people."

"Say" and "write" are at the head of the list to which the convention applies. Other candidates are: reply, respond, argue, declare, announce, remark, whisper, read. It's impossible to give a complete list, and perfect consistency, agreeable though it might be, is probably impossible as well. Don't lose sleep over it. The scholarly writer will not, I hope, include in her list such words as "groan," "snort," "sigh," and "gasp." These words take only cognate objects ("sighed a sigh") except in vulgar fiction.

In standard order, the comma comes right after the verb:

> Jonson [6] wrote, "Where it ends a former syllable it sounds longish."

A word or a phrase may intervene:

> Graves wrote in his *Spiritual Quixote* [9], "Go to the tavern, and call for your bottle and your pipe and your Welsh rabbit."

In inverted order, the comma slides under the quotation marks (as you already know a comma should):

> "Under our garb He took our nature," wrote Grosseteste [15].

In a split quotation there are two commas, one separating the verb from the part before, one separating it from the part after:

> "Well ink," says Palmer, "is the plant *V. Beccabunga.*"

The comma-quote convention applies only to full-sentence quotations:

▷ He writes, "a Mindy weeke" after every accounting, so we assume that Sunday was still thought of as the last day in the week.

He writes "a Mindy weeke" after . . .

The convention applies only to verbs, not to infinitives, participles, and gerunds:

▷ To say, "I think not" is all very well for the non-specialist.

To say "I think not" is . . .

▷ Writing, "Nothing may come of this" more than once in his diary [6], Cavendish nevertheless plunged ahead.

Writing "Nothing may come of this" more . . .

▷ Saying, "Dress and tonsure profit little" did not prevent his wearing a habit.

Saying "Dress and tonsure profit little" did . . .

And the convention requires a comma only between verb and quotation, not between the quotation and the rest of the sentence:

▷ Chaucer wrote, "Fare now well mine own sweet herte," during this Farnsworth period.

Chaucer wrote, "Fare now well mine own sweet herte" during his Farnsworth period.

The comma-quote convention is suspended for sentence quotations of one or two words, but only for those in normal order:

She said "Bosh" to his arguments.

"Bosh," she said to his arguments.

It is also suspended when you switch into the imperative, a rare occurrence in scholarly prose:

Say "Nothing begets nothing" ten times aloud before looking at Elliott's metaphysics.

## Colon–Quote

Use a colon to introduce a quotation only at the end of a sentence. The following example may be technically correct, but it's hideous to look at:

▷ Motley [43] wrote: "As long as he lived, he was the guiding-star of a whole brave nation, and when he died the little children cried in the streets," immortalizing himself as well as William.

Motley [43] immortalized himself as well as William when he wrote: "As long as he lived, he was the guiding-star of a whole brave nation, and when he died the little children cried in the streets."

## Formatted Quotations

What do you do if your quotation crosses a paragraph boundary? Ignore it, unless the paragraphing has a strong impact on the quotation. If it has, display the paragraphs:

> Crayne's tirade continued unabated:
>
> You are the most miserable excuse for a son any father ever felt shame over. You are scarcely human, scarcely an animal.
> You are a stone.

What do you do if your quotation crosses a verse boundary? Use slashes to show the lines in short, inlaid quotations:

> It is difficult to believe that a major poet could write, "Pleasures newly found are sweet / When they lie about our feet."

Display the verses of longer verse quotations:

> The sickly greens at dinner were blamed on the local shop, and the "Song Against Grocers" [19] resulted:
>
> God made the wicked Grocer
> For a mystery and a sign,
> That men might shun the awful shop
> And go to inns to dine.

With complicated poems, you may be able only to approximate, but do the best you can to follow the format of the original. A copy of the original will be more help to a typist or a printer than your version; make a clean photocopy and insert it in your text.

As for other kinds of format, letterheads, titles, captions, headings, and such, display is seldom satisfactory.

▷ It was some time before Voltaire wrote again:

Aix-la-Chapelle

6 February 1770

My dear le Riche:

The number of the wise will always be small. It is true that it has been largely increased, but it is nothing in comparison with the number of fools, and unfortunately they say that God always favors the heaviest battalions.

With a little caginess, you can avoid the problem:

It was the 6th of February 1770 before Voltaire wrote again to le Riche, this time from Aix-la-Chapelle:

The number of the wise . . .

## Changes in Quotations

### Changes You Should Not Show

Occasionally a scrupulous fit will come over a young scholar and produce monstrosities of false conscience. Let's imagine that our scholar is quoting from a passage by Emma Goldman:

Anarchy stands for the liberation of the human mind from the dominion of religion; the liberation of the human body from the dominion of property; liberation from the shackles and restraints of government.

Our scholar produces this:

▷ Goldman's description of anarchy as ". . . the liberation of the human body . . ." referred as much to the wage-earner as to the slave. "[L]iberation from the shackles and restraints of government" meant liberation into the family of humankind, and when she wrote that "[a]narchy stands for the liberation of the human mind . . ." she meant the mind of the factory worker, not the academic.

Not one of those ellipses is needed. The ellipsis is for omission from the middle of a quotation, not from either end. Nor are the brackets around the upper-case "L" and the lower-case "a" necessary. Bringing a quotation into conformity with the quote-cap convention does not constitute altering it, and bracketing such changes looks not punctilious but weird.

Goldman's description of anarchy as "the liberation of the human body" referred as much to the wage-earner as to the slave. "Liberation from the shackles and restraints of government" meant liberation into the family of humankind, and when she wrote that "anarchy stands for the liberation of the human mind" she meant the mind of the factory worker, not the academic.

In quoting titles, you will often need to alter capitalization and punctuation to fit your style; these changes, too, are conventional and need not be set off with brackets. Suppose that you're talking about a journal that styles itself all in capital letters:

▷ *THE AMERICAN HERPETOLOGIST.*
▷ *T[he] A[merican] H[erpetologist].*
  *The American Herpetologist.*

Pushing commas and periods onto the ends of quotations and demoting double quotes to single ones for quotation within quotation are two more conventional changes. Proceed blithely.

## Omission

Show omission from the middle of a quotation with an ellipsis, jocularly known as a dot-dot-dot. These dots are periods. Do not position them above the line; do not substitute asterisks.

The ellipsis is an ugly mark of punctuation, and the conventions of ellipsis owe more to a recognition of this ugliness than to logic.

Here is a passage (from John Wesley's journal) on which to practice ellipsis:

> Thence I rode to Cardiff, and found the society in as ruinous a condition as the castle. The same poison of Mysticism has well-nigh extinguished the last spark of life here also. I preached in the Town-hall, on "Now God commandeth all men every where to repent." There was a little shaking among the dry bones; possibly some of them may yet "come together and live."

Ellipsis from the middle of a sentence:

> The same poison . . . has well-nigh extinguished the last spark of life here also.

For ellipsis from the beginning of a sentence that falls in the middle of your quotation, cap the first word of the rest of the sentence if you want the rest read with sentence intonation:

> The same poison of Mysticism has well-nigh extinguished the last spark of life here also . . . Possibly some of them may yet "come together and live."

Notice that the sentence period evaporates under the influence of the ellipsis:

> ▷   also. . . . Possibly
>     also . . . Possibly

Ellipsis from the end of a sentence that falls in the middle of your quotation:

> I preached in the Town-hall . . . There was a little shaking among the dry bones; possibly some of them may yet "come together and live."

The same three dots indicate an omission of any size:

Thence I rode to Cardiff . . . There was a little shaking among the dry bones; possibly some of them may yet "come together and live."

Never double up on ellipses, no matter how much logic seems to demand it.

Enough John Wesley. Never use an ellipsis at the beginning of your quotation:

▷ Lewis [27] finds at the heart of comedy ". . . the observations of a thing behaving like a person."

Lewis [27] finds at the heart of comedy "the observations of a thing behaving like a person."

Use an ellipsis at the end of your quotation only to show breaking off mid-thought, where the ellipsis means "and so on":

The line is frequently rendered "In the sweat of thy brow shalt thou eat bread," but what we actually have in the King James is "In the sweat of thy face . . ."

In case you happen to see it some time and wonder about it, the ellipsis is sometimes used as a mark of final punctuation to indicate trailing off:

▷ If they only knew what madness lies behind this apparently normal mask . . .

But it's a shabby device and has no place in scholarly prose. Therefore the arrow.

An ellipsis may indicate that you've left out a word, a phrase, a sentence, or a paragraph, and there's no way for your reader to tell how much is gone. It's bad form to use an ellipsis for a large omission; stop the quotation and then start up again:

▷ Harman [14] writes in her memoirs, "The first charge against me was that of stinginess . . . I had discovered that distasteful food presented less hardship to the purse than delicious, well-cooked meals."

Harman [14] writes in her memoirs, "The first charge against me was that of stinginess." She lends some weight to the charge when she boasts in a later chapter, "I had discovered that distasteful food presented less hardship to the purse than delicious, well-cooked meals."

The ugliness of the ellipsis reinforces my contention that you should quote as little as you can to start with and as whole as you can when you do quote. On the other hand, the judiciously placed ellipsis can make the difference between an apt, entertaining quotation and one that meanders off on its own track, ignoring the purpose you had in mind. Use ellipses to help knit quotations firmly into the fabric of your own prose, and only for that reason.

## Alteration

Show alteration within a quotation by bracketing the material that is yours. Your contributions may be addenda or substitutions.

Adding a short explanation is always acceptable:

Darwin then goes on, "I also crossed a bard with a spot [*C. livia*], which is a white bird with a red tail and red spot on the forehead, and which notoriously breeds true."

But a long explanation is better off in a sentence by itself:

▷ The *Missouri Monthly* [24] reports, "Grapes [from which wine is produced in Gasconade and other central and north-central counties] are grown in the Ozark region, and Missouri is second only to California in viticulture."

The *Missouri Monthly* [24] reports, "Grapes are grown in the Ozark region, and Missouri is second only to California in viticulture." Wine is produced from the Ozark grapes in Gasconade and other central and north-central counties.

Brackets also indicate substitutions. You may, for instance, want to substitute a noun for a pronoun. In this example, the original reads "he":

According to Macaulay [22], "In order that [Frederick the Great] might rob a neighbor whom he had promised to defend, black men fought on the coast of Coromandel and red men scalped each other by the Great Lakes of North America."

If the pronoun falls first in the quotation, make your substitution outside:

▷ *Time* said that "[Gorbachev] believes that the party, whatever its internal divisions, still has the most effective organizational structure for promoting reform."

*Time* said that Gorbachev "believes that the party, whatever its internal divisions, still has the most effective organizational structure for promoting reform."

There are other reasons for making substitutions. In descending order of advisability: You may want to alter the syntax of a quotation to fit in with the point you're trying to make. You may wish to replace an unfamiliar word or usage. Or you may wish to correct the author whom you're quoting. Question even the simplest of such substitutions.

For instance, Edwards obviously referred to himself in the first person and in the present tense:

▷ Oliver Edwards told Dr. Johnson that he had "tried too in [his] time to be a philosopher: but [he didn't] know how, cheerfulness was always breaking in."

The use of the brackets is technically correct, but why mangle the quotation? The author reveals no overriding design of her own and should instead have written:

Oliver Edwards told Dr. Johnson, "I have tried too in my time to be a philosopher: but I don't know how, cheerfulness was always breaking in."

Replacing the unfamiliar is all the more questionable. Here the original read "scumble":

▷ "This done," Dugdale says, "he did [soften] the offense with
  pretty words and wailings."

Any such alteration is better handled as an addition than as a
substitution:

> "This done," Dugdale says, "he did scumble [soften] the
> offense with pretty words and wailings."

Trying to correct the author you're quoting is the most dangerous
of all. Here the original used the coy sobriquet "Caledonians":

▷ We read in Chambers [6], "It appears that during these
  events the [Scots] had again become formidable."

Or again, Disraeli said "myself" here where the grammar of reflex-
ives won't permit it:

▷ Disraeli then stepped back, according to observers [16], let
  his hands fall to his sides, and spoke very simply. "Lord
  Salisbury and [I] have brought you back peace—but a peace I
  hope with honor."

The Chambers is no longer quotable once it's been sanitized. Either
conquer your squeamishness and quote it whole or paraphrase it
instead:

> We read in Chambers [6], "It appears that during these
> events the Caledonians had again become formidable."

or

> We read in Chambers that during these events the Scots re-
> gained their strength.

And the alteration of Disraeli's words is outrageous. "Myself" for
"I" or "me" is an error, but an error of a particular kind. It indicates
unsureness, timidity. Disraeli was a stylist; as anyone writing about
him should know, he was perfectly capable of sacrificing grammar
to rhetoric. What was it that made observers say he spoke simply?
His manner, his posture, his tone of voice—and that foxy "myself."

The author who takes it upon herself to correct her betters is on mighty shaky ground.

At the risk of being repetitious: Quote seldom; quote whole.

## Modernization

Quotations for old sources will be easier to read if you modernize difficult punctuation and spelling. The longer the quotation, the more help your reader can use; archaic spellings that seem colorful and charming in a brief quotation become fatiguing in a long one. The mere modernization of spelling and punctuation need not be shown with brackets; an explanation of your policy early in your text (perhaps in a content footnote) covers all cases. Work with a light hand.

This is the moderate position on modernization. Two sterner views exist.

One argues against any modernization whatsoever, invoking the principle of unswerving fidelity to sources and the harsh demands of the scholarly calling. Writers of this persuasion are fond of reproducing photocopied documents for us to read, and the nastier the handwriting the better they like it.

The other view on the subject demands total modernization—no old-fashioned usages, even the ones that are amusing and easy to read; no outdated syntax; no obsolete vocabulary. Proponents of this cause argue that the original author saw nothing colorful in the mechanics of her writing, so neither should we. They regard antiquarian interests as prurient.

Steering between these two extremes requires taste and wit. Your readers will bless you for it. Take as an example a passage from Thomas Dallam's book about his visit to Turkey in 1599. Here is how the alter-nothing school would give it:

▷ Yow ar come hether wythe a presente from our gratious Quene, not to an ordinarie prince or kinge, but to a mightie monarke of the worle, but better had it bene for yow yf it had bene sente to any Christian prince, for then should yow have bene sure to have receaved for yor paines a greate rewarde; but yow muste consider what he is unto whom yow have broughte this ritche presente, a monarke but an infidell, and the grande Enemye to all Christians.

Even for his day, Dallam was a poor hand at spelling. Here is how the alter-all school would give the same passage:

▷ You [have] come [here] with a present from our gracious Queen, not to an ordinary prince or king, but to a mighty monarch of the world. [Still, it would have been better] for you if it had been sent to [a] Christian prince, for then . . . you [would] have been sure to [receive] for your pains a great reward. But you must consider what [kind of person] he is [to] whom you have brought this rich present—a monarch but an infidel, and the [foremost] enemy [of] all Christians.

Midway between the two is this version:

You are come hither with a present from our gracious Queen, not to an ordinary prince or king, but to a mighty monarch of the world. But better had it been for you if it had been sent to any Christian prince, for then should you have been sure to have received for your pains a great reward. [Instead] you must consider what he is unto whom you have brought this rich present—a monarch but an infidel, and the grand Enemy to all Christians.

The object is to retain the flavor that makes the passage worth quoting instead of paraphrasing, and to retain only the flavor, not every gristly bite.

## Americanization

Unfortunately for quoters, there are three small, mechanical issues on which the United States parts company with the rest of the English-speaking world. We have our way of spelling a number of disputed words, our way of abbreviating personal titles, our way of punctuating quotations; they have theirs. Which way should you follow when you quote them? Either, as long as you're consistent.

Suppose you wish to quote the following passage, which illustrates all three differences:

The kerbstone broker delivered up his judgement. 'Our organisation's not up to it, Mr Mawkers', he said sadly. 'It'd be an honour, but the answer's no.'

Here are the points to notice: "kerbstone," "judgement," single quote as the mark of primary quotation, "organisation," "Mr," comma outside the close-quote, "honour." If you decide not to Americanize, you must Americanize nothing. The quotation will look exactly as it does above:

> Ramshaw depicts the scene with his customary gentle humor:
>> The kerbstone broker delivered up his judgement. 'Our organisation's not up to it, Mr Mawkers', he said sadly. 'It'd be an honour, but the answer's no.'

(The quotation qualifies as hard and should be displayed.) If, on the other hand, you decide to Americanize, you must Americanize everything except titles and proper names. "Ageing and the Desire for Immortalisation" is so spelled even when you Americanize; the Centre for Industrialisation is so spelled even when you Americanize; but anything that's not either a title or a proper name gets fixed. The Americanized version of the quotation will look like this:

> Ramshaw depicts the scene with his customary gentle humor:
>> The curbstone broker delivered up his judgment. "Our organization's not up to it, Mr. Mawkers," he said sadly. "It'd be an honor, but the answer's no."

Notice: "curbstone," "judgment," double quote as the mark of primary quotation, "organization," "Mr.," comma inside the close-quote, "honor."

Choose the method you find easier (neither is a breeze) and stick to it through the course of any one paper.

## "Sic"

"Sic" is Latin for "thus." Enclosed in brackets, it is inserted into a quotation after a questionable expression to assure the doubtful reader of its accuracy.

Sperling's daughter wrote an affectionate note to him after his appointment: "You old crumudgeon [sic], give 'em 'ell," she said, and went on to point out such practical details as the new wardrobe that the tropical climate would necessitate.

"Crumudgeon," a small family joke, supports the author's assertion that the communication was affectionate; without the "sic" the reader might assume the word was a typo. This is an unsneering use of "sic."

In general, however, "sic" is hostile. To correct an error in a quotation is merely condescending; to leave it in and sic it is an attack. Be warned, and do not take up arms unknowingly. Avoid using "sic" to show how precise and knowledgeable you are, and above all make sure that the error you point out is really wrong.

> She who sics the blameless phrase
> Hoping she will gather praise
> Makes herself a double fool,
> Wrong and pompous. Mind the rule:
> Sic less, and you won't be sorrier;
> Sic more, and *sic transit gloria*.

If on consideration you choose to slip the gimlet "sic" between the ribs of your enemy's words, go to it. Serious quarrel in high style is one of the joys of the scholarly life.

## "Italics Mine"

One way to fit a quotation to your purposes is to emphasize the part you're most interested in by putting it in italics or underlining it. You must then declare that the emphasis is yours by inserting "italics mine" in brackets at the end of the quotation. Use the expression for both italics and underlining; everyone recognizes the two as interchangeable. That's how to do it; but don't.

Go easy on italics everywhere. They have a thoughtless air about them, an "Oh, I can't be bothered to rework this, I'll just italicize it and let you figure it out." They are ugly to look at and difficult to read. They lend themselves easily to abuse, to attempts at wrenching stress from syntax that won't permit it. These are reasons for questioning any old italics, and adding italics to quotations has other dangers as well. Almost always, you should be paraphrasing or quoting only the part that interests you rather than italicizing. If a pious respect for other writers' words doesn't persuade you, consider the possibilities for unconscious humor:

▷ As late as Hazlitt's time it was still possible for him to write, "You will hear more good things on the outside of *a stagecoach from London to Oxford* than if you were to pass a twelvemonth with the undergraduates, or heads of colleges, of that famous university [italics mine]." So little had the science of equine management advanced that the journey was likely to be made in a single run; the practice was still common of driving horses out to their limit, and eventually to the grave.

The author who unwittingly reveals that Hazlitt's words are no more to her than data for a history of animal husbandry must forgive us if we smile at her. We are all fanatics about our subjects, but we should try to keep fanaticism in check:

As late as 1810 it was still possible to take a stagecoach from London to Oxford [15]. So little had . . .

## Changes in Epigraphs

Choose epigraphs that require no omission or alteration. An epigraph is a cheerful little kite flying over the solid earth of your prose. Don't weigh it down with ellipses and brackets.

## No Brackets

Even in student papers, parentheses may not be used for indicating interpolations into quoted matter. If your keyboard has no brackets, draw them in by hand:

```
Mill believed that "advice, instruction,
persuasion, and avoidance by other
people . . . are the only measures by which
society can justifiably express its dislike or
disapprobation of [an individual's] conduct.
```

# Permission to Quote

In general, you do not need permission to quote for scholarly purposes from published material. Permission to quote from unpublished material is a matter for negotiation, diplomacy, and sometimes law. If you run into difficulty, seek advice from your publisher or from some older, cooler head with experience in your field.

Be aware that most publishers and journals consider getting permission to quote the author's responsibility. A manuscript that lacks permissions may be rejected out of hand because it's too much of a headache to contemplate all the negotiations that would be necessary to publish it.

One of the conditions of permission to quote is usually that you send a copy of your work to the original author; whether or not you're required to, it's always a courteous gesture.

# Other Uses for Quotation Marks

Despite their name, quotation marks have other uses besides marking off quotations, which it seems wise to describe briefly for the sake of completeness.

Quotes and italics are interchangeable for setting off words considered as words:

The "rack" of "rack and ruin" is like "wreck."

Italics are preferable to quotation marks for lists of such words. Sometimes you can avoid either because of the way you construct your sentence. The object is to save your reader from any slight confusion; when no confusion is possible, no quotes or italics are needed:

▷ The infant's first ten words, in order of acquisition, were: "mama," "juice," "airplane," "Jane," "noisy," "kitty," "cracker," "bad," "fan," and "stink."

The infant's first ten words, in order of acquisition, were: mama, juice, airplane, Jane, noisy, kitty, cracker, bad, fan, and stink.

Quotes may set off the first occurrence of an unfamiliar word or expression when a definition follows at some distance:

> Tukey's technique is to "slash" the outlying numbers—to subtract from the positive outliers or add to the negative ones the mean value of the set.

Do not set off the word with quotes after the first occurrence. No quotes are needed when the definition comes immediately after the unfamiliar word:

> Lamport suffered from hidrosis, excessive sweating, which the doctors of the time thought of as a fatal sign.

Quotation marks and expressions like "so-called" and "alleged" are interchangeable (not overlapping) for setting off words used with ironic force:

> Then these "morons" suddenly became able to read and write, to calculate, and to take up school subjects. One of them later became a teacher herself.

Finally, you may see in other people's writing quotation marks used to set off colloquialisms—in other people's writing but not yours. If you use a word, use it wholeheartedly. Don't condescend to it. If it's not a good word, find another.

▷ Margaret showed a marked tendency to "fly off the handle" in these crises.

Why pass on to your reader an expression you feel you have to handle like a dead fish?

> Margaret showed a marked tendency to get excited in these crises.

or

> Margaret showed a marked tendency to fly off the handle in these crises.

In all of these uses, quotation marks follow the standard patterns for fitting in with the punctuation of the surrounding sentence. Periods and commas slide under the close-quotes, other marks stay outside.

## Quotations in Draft

Repeated copying of quotations invites errors. If you are working with a pen or a typewriter, hold off on transcribing a quotation until you're doing your final draft, and then copy it straight from the original. All you need in previous drafts is a reminder about what you intend to quote. If you're working with a computer, make your transcription once, directly from the original, and copy it thereafter.

# The Content Footnote

Although the new way of doing citation and reference jettisons the bibliographic footnote, the content footnote is another story. When you hear the comment "The best part was the footnotes," you can be sure that doesn't mean the ibids and op. cits.

The content footnote can be abused, of course. There are scholars who footnote compulsively, six to the page, writing what amounts to two books at once. There are scholars whose frigid texts need some of the warmth and jollity they reserve for their footnotes and other scholars who write stale, dull footnotes like the stories brought inevitably to the minds of after-dinner speakers. There are scholars who write weasel footnotes, footnotes that alter the assertions in their texts. There are scholars who write feckless, irrelevant footnotes that leave their readers dumbstruck with confusion.

The footnote should never be your first choice for expressing an idea. Integration is a powerful virtue in prose—"seamless masterpiece" didn't get to be a cliché for nothing. Never footnote without first asking yourself whether, with a little more skill and a little more foresight, you might not be able to work the idea into your text.

On the other hand, vitality is a greater virtue than unity any day. The content footnote is an awkward tool, inelegant, all thumbs, but it has the breath of life to it. In many contexts the appearance of a footnote parallels the moment when we draw our chairs closer to a speaker and bend forward: Now we're getting to the good stuff, now we're getting to the heart of it. Clumsy and halting though footnotes undoubtedly are, they've given us too much enlightenment and pleasure for us to turn our back on them now. By using footnotes judiciously you can fill your reader in on general information she lacks, satisfy her curiosity about fine points, whisper delicious tidbits in her ear, and share with her an occasional small frolic.

No scholar should be ignorant of the two classical works on the subject of footnotes:

Robert Benchley.
Shakespeare explained.
In *The Benchley Roundup,* pages 33–35. Harper & Brothers, 1954.
University of Chicago Press edition, 1983.

Frank Sullivan.
A garland of ibids for Van Wyck Brooks.
In Robert P. Falk, editor, *The Antic Muse,* pages 55–58. Grove Press, 1955.
Originally published in *The New Yorker,* 19 April 1941.

## Fundamentals

Footnotes are parentheses. Your text must be grammatically and logically detachable from your footnotes; the footnotes needn't be detachable from the text. Here is a footnote that makes no sense without the text:

and it was Kemble's wish to establish a system so that his letters to Mrs. Siddon* might be preserved against

---

* Who was no mean correspondent herself, her letters for the period 1805–07 alone having been collected in three volumes [27].

While that scarcely merits accolades for beauty, it is acceptable footnote style. But here is an unacceptable footnote, one that the text attempts to depend on:

▷ that Edward Manette and the Duke of Burgundy had done for the sake of the King.* She was of a mind to allow

---

Bad examples are marked with an arrowhead (▷).

---

\* Charles's consort at the time was a bourgeoise, one Amite Duvalle. Her father, a clothier in Amiens, cut her off for the immorality he would certainly have welcomed had the family been of either better or worse birth.

The "she" in the text cannot take its referent from the footnote; the text must read independently. When the error is grammatical, it's fairly easy to catch. But the text must also be logically independent of footnotes. Here is an example of information too important to be relegated to a footnote:

▷ for the thirty-six subjects\* who participated throughout this

---

\* Volunteers predominated in this group. Only two of the conscripts stayed the course.

To slide essential qualifications into a footnote is at best bad form; at worst, dishonesty. Your reader should be able to take your text without the footnotes and understand its weaknesses as well as its strengths. The prospect of making bold statements in text and then correcting them in cautious footnotes tempts some young scholars; in the words of St. Paul, be not deceived.

How long is a footnote? Longer than a word or two, which you could simply slip into your text in parentheses; shorter than half a page. If a footnote threatens to run longer than half a page, do something to it. Perhaps you should incorporate it into your text; perhaps you should turn it into an appendix and mention the appendix in your text; perhaps you've just run away with yourself and what you need to do is cut.

Footnotes should not include tabular material or material with subscripts or superscripts because they will eventually be set tight— single spacing on a typewriter, small type with letter leading (space between the lines) in print, Some people get around this restriction by incorporating their footnotes into their texts and calling them remarks:

although the midmean in this instance is defective.
*Remark:* A correction can be made with $\frac{1}{2} x^2 y^2 z$ in most
cases.

The wing variables remain unstable. Until more of the

Remarks are not so flexible as footnotes—you can't put a remark in the middle of a sentence, where an asterisk or a dagger would do no harm. But they are a handy option to consider if your subject requires fancy notation.

Modest displays can occur in footnotes by means of double-indenting:

> in June on the occasion of the King's official birthday.* His health was beginning to fail and he was

---

> \* No one else liked George either. Byron has a farcical description of him in heaven memorizing the hundredth psalm, and E. C. Bentley wrote the unkind couplet.
>
>> George the Third
>> Ought never to have occurred.

But don't try anything complicated in laying out your footnotes; they will only look chintzy and embarrass you.

Footnotes or endnotes? In the old-fashioned style, when nine out of ten notes were bibliographic, the shift to endnotes made good sense. The reader who had constantly to readjust her eyes for no better reward than a loc. cit. or an ibid. passim was just as happy to have all the notes bunched at the end. With the elimination of the bibliographic note, footnotes come into their own again. Even the tired-eyed, astigmatic reader is happy to glance down from time to time if she knows that your footnotes are informative and amusing and if you don't ask her to do it too often.

"Not too often" is begging the question, of course. How often is too often? Footnotes that could have been gracefully incorporated into your text try your reader's patience; so do footnotes of slim relevance unless they're really funny. A useful corrective to excessive footnoting is financial: A typed page with a footnote on it costs about half again as much as one without. The ratio in printing is not quite so punitive, but if you are doing your own typesetting with a computer system you should be prepared to discover that footnotes are its soft underbelly. There are no absolute standards, but think twice before you decide to footnote.

Citation occurs in footnotes as it does in text, by means of bracketed numbers. These numbers do not carry over from text to footnote, from footnote to text, or from one footnote to the next. If you use the same source for text and footnote, cite it twice:

in the fossil dinoflagellates of the Mesozoic and the Cenozoic [12].* Paleontologists currently think that

---

> \* Ehrenberg also laid the groundwork for later investigations of the acitarchs [12].

The repetition may feel odd to you, but it's necessary. Your reader has no way of knowing that both text and footnote are attributable to the same source unless you tell her so explicitly.

Unlike bracketed numbers, footnote symbols follow punctuation:

▷ until no new geological information\*, no matter how much
until no new geological information,\* no matter how much

## Explanatory Footnotes

### Definitions

Before you footnote a definition, there are two tests to apply. Can you substitute a more familiar term?

▷ his paronomastic\* facility resulted in his being asked

---

> \* Word-shunting, making jocular or suggestive use of similarity between different words or of a word's different senses.

his facility at puns resulted in his being asked to give

The line between linguistic exuberance and showing off is narrow, but it should be observed. If you cannot replace the term, can you incorporate the definition into your text?

▷ converting the semivowels\* to true consonants in all

---

> \* The letters *w* and *y*.

converting the semivowels, the letters *w* and *y*, to true consonants in all but the heightened speech of the class

Use footnotes only to define irreplaceable terms and only when the definitions cannot be fitted into your text:

▷ down the Ophel* in the direction of the Pool of the Cap

---

  * A swelling on the southern slope of the Mount of the Temple—a long, narrow, rounded spur between the mouth of the central valley of Jerusalem and the Kidron.

Definitions must occur at the first use of the term, not later:

▷ reverted to the terza rima* in his version of the classical

---

  * Lines of five iambic feet with an extra syllable rhymed *aba, bcb, cdc,* and so on. The last tercet is usually converted by an extra line into a quartet, *yzyz,* to avoid leaving a line unrhymed.

The clue here is "reverted" in the text; if you catch yourself defining a term midstream, you must search back for the first use and insert the definition there.

## Equivalent Measures

In dealing with unfamiliar measures and coinage, you should always help your reader get her bearings. Don't, however, automatically reach for a footnote. Sometimes you can simply substitute a more familiar term:

▷ indented a mut quad* on either side and leaded out to

---

  * A variable unit of measure the width of the capital *M* in the alphabet under consideration.

▷ indented an em on either side and leaded out to a full

Sometimes you can work an explanation into your text:

▷ swigging pint* after pint of home brew. They turned

---

  * The imperial pint is twenty ounces.

    swigging pint after pint of home brew—and the imperial pint is twenty ounces. They turned the evening

Reserve footnotes for complicated explanations. Coinage, for instance, seldom lends itself to facile equivalents:

> paid for with three solidi* and delivered to her home

---

\* Estimates of the value of the solidus vary from three dollars [14] to twenty-five dollars [36]. One solidus was enough to buy food for the family of a freed slave for a day [28] but not enough to pay for Orideon's reading the omens [19].

## Identifications

Footnotes can identify minor figures in your cast of characters, especially those who make only one appearance:

> engaged to Gerta Kirchhoff* only the year before. A shameless flirt, he had some impact on the life of the

---

\* Gerta Kirchhoff (1824–87), German physicist who, with Robert Bunsen, developed spectrum analysis. She never recovered from Sandor's jilting her and made him another offer of marriage after the death of his second wife, when they were both in their seventies.

> figures such as Torelli* who were better known at court

---

\* Pompeo Torelli (1539–1608), Italian dramatist. His *Merope* (1589), the first treatment of this subject, was later taken up by Voltaire and Matthew Arnold.

## Translations

In order to satisfy all your readers, you should, in general, provide both the original and a translation for any passage you quote that was written in a language other than English. Omit the original only when it is of no literary or linguistic interest; omit the translation only for student papers or manuscripts circulating in draft among your colleagues. Never omit the translation in anything that's being published. (An exception might be made for a foreign tag or a pun or joke.)

Footnotes are the best way to meet this obligation. It's up to you whether to put the original in the text and the translation in a footnote or vice versa.

Ma 'l suon che di dolcezza i sensi lega,
col gran desir d'udendo esser beata,
L'anima, al dipartir presta, raffrena.*

---

* In Hilbertson's translation [26]:
    But to my joy-besotted soul the sound
Carries a hope for heaven now
And holds my soul earth-bound.

the words of the Secret, "so that it may become acceptable by
her merits, in whose honor it is offered."* The tradition of
mediation is very powerfully felt in

---

* "Ut in cujus honore solemniter exhibetur, ejus meritis efficiatur accep-
    tum."

If the translation is your own, you needn't give a citation for it
unless you've published it elsewhere.


## Glosses

Brief glosses on prose quotations fit well into the text if you enclose
them in brackets; use footnotes only for lengthy glosses.

wrote, "It seems, Mother [Mrs. Bixler, his stepmother], that
the time has come for me to set out again on my own and

said, "The redeemed language* of the speeches she gave to

---

* Allenby seems to use this expression in a causal way, with no reference to
    the technical terminology of Augustinian criticism.

Even very short glosses on poetry or verse should appear as footnotes:

It shall not touch, with breath of bale,
The pleasance* of our fairy-tale.

---

* Alice Liddell's middle name was Pleasance.

You make me marvel wherefore ere this time
Had you not fully laid my state* before me

That I might so have rated my expense
As I had leave of means

---

* Variant *place*.

The same is true of glosses on tables and graphs. Here the population of the whole table except one entry is twenty:

| 13.44 | 13.22 | 8.19 | 12.65 | 13.19 |
| 10.81 | 9.37 | 10.13 | 9.91 | 10.12 |
| 4.66* | 10.87 | 9.49 | 10.14 | 11.59 |

---

* $N = 15$.

## Special Notation

Do not combine footnote symbols with special notation. Put explanations of special notation in your text, not in footnotes:

$\triangleright$ $\sigma(f)^* = \{\, h \mid \text{for all } x \text{ in } C^+ \; h(x) = \text{o iff } f(x) = \text{o} \,\}$

---

* The operator $\sigma$ (said "sameroots") represents the case where we need to know only whether $f(x)$ is zero.
†C denotes the set of complex numbers.

$\sigma(f) = \{\, h \mid \text{for all } x \text{ in } C, \; h(x) = \text{o iff } f(x) = \text{o} \,\}$
The operator $\sigma$ (said "sameroots") represents the case where we need to know only whether $f(x)$ is zero. C denotes the set of complex numbers.

## Enlargement

The use of footnotes for detail usually results from the attempt to write for two audiences at one time. The general reader, our scholar reasons, is interested in results; the specialist is interested in method. So, put the results in the text and the method in footnotes, have your cake and eat it too.

There are people who can pull this trick off perfectly, and others who muck it up. What are the guidelines for success?

First of all, these footnotes must only enlarge, never mitigate. To make flat statements in your text and then qualify and soften them in footnotes is to treat the general reader with a contempt she readily identifies and returns.

Second, this use for footnotes precludes all the other explanatory uses. If you think about it, all of the other explanatory footnotes are intended to lend a hand to the reader who lacks specialized knowledge. Intermingling these with footnotes intended to segregate specialized knowledge is confusing and disruptive. If you want to use footnotes for information of interest only to your colleagues, you must incorporate all your helps to the general reader into your text. Begin your first footnote with an explanation of the scheme you intend to follow: "The footnotes in this article are meant for specialists." That way both kinds of readers know what to expect and can proceed intelligently.

## The Footnote Aside

The best-loved footnote is the aside—the tidbit, the comment, the sidelight, the joke. Most of the delight of these footnotes comes from their context and their content, but it is possible to give a few general tips.

Avoid the cultivation of a schizophrenic style. The author of the text and the author of the footnotes should be recognizably the same person. Picture the desiccated scholar who raises her eyes from the crumbling yellow pages of her notes, peers dimly over her glasses, smiles a vague, wan smile—and suddenly turns a cartwheel. Her audience is disconcerted and distressed. Young scholars sometimes adopt an artificially prim style in their texts and then, in their footnotes, let their natural high spirits get the best of them. Neither the lackluster text nor the frenzied footnote is a goal to strive after, and the combination of the two is dreadful.

Length should continue to serve as a rough guideline for whether a remark belongs in the text or a footnote. An aside of a word or a phrase or a short sentence belongs in the text, often in parentheses. Save your footnotes for longer excursions, remembering that consciousness is everywhere a virtue, but especially in jest.

Don't pull your punches. Avoid all introductions if you can; avoid like the plague introductions that use the impersonal pronoun and the passive voice:

▷ which the downward-sloping demand* seems to require in

_____

* One is irresistibly reminded of Anthony Hope's "Economy is going without something you do want in case you should, some day, want something you probably won't want."

which the downward-sloping demand* seems to require in

_____

* "Economy is going without something you do want in case you should, some day, want something you probably won't want"—Anthony Hope.

The aside, like the epigraph, should not be weighted down with heavy, irrelevant citations. If you're quoting someone in an aside, give a brief, unscholarly description of the source and let it go at that.

## The Acknowledgment

A special use for the footnote aside is to thank a colleague who's done you a good turn. Help on an entire manuscript is usually acknowledged in a section at the beginning or at the end of the text, but help on a single point can be mentioned in a footnote.

It is virtually impossible to express gratitude without using the first-person singular. You will only sound stilted and unappreciative if you try:

▷ possibly by olfactory clues.* When male pairs are joined

_____

* This suggestion was first brought to the author's attention by Gretchen Pritchard, whose assistance is acknowledged with appreciation.

possibly by olfactory clues.* When male pairs are joined

_____

* My thanks to Gretchen Pritchard for this suggestion.

## The Quibble

An important use for footnote asides is segregating quibbles. It's unattractive to clutter up your text with split hairs; finick in your footnotes:

*Debutante,* with Rex Harrison.* Her subsequent career

---

* Harrison was born in 1908 and christened Reginald Carey, not "Reginald Cary" [13], not "Reginald Carew" [26], and certainly not "Rex Carew" [18].

The only trouble I foresee about this advice is that all the mean-spirited, jesuitical fussbudgets I have ever known always see themselves as perfectly reasonable, just a little more fastidious than the common run of persons, that's all. Relegating quibbles to your footnotes requires that you recognize them.

## Footnotes in Draft

If you are doing your own typesetting, this is the time to find out whether your typesetting system handles footnotes automatically the way you want it to. If it doesn't, don't attempt to coerce it; go out and get another.

If somebody else is doing your typesetting for you, do not use any footnoting features your word-processing software may provide. The best system for handling footnotes in draft is to run them in with your text, double-spaced, marking the division with bars:

helped Heath with his work.* Bennett was at the end

---

* Major General Heath's chief preoccupation at this time was a proclamation on sniping during the invasion. The manuscript survives in a dozen drafts, which must have taken weeks of Bennett's time. The invasion never took place and the famous proclamation never saw the light of day.

of his patience with his family, and his financial situation was endangered by the Army's peculiar

Signal draft footnotes with the following symbols in order, starting over on each new page:

* † # ** †† ##

Avoid signaling a footnote with a symbol you're using for some other purpose. If you're using the asterisk to talk about Kleene* (a mathematical function; the name is pronounced, whimsically, cleanie-star), banish the asterisk from your list of footnote signals— even if Kleene* appears on only one page of your text.

# Scholarly
# Peculiarities

The list that follows is neither exclusive nor comprehensive. Other kinds of writing share many of the failings described here, though they turn up more often in scholarly prose; and scholars have, heaven knows, other faults than these. But even so sketchy and incomplete a listing owes a debt to the masters. It would be churlish to neglect to thank them and irresponsible to fail to recommend them to you.

Since Oxford University Press first published H. W. Fowler's *A Dictionary of Modern English Usage* in 1926, the book has been the stern teacher and kindly guide to all who wish to write well. What can I say about Fowler? What can the minnow say in praise of the whale? Go out and buy a copy today, read through one letter a week, and in half a year you will have made a friend for life.

And then there's the little book, *The Elements of Style* by William Strunk, Jr., and E. B. White (Macmillan, 1959, and in print ever since). If you are condemned to a desert island and allowed only one book to help with composing notes to send out to sea in bottles, choose Fowler. If you're allowed another, take Strunk and White.

Fowler never treats words as fetishes; Strunk and White seldom do. But most other people who give advice on writing attach totemic significance to individual lexical items, often summoning up a dark vision of the end of the English language if this or that word changes its meaning or means something that they don't want it to mean or gets used in some way they don't want it to be used. Young writers who fall into the clutches of these word-fetishists often develop a special form of writer's block, one in which every sentence appears to be a minefield of potential usage errors. An excellent corrective to this frame of mind is Thomas Creswell's

*Usage in Dictionaries and Dictionaries of Usage* (American Dialect Society, University of Alabama Press, 1975). Creswell on usage-mongers is brilliant and scathing. If you read his monograph, you will enjoy a good laugh and breathe easier thereafter.

It's hard to think about the construction of a sentence if you don't know the names of its parts; a grammar can teach you those names. In 1990 Collins, an English publisher, brought out John Sinclair's *Collins COBUILD English Grammar,* a radically new grammar based on the analysis of a huge corpus of machine-readable text. The book has two disadvantages: It's intended for people who are learning English as a second language, and it's English English, not American English. But its virtues far outweigh these difficulties. The book is grounded in the actual practice of people who write and speak English rather than in hypothetical questions about what we might be able to say if we tried. And its emphasis on production—when you want to express this, try putting it this way—gives it a cheerful, muscular tone. I do not yet know it as well as I intend to, but I know it well enough to urge you to get a copy for yourself.

# The Abstract Abstract

The purpose of an abstract is to summarize, not to tease. Many authors find it painful to trot their results out naked before the world; they want to seduce, to captivate, to tantalize. What results is the abstract of the seven veils:

▷ An advance in the definition of certain operators is made possible by the application of several recent results in complexity. Full details are supplied, and illustrative examples are included. Data on related findings are presented in the final section along with implications for further research.

In other words, what's in this paper is a secret. A good abstract should be concrete:

---

Bad examples are marked with an arrowhead (▷).

The operators Shift, Reply, and VVX [5,14,9] are not so weak as they first seemed. An application of Browning's Theorem [2] and his more recent work on conjunctivity [1,3,4] suggests that these operators impose hidden constraints on their members, which may constitute a uniform but as yet undefined set.

Notice that an abstract can use pointers to your reference list; an abstract published separately from the paper it abstracts can have its own short reference list.

## Acknowledgments

Not even the most heartfelt sentiment can survive stale language. Many an advisor before yours has been thanked for understanding and guidance, many a colleague for useful contributions, many an assistant for accuracy and neatness, many a spouse for patience. Not one has escaped gratitude for services above and beyond the call of duty.

As always, specificity is the best cure for cliché. Yes, your advisor was, like all others, kind, helpful, firm, and encouraging; but who else suggested a way out of the bind you got yourself into in chapter 6? Yes, your spouse was, like everyone else's, stoic, Job-like, and emotionally and financially supportive; but who else coded up your recursive functions?

▷ I am also grateful to my colleagues Paula Hibbin and John Hershberger for their helpful comments.

I am also grateful to Paula Hibbin for telling me about the work of the Syracuse group and to John Hershberger for finding over a hundred typographical errors in my manuscript.

## "Among" and "Between"

There's an old rule of thumb that "between" is for two and "among" is for three or more.

As rules of thumb go, it's not a bad one. I divide each cupcake between two children but the cookies among all six of them. Margaret and I have a secret between us; Mark and Margaret and I have one among us.

As a description of the distinctions we actually make, however, the rule of thumb leaves much unsaid. I can sit between two lakes but not among three of them. An object in a room is between the floor and the ceiling, but it is not among the four walls. There's a difference between two things but not among three of them. And an agreement might be either among or between three people, depending on its nature.

Both "between" and "among" can be used to talk about space and about abstract relationships; only "between" can be used to talk about time.

When we're talking about space and we mean two, we say "between two" rather than plain "between":

▷ The house stands between farms.

The house stands between two farms.

When we're talking about space and we say "among" with no number, we mean "surrounded by," not just "among more than two." If an advertisement says, "The house stands among farms," and around it there are three farms and fifty-six tract houses, the "among" is false advertising. Nobody ever actually says:

▷ The house stands among three farms.

We use some other form: The house has three farms around it; the house stands between two farms and in front of a third; the house has farms on three sides—whatever. Or we use "between":

The house stands between three farms.

When we use these prepositions to talk about abstract relationships, "between" specifies one-to-one relations, "among" specifies many-to-many or many-to-one relations. Thus when there are only two members, "between" is the only possible word. When there are more than two, however, the two words stress two different things. "Between" stresses the relationships of the members to one another:

*A* with *B, A* with *C, B* with *A, B* with *C, C* with *A, C* with *B*. "Among" stresses the relationship of the members to what's in common: *A, B,* and *C* all stand in the same relationship to *X.*

> The only hope for reunification was a series of treaties between Germany, Poland, and Czechoslovakia.

> Germany, Poland, and Czechoslovakia agreed among themselves to ignore the question of refugees.

"Between" is the word for the meaning "under threat of inundation by" regardless of number. We say, "Between cooking and cleaning, I haven't had time to eat" but also "Between cooking and cleaning and washing and ironing and sending the mail, I still haven't had time to eat." "Among" is not English in this construction. But I remember seeing a very graceful writer once retain the echo of duality in this "between" by using a series of pairs as its object: "Between government and conquest, literature and the arts, fashion and gourmandism, Louis might appear to have little time left for Madame de Maintenon."

What about using "between" for only one thing? If you examine these sentences closely, you'll discover that the object of "between" is singular in both cases:

▷ They've put a lighted driveway between every house in that subdivision.

▷ You can choose between staying here or going home in somebody else's car.

"Between every" and "between all" work well in spoken English, but not in writing. Editing them, however, seems hard. I have seen practiced writers change "every" to "each," or "between" to "among," or both, and then scratch their heads over the resulting mess.

The problem seems to be that the original version is quite some distance away from the edited one:

> They've put a lighted driveway between every two houses in that subdivision.

Now, that's only one word and one suffix different from "between every house," but the mental distance is obviously much more. Introspection leads me to believe that when we say "between every house" we're picturing some kind of continuous interweaving of houses and driveways. It's a leap to get from there to the realization that the same relationship can be seen as filling the interstices between pairs, and it's a conceptual leap, not a linguistic leap.

The fix for "between $x$ or $y$" is not hard to make: Change the "or" to "and." But there are complications when the members contain compounds, and there are complications when you want emphasis.

▷ You can then choose between PF and PIE and AF and AIE.

Unless your reader already knows what you mean, she's unlikely to understand it from that sentence. The colloquial solution is economical:

You can then choose between PF and PIE or AF and AIE.

If you're in a situation where the colloquial solution won't do, you'll have to sweat a bit:

You can then choose between, on the one hand, both PF and PIE and, on the other, both AF and AIE.

or

PF and PIE represent one choice; AF and AIE, the other.

or

There are two choices: PF and PIE; AF and AIE.

# Bending Over Backwards

Most of us had, in the sixth or seventh grade, a schoolteacher who tried to give us "grammar." Either she didn't know what she was talking about or we were fooling around and looking out the window, because there are several errors common in otherwise educated writing that seem to result from her teaching. Distinctions have been garbled, and a mystical significance attaches to some words.

## "As" for "Like"

Yes, you must not use "like" for "as":

▷ Blottoes smoke good like a cigarette had ought to.

That is the uneducated error you were warned against. But the educated error, "as" for "like," is just as bad:

▷ In their haste and confusion, the city officials were acting as children.

If the word links to a noun or a pronoun, it's "like"; if it links to a whole clause, it's "as." Here's the case with a noun or pronoun:

> In their haste and confusion, the city officials were acting _____ children.
>
> children = noun
>
> In their haste and confusion, the city officials were acting like children.

And here's the case with a clause:

> In their haste and confusion, the city officials were acting _____ children do.
>
> children do = clause
>
> In their haste and confusion, the city officials were acting as children do.

But notice that "as . . . do" is nothing more than a dodge for the dreaded "like."

## "If It Were" for "If It Was"

There are two kinds of conditional clauses, simple conditions and conditions contrary to fact. Constructions of the "were/had been" variety are used only for conditions contrary to fact. Test the clause in question by adding an imaginary parenthetical statement of fact. If the parenthesis begins with "but," the condition is contrary to fact; if the parenthesis begins with "maybe," the clause is a simple condition. Here's the case where the parenthesis begins with "but":

> If there _____ no alternative to interviews, we would have gone ahead with that lengthy and inaccurate technique.

> If there _____ no alternative to interviews (but there was)—condition contrary to fact.

> If there were no alternative to interviews, we would have gone ahead with that lengthy and inaccurate technique.

And here's the case where it begins with "maybe":

> If there _____ no chance for appeasement, Talleyrand had a plan for victory.

> If there _____ no chance for appeasement (maybe there was, maybe there wasn't)—simple condition.

> If there was no chance for appeasement, Talleyrand had a plan for victory.

## "May" for "Can"

Yes, it's "may" rather than "can" for granting permission:

▷ Can I eat a piece of cake?

I can hear my grandfather's voice. "Oh yes, you can. You have a mouth, tongue, teeth, a good digestive system. Certainly you can. You *may* not."

But the words are linked in another way that has nothing to do with let and license. "Can" is at one end of the continuum of possibility, with no nuance:

> The normal child of six can handle a spoken vocabulary of about fifteen hundred words.

"May" is somewhere in the middle; it has a "maybe" or a "perhaps" built into it:

She may read as many as two hundred words.

At the far end, "might" is dubious; it suggests that the chances are fifty-fifty or less:

She might even write her own name.

It's important, then, when you're talking about possibility rather than permission, to reexamine the knee-jerk preference for "may." Using it in place of "can" casts doubt on perfectly straightforward statements:

▷ The reader may find a fuller explanation of irreducibility in chapter 4.

Can she or can't she? Surely there shouldn't be any doubt.

If you've been so traumatized that any "can," even a blameless one, gives you the jimjams, remember that "will" is at the same end of the continuum.

The reader can find a fuller explanation of irreducibility in chapter 4.

or

The reader will find a fuller explanation of irreducibility in chapter 4.

### "Well" for "Good"

Yes, the use of "good" as an adverb is a vulgar error:

▷ That kid sure done good.

But the use of "well" as an adjective for anything but health is the educated version of the error:

▷ It would be well for us to examine these assumptions more closely.

The copula—the verb "to be" and its analogs—link their subjects with adjectives, not adverbs. Test the verb in question. If it's analogous to "be" or "seem," it's a copula, and you need the adjective, "good"; if the verb is analogous to "do," you need the adverb, "well." Here's the case with a copula:

As a result, she sounded very _____ that night.

"sounded," like "seemed"—a copula

As a result, she sounded very good that night.

(Of course, if you meant she sounded healthy, you would say "sounded well"; we're thinking about the "well" that contrasts with "badly," not the one that contrasts with "sick.") Here's the case with a verb that's not a copula:

As a result, she sang very _____ that night.

"sang," like "did"—a copula

As a result, she sang very well that night.

So you can correct "well" for "good" by substituting "good":

It would be good for us to examine these assumptions more closely.

Or you can keep "well" and attach it to a verb that's not a copula:

We would do well to examine these assumptions more closely.

## "Whom" for "Who"

This is my favorite bending-over-backward mistake, because I went to a school where we were required to render the cheer "Two, four, six, eight, whom do we appreciate?" Yes, "who" for "whom" is a mistake, but the reverse is worse:

▷ There was a good deal of speculation as to whom the representatives appointed from the wards with elections in dispute might be.

▷ Mallowby spoke for the justice of the cause of the Pretender, whom, as he averred, everyone in the kingdom knew was honest, modest, and wise.

To tell "who" from "whom," you need to work out what role the word is playing in the smallest enclosing clause. Here are a group of fake sentences demonstrating all the possible roles. Subject (the smallest enclosing clause is "who does it"):

She is the one who does it.

Direct object (the smallest enclosing clause is "whom we need"):

She is the one whom we need.

Another kind of direct object—here the verb in the smallest enclosing clause ("whom we call 'Red'") takes two objects, one of them our "who"/"whom" word and the other an objective complement (also known as a predicate objective):

She is the one whom we call "Red."

Here it's the indirect object; "gave" is the verb, "the award" is the direct object, and "whom we gave the award" is the smallest enclosing clause:

She is the one whom we gave the award.

Here it's the object of a preposition; "to" is the preposition and "to whom we gave it" or "whom we gave it to" the smallest enclosing clause:

She is the one to whom we gave it.

or

She is the one whom we gave it to.

Here it's the complement of a copula (a.k.a. a predicate nominative); "might be" is the copula and the smallest enclosing clause is "who it might be":

She is the one who it might be.

Here it's the subject of an infinitive; "to go" is the infinitive and the smallest enclosing clause is "whom we want to go":

She is the one whom we want to go.

That's it—those are all the cases.

Of course, most of these examples are thoroughly fake. We don't actually talk that way. If you walk around saying things like "She is the one whom we gave the award," either you are a foreigner who has received very bad advice or you suffer from severe gastric distress. In short sentences we usually delete the "who"/"whom" word if we can: "She is the one we need," "She is the one we want to go." In speech, we use "who" regardless of the construction if the word is fronted, placed first in the smallest enclosing clause: "She is the one who we gave it to." Only in rather formal writing do we maintain the "who"/"whom" word even when it could be deleted; only in rather formal writing do we use fronted "whom."

So when we do engage in formal writing, we haven't many instincts to guide us. It's easy to focus on identifying the smallest enclosing clause when you should really be thinking of something else:

▷ There was a good deal of speculation as to whom the representatives appointed from the wards with elections in dispute might be.

The main clause of the sentence is "there was speculation." "As to" etc. is a prepositional phrase modifying "speculation." "Who/whom the representatives" etc. is a noun clause that's the object of the preposition "as to." "The representatives" is the subject of that noun clause; "might be" is the verb, and it's a copula; "who" or "whom" is the complement . . .

No. No! Correcting "whom" to "who" is not the answer to a convoluted, misshapen sentence. The answer is rewriting.

The wards with elections in dispute were to have representatives appointed, and there was a good deal of speculation as to who the representatives might be.

# Capitalization

Is it because so many of our scholarly folkways are German in origin that scholars tend to overcapitalize? The names of academic disciplines do not need capitals unless they are being used as shorthand for administrative departments. So we have:

> Geology and Geophysics is at war with Biology over the lecture hall at the end of the corridor.

but

> No discovery in geology and geophysics has had greater impact on the lives of ordinary people.

The use of capitals to personify and solemnize rapidly becomes tedious:

> ▷ Thus Art, her raiment torn and bedraggled, once more took up the Sword against the traitor Craft.

Most nouns and adjectives derived from proper names lose their capitals; to retain them is pedantic:

> ▷ Lamport ate his way noisily through an entire tray of Napoleons and fell asleep.

A sound, conservative dictionary is your best guide to the use of capital letters. (I'd recommend the Random House 2nd.) Articles ("a," "an," and "the") are capitalized at the beginnings of sentences, sentence quotations, and titles. They are not capitalized when they attach to proper nouns:

> ▷ This work was supported by a grant from The National Science Foundation.

> This work was supported by a grant from the National Science Foundation.

# The Cliché Redivivus

There is a certain kind of dry, scholarly humor that delights in tinkering with saws and sayings:

> George was unable to see the European forest for the English oak.

> In the conference on metrification, Lavoisier was every inch a diplomat—or, as it became, every centimeter.

I have nothing against this practice; it tickles me. But if you too enjoy it, remember that a little goes a long way and beware of twisting your exposition out of shape just for the chance of getting off a good one.

# Coherence

Some scholars seem to distrust ordinary discourse coherence. Every sentence, every fresh clause, must begin with a connective: thus, thence, whence, whither, therefore, hence, and, then, so, again. In advanced cases you get combinations: "And so, then, these results are therefore . . ." If you have fallen into this habit, try excising all connectives and then restore only those you need for emphasis. Take it as a general rule that no sentence is allowed to fly off from its predecessor willy-nilly. If it has taken flight, no amount of glue in the form of adverbs and conjunctions will hold it down.

# The Colonated Title

Pick a scholarly work, any scholarly work. What's its title? Something-something, *colon*, something-something-something. Am I right? The use of title and subtitle is justified by the desire to be both catchy and precise:

> *Nose to the Grindstone: A Life of Arnold Bennett.*

Setting a context is another justification:

> The Manley Clinic sleep treatment: A study of drug abuse
> among physicians.

But the habit can become so ingrained that scholars reach for colons
automatically where none are needed:

▷ The economy of the French capital: Paris, 1750–1800.

  The economy of Paris, 1750–1800.


## Conclusions

Begin at the beginning and go on till you come to the end; then stop.
That's excellent advice, and every scholar should heed it. There is
no rule of composition that says you must end with a summary of
everything that's come before—honestly there isn't. The mark of a
good summary is revelation: "Remember this, reader? And that?
Well, here's how they fit together." If you have revealed all before
you start to summarize, then stop.


## Emphasis

Because so much scholarly writing is calm, deliberate, and mea-
sured, some scholars overdo it when they want to be forceful. The
ideal is for all emphasis to be structural, none mechanical—for the
shape and motion of your sentences to carry your stress all by
themselves. When you feel yourself itching for italics or an underline, look first to see whether the passage shouldn't be rewritten:

▷ During this phase, some of the internal *and external* stimuli
  to which the females were exposed affected their behavior.

  During this phase, both internal and external stimuli affected
  the females' behavior.

or

During this phase, some of the internal stimuli to which the females were exposed affected their behavior, but external stimuli also began to affect them.

or

External as well as internal stimuli began to affect the females' behavior.

When you must italicize, choose a key word or two; italicizing a whole passage actually de-emphasizes it by making it more difficult to read:

▷ The student should realize that *the fundamental bias of this work is theoretical* and that *applications are merely sketched, not worked out in detail.*

The student should realize that the fundamental bias of this work is *theoretical* and that applications are merely sketched, not worked out in detail.

(Better yet, do away with italics altogether.)

Underlining and italics are interchangeable conventions for emphasis. Total caps, on the other hand, should never be used for stress:

▷ This approach is the WORST possible and induces fluctuations beyond the capacity of most measuring instruments.

(Use italics or an underline, or do away with the mechanical emphasis altogether and let the sentence stand on its own.) Capitalizing "the" or "a" for stress is a barbarism:

▷ Elizabeth was, after all, The Queen, and her mere motion was sufficient for the deed.

(Use an underline or italics if you insist, but be aware that the effect is paltry.)

Except in the rendering of dialog, exclamations are rare in writing, and scholarly writing is the least exclamatory of all. Adding an exclamation point to a plain declarative sentence makes it not emphatic but pathetic:

▷ There has been, up to now, no complete account of the acquisition and disposition of some 216 millions of acres of public
   lands in Texas!

(Start the sentence with "surprisingly" and end it with a period;
better yet, ask yourself whether it really is such a surprise.) If you
are ever in doubt about whether a sentence merits an exclamation
mark, try shouting it out the window. There will be virtually no
correct uses in scholarly writing.

## "Hopefully"

The story on "hopefully" is one of the strangest in modern English.
   "Hopeful" has had two senses ever since it first appeared in the
language late in the 16th century. A person could be hopeful (expectant, eager, desirous); or a situation could be hopeful (promising,
auspicious, bright).
   As with most adjectives, both of these "hopeful"s regularly produced "-ly" adverbial forms, but the kind of hopefulness that means
expectant and eager produced adverbs more readily than the kind
that means promising and bright. There's nothing mysterious about
that difference in frequency. A person can carry herself hopefully or
eye a desirable object hopefully or prepare herself hopefully for a
possible future. Impersonal substantives, on the other hand, serve
less often than personal ones at the head of the kind of active verbs
we modify with adverbs of manner. Nonetheless, a wager can be
shaping up hopefully; a day can begin hopefully; the omens can
augur hopefully. All perfectly straightforward and normal. The first
OED citation for "hopefully" in this second sense is from 1637.
   Early in the 1930s, this second sense of "hopefully" began to
appear in a different kind of construction, as what's called a sentence adverb. Sentence adverbs are part of a class of expressions that
can modify whole clauses; such expressions are called absolutes.
Look at some sentence adverbs at work:

Interestingly, most mathematicians failed to notice the correspondence.

Presumably he knows what he's doing.

Regrettably there is no remedy for this kind of infection

Fortunately we managed to get out before he noticed us.

Hopefully the weather will clear up before it's time to leave.

Then in the early 1960s attacks against "hopefully" began to appear in print.

The attacks were by and large astoundingly ill-informed. Some managed to convey that it was "hopefully" as a sentence adverb to which they were opposed but lacked the technical vocabulary with which to express the idea. Some opposed both "hopeful" and "hopefully" in the sense promising(ly), auspicious(ly), bright(ly). Most bizarre of all, some took it upon themselves to oppose all sentence adverbs.

The authors of these attacks presented themselves as defenders of the purity of the language against the onslaught of wicked barbarians. They asserted (apparently without ever feeling the need to check the evidence) that the objects of their attack were very recent additions to the language—true in the case of "hopefully" as a sentence adverb, but not true at all of impersonal "hopeful" and "hopefully," and completely zany when it comes to sentence adverbs in general. (In five minutes with the *OED* I was able to find "certainly" being used as a sentence adverb in 1300.) One came to see that these self-proclaimed language defenders knew nothing of even the most elementary tools of the trade.

So, what should we do? Ignore the ignorant bully-boys or knuckle under?

When I was young I once attended a school at which one group of girls declared that anyone who wore yellow on Thursday was a freak. The rest of us recognized the interdict as arbitrary, irrational, and mean. Its only purpose was to wound. We talked about it among ourselves, and we tried to fire ourselves up to wear yellow on the fatal day. But there were sixteen lonely hours between last study hall on Wednesday and getting dressed Thursday morning. Nobody owned very many items of yellow clothing anyway; quite likely they were already in the laundry. And yellow's not a flattering color in the morning light. Not at all flattering. Tends to make the wearer look green.

I moved in the middle of the year, so I have no idea whether some brave child eventually wore a yellow blouse, or yellow socks, or a yellow handkerchief to that school on a Thursday. Hopefully there was more than one; hopefully the girls who laid down the original rule saw how jaunty the rebels looked in their yellow outfits; hopefully—oh, devoutly to be hoped—they all became best friends and behaved beautifully to one another and never did anything petty or malicious again as long as they lived.

# Hyperqualification

Most scholarly prose is hedged round with caution and qualification, as well it should be; the world of scholarship is no place for hysterical exaggeration. But doubling and tripling up on qualifications gives your writing the texture of an unmolded custard, soft and runny at the edges. To be both accurate and forceful requires ingenuity:

▷ Many of the members of the sample population showed some tendency in the direction of being not very stable.

The sample tended toward instability.

▷ One of the chief preoccupations of most if not all of the representatives was the likelihood of some kind of reform in a rather short time.

Reform was in the wind.

▷ It is almost certain that the greater number of the semiconductors will eventually prove to be of almost no commercial value, but for many the strong possibility remains that they will seem rather interesting to the theoretician and continue for some time to attract a great deal of attention in many laboratories.

Most semiconductors may be useless, but they are fascinating.

Two qualifiers require special attention, "relatively" and "comparatively." In sentences where the terms of the comparison are stated, they are redundant:

▷ The interest of the older children was relatively greater and more sustained.

The interest of the older children was greater and more sustained.

▷ Nitzler was comparatively inexperienced for a district official.

Nitzler was inexperienced for a district official.

In sentences with no terms of comparison, they are meaningless:

▷ Knowlton had hit on a relatively inexpensive solution to the problem.

Relative to what?

Knowlton had hit on an inexpensive solution to the problem.

or

Knowlton had hit on a solution to the problem that cost less than any previous solution, but it was still too expensive to put into production.

or

Knowlton had hit on a fairly inexpensive solution.

Correct, sensible uses for these words are few and far between.


# Hyphens

The car. The car body. The car body repair. The car body repair kit. The car body repair kit cover. The car body repair kit cover fastener. We know how to say these things, but not how to write them.

Have I told you the story of the Indian gardener? (My father taught me this story when I was very small, along with other useful information about using a #2 pencil to correct galleys and never putting water in whiskey.)

Once upon a time there was an Indian gardener who had a terrible problem with snakes. Her neighbors advised her that the only solution was to get a mongoose, and they told her the name of the regional official responsible for providing gardeners with government-supported pest control. She decided that her garden was so large and the pesky snakes so numerous that she would ask for a pair rather than just one mongoose. So she began her letter:

Dear Friends: Please send me two mongooses.

That sounded ridiculous. So she tore up the letter and began again:

Dear Friends: Please send me two mongeese.

That sounded even worse. So at last she wrote:

Dear Friends: Please send me a mongoose. Sincerely yours, etc.
P.S. Please send me another.

According to my father, the mongoose is the mascot of all working writers. Use the mongoose solution for hyphens:

▷ the car-body-repair-kit-cover fastener
   the cover fastener for the kit for making repairs to car bodies

## Initialisms and Acronyms

With initial mania everywhere, it would be surprising if no scholars were infected. Treat the disease with a dose of plain, old-fashioned words:

▷ Negotiations then began between the Cooperative Wholesalers Society (CWS) and the Milk Producers Revenue Board (MPRB). The CWS wanted price supports; the MPRB wanted free competition.

Negotiations then began between the Cooperative Wholesalers Society and the Milk Producers Revenue Board. The wholesalers wanted price supports; the producers wanted free competition.

# Introductions

If you find yourself writing an introduction that seems to be nothing more than a table of contents, why not substitute a table of contents?

▷ The first section reviews the current literature on aphasia. The second section discusses melodic therapy techniques. Then in the third section there are three case histories. Finally, the fourth section brings up open questions for future research.

1. Review of the Literature on Aphasia     1
2. Melodic Therapy Techniques     8
3. Three Case Histories     17
4. Future Research     22

The table of contents says everything the introduction did and more—it has page numbers too.

# Inventing Terms and Notation

The topic at hand is assigning names to new discoveries, not foolishness like "sendee" for recipient.

Be sure that what you want to name is really new. A discovery at the far edge of your area of specialization may be a commonplace in someone else's. Rediscovery leads to a proliferation of terms and obscures the unity of knowledge across fields.

Be sure that your discovery is worth naming. Although it's difficult to foresee the results of your work, the stony truth is that nine out of ten new concepts never get much further than their author, a colleague or two, and a few graduate students. There's no point in beating your brains out over a great name for something with no applicability to anyone's work but your own. "This technique," "this result," "my finding," "my approach," "the new variable" may be sufficient.

Consider the local definition. Suppose, for instance, that your Type 4 behavior is, in common language, fear. Rather than call it "Type 4" or, worse still, "phobic disquietation," you can in an introduction define "fear" as nothing more or less than Type 4 for the length of this paper. Your reader will be able to keep it straight from Types 1, 2, 3, and 5, and you will have struck a blow for modesty and common sense in nomenclature. In a long paper, you would be wise to remind your reader now and then that by "fear" you mean only Type 4, lest she get confused and think you're talking about the general phenomenon.

Consider the context. You are not Adam and Eve in the Garden of Eden. If there already exist three phenomena called lutes, flutes, and oboes, calling the fourth member of the family a wheelbarrow is cloddish. Give some thought to the verbs that cluster around any noun you're considering. We're stuck with such monstrosities as "to walk a tree" and "to stack a goal," but we certainly don't need more.

Don't jump in. Hold off on naming a new idea until it has assumed its full shape in your mind. A poor name, hastily chosen, can mislead your readers and can even subtly restrict your own ability to realize the extent of your invention.

Keep it simple. A moment's thought should convince you that "dumping" is a better way to describe a dumping sort of concept than "geotropic activation," better, catchier, and more likely to make a name for you. Simplicity is especially important in inventing new notation. I once saw a paper with $w$, $\underline{w}$, $\underline{\underline{w}}$, $w'$, $w''$, $\underline{w}'$, $\underline{w}''$, $\underline{\underline{w}}'$, $\underline{\underline{w}}''$ — shall I go on? If you care nothing for your reader's weary eyes, think of wresting the same symbol set from successive typesetting programs for the rest of your life.

Always give your reader some indication of how you intend a new notation to be said aloud. There's nothing more tiresome than reading through an entire paper subvocalizing "little left squiggle, straight bar, little right squiggle."

Don't blow your own horn. If you're Sweeney, leave it to someone else to call your technique Sweenification.

Get help. Any philologist worth her salt will be overjoyed to help you with prefixes and suffixes and roots from Greek and Latin. She suffers, after all, much more than you do from words like "calmative," "nounal," and "cavitron."

# Inversion

There is a common delusion among scholars and other people who write formal prose that relatives and comparatives require inversion afterwards. They do not. Here are two inverted sentences:

> This proposal won more favor than did its predecessors.

> The polyvalent functions have as many uses as have the bivalent ones.

Here are the same sentences uninverted:

> This proposal won more favor than its predecessors did.

> The polyvalent functions have as many uses as the bivalent ones have.

The inverted versions are not bad enough to require stars, but a comparison with ordinary, everyday diction makes it clear that the versions in natural order are better:

> ▷ She's twice as smart as am I.

> She's twice as smart as I am.

In many cases, the periphrastic verb, the one that repeats the verbal idea, can simply be omitted:

> This proposal won more favor than its predecessors.

> The polyvalent functions have as many uses as the bivalent ones.

# "Let's"

There are three different kinds of "let" to think about:

1. One is the transitive verb "let," meaning allow, permit, cause:

> I let it happen, you let it happen, she lets it happen, we let it happen, they let it happen

yesterday I let it happen, I'm letting it happen, I've let it happen

Here's that verb in the imperative:

Let the surgeon have the biggest piece of cake.

Let her pass.

Let him breathe.

And here's that verb in the imperative with "us" as its direct object:

Let us through.

2. The second is the optative particle "let." Optative means wishful and a particle is a nonlexical word, a little bit of grammatical information that is realized as a separate piece of stuff rather than as an inflection on a word, but essentially a grammatical rather than a lexical kind of thing. Here's the particle at work:

Let the world take note.

Let love abide everlastingly.

Let there be light.

Notice that this "let" is very formal diction; it is at home in church and at graduation and not many other places. (This "let" is also the one we use in the formulaic "Let *AB* be equal to *CD*.") Here's the optative particle "let" followed by "us":

Let us then renew our bonds and take up our burdens.

3. The third is the modal auxiliary "let's."

The central auxiliary verbs, or helping verbs, are: be, have, and do; can, may, will, shall, could, might, would, should, and must. These central auxiliaries have a number of features in common: In forming negative finite clauses, the first auxiliary goes before the "not"; auxiliaries have contraction equivalents; auxiliary operators admit inversion; they can carry nuclear stress; auxiliaries can function as operators in reduced constructions; etc. etc. etc.—you don't want to know all this stuff.

What you do want to know is that auxiliariness is a ramp, not a cliff. Besides the central auxiliaries there are a number of others: dare, need, ought to, used to, had better, would rather, etc. "Let's" is one of those others. Here it is exhibiting its auxiliariness:

> Let's give her another chance.
>
> Let's not be late.
>
> Shall we go? Let's.

This is ordinary, everyday diction. As you can see, when somebody tells you that "let's" is a contraction of "let us," she's dead wrong.
As this "let's" gets more colloquial, it gets more auxiliary:

> Don't let's tell him more than we have to.
>
> Let's don't go tomorrow.
>
> Let's us go upstairs while the rest of you stay here and wait.

(English sources tell me that "let's don't" and "let's us" are Americanisms.)
And what implications have these three "let"s for writing?
The auxiliary "let's" is not a contraction of the optative particle "let" plus "us." (Neither is it a contraction of the transitive verb "let" plus the direct object "us," but I doubt that anybody ever thought it was.)
Suppose you want to say something like:

> Let's consider three possibilities.

And suppose you're uncertain about whether that will make you sound serious enough and respectful enough. You might be tempted to try substituting:

> ▷ Let us consider three possibilities.

Don't do it. If you use the optative particle "let" in anything other than the formula "Let *a* be equal to four times *b*" you are going to sound stiff. Serious is OK; respectful is OK; stiff gets in the way of your reader's ability to attend to what you're saying. If the auxiliary "let's" is not appropriate, you have to do something else altogether:

There are three possibilities to consider.

or

As you will see, there are three possibilities.

or

Three things seem possible.


# A Little Latin

**AD; BC** (*anno Domini,* **in the year of the Lord; before Christ**) Few
works are of such vast historical scope that these abbreviations are
necessary. But if your period is 35 BC to AD 76 then you should
notice that "BC" goes after the year and "AD" goes before it. If you
prefer, you may write the abbreviations "B.C." and "A.D."

No one objects to "the third century BC" on grammatical
grounds, but there are some pernickety people who will not allow
"the third century AD" because *annus* means year. Well, so it does,
but it also means age or time or season. Since we have no other
handy way of expressing the idea, using "AD" with centuries seems
a harmless sort of shorthand. "CE" has been proposed (for
"Christian Era" or "Common Era"), but because it has never become popular it slows the reader down instead of speeding her
ahead as shorthand should.

**A.M.; M.; P.M.** (*ante meridiem,* **before noon;** *meridies,* **noon;** *post
meridiem,* **after noon**) By this system, noon is 12 M. and midnight
is 12 P.M. But there are also people who write noon "12 N." and
midnight "12 M." And on the 24-hour clock, noon is 12 and midnight is either 0 or 24. To avoid confusion, write out the words
"noon" and "midnight."

**C., c** (*cum,* **with**) Use these only in notes to yourself, not in writing
for other people to read.

▷ Silicon is found mainly c oxygen as $SiO_2$.

Silicon is found mainly with oxygen as $SiO_2$.

**C., ca.** (*circa,* **about**) The use of these expressions with approximate dates and figures is justified only in parenthetical dating and in lists and tables. Avoid them in ordinary sentences:

▷ An amnesty was declared at the time of his death c. 1542.

An amnesty was declared at the time of his death, in about 1542.

▷ The distance was ca. three hundred miles.

The distance was roughly three hundred miles.

In parenthetical dating, you may also use question marks:

Edward George Bateman (ca. 1790–1864).

or

Edward George Bateman (1790?–1864).

On lists and tables, you may also use the ~ sign:

| 3,114 | 4,228 | 5,109 | 1,134 | c. 4,500 |

or

| 3,114 | 4,228 | 5,109 | 1,134 | ~4,500 |

If all the figures on a table are approximate, you'll say so in the heading and have no need for marking off individual numbers.

Round off figures that you must give as approximations:

▷ Ca. 1.482 atmospheres.

Ca. 1.5 atmospheres.

**E.g.** (*exempli gratia,* **for the sake of example**) Natural, unabbreviated English words make for more graceful expression:

▷ The American Romantics, e.g. Burchfield and Stettheimer, thought of themselves as rebels.

The American Romantics, such as Burchfield and Stettheimer, thought of themselves as rebels.

**Etc.** (*et cetera,* **and so on**) The least of the objections to "etc." is
that it is a foreign expression for which you can easily substitute
unabbreviated English. Its sloppy vagueness is unsuited to the rigor
and precision of scholarly thought, and it is addictive at the ends of
lists, even when it makes no sense:

> ▷ Many of these back-formations (for example, "ethic," "bur-
> gle," etc.) serve useful functions.
>
> Many of these back-formations (for example, "ethic" and
> "burgle") serve useful functions.

"For example" gives notice that only some members of a set are to
be mentioned; "etc." then drags in all the other members. The two
expressions are at loggerheads.

If you never use it carelessly, "etc." can convey a nice dismissive
effect:

> Bowtha's ability to attend to the sense of an appeal began to
> deteriorate with her growing fixation on individual words—
> "disinterested," "enormity," "flaunt," "infer," etc.

**I.e.** (*id est,* **that is**) There are few settings in which simple apposition will not do the job, and do it less stiffly:

> ▷ In her masterpiece, i.e., *The Age of Innocence,* she overcame
> these tendencies.
>
> In her masterpiece, *The Age of Innocence,* she overcame
> these tendencies.

When apposition is not enough, "that is" is better than "i.e."

**N.B.** (*nota bene,* **note well**) In general, your writing itself should
help your reader to note well what you're saying, without any need
for flags and arrows. In those few cases where you need a flag, there
are other expressions with more impact than "N.B."

> ▷ The reaction then occurs very quickly. N.B.: The resulting
> gas is fatal in concentrations as low as one part in ten billion.

The reaction then occurs very quickly. Warning: The resulting gas is fatal in concentrations as low as one part in ten billion.

**Viz.** (*videlicet,* namely—from *videre licet,* it is permitted to see) This expression is archaic and should be used only for humor. But be cautious about using such effects. Some young scholars adopt a half-mocking tone when they set out to write—archaisms, convolutions, the excessive use of "one," all of it conscious, all of it arch. Sometimes this style can be funny, but more often it's sad. The message comes through: "I'm not sure just where I stand on this, so I'm going to pretend it's all beneath me."

The search for an authentic voice in which to write is very difficult if you go at it directly. Concentrate instead on getting your subject across to your reader. That job is hard enough to eradicate self-consciousness and the need for defensive irony.

# Motivation

"Motivation" is the term mathematicians use for the context of a piece of work, where it comes from and what it leads to. Motivation is the mortar around bricks in the scholarly edifice, and every article needs some.

Often the use that you make of your secondary sources will indicate where your work fits. When explicit motivation is necessary, be on guard against grandiose, far-reaching statements. Early in my career, I had the task of correcting an extraordinary essay from a student that began, "All the world is turning to thoughts of mortuary science." All the world need not be turning to thoughts of your subject, but neither should you present it in a vacuum.

▷ One of the most pressing problems facing us today is the identification of the locus of histamine reactions.

▷ The locus of the histamine reactions is unknown.

If we knew the locus of the histamine reactions, we would be a step closer to preventing allergies.

▷ Who has not, on reading Milton, been struck by the impact of recessive accent on his meter?

▷ Milton's meter displays certain characteristics of recessive accent.

Recessive accent accounts for much of the "figured bass" effect that observers have noted in Milton's meter.

The examples are exaggerated for the sake of brevity; motivation usually resides, not in any individual sentence, but in the attitude that informs a whole piece of work.


## "Nor"

Since scholarly writers have a corner on the "nor" market, they bear the responsibility for keeping the word in working order. There are only two constructions in modern English in which "nor" can occur. The first is in partnership with "neither."

Neither Knowles nor Sunderman makes this distinction [12,35].

The second is as a clause-level coordinating conjunction, meaning approximately "and . . . not" or "and . . . no."

Frick was disenchanted with the railroads, coal, and oil, nor had he any interest in the money market for itself.

The clause that follows this "nor" is inverted, "had he any interest" rather than "he had any interest." If you stick to these two uses for "nor," you'll be in good shape.

Below the clause level, "nor" cannot appear without "neither."

▷ The mixture does not settle nor go into solution.

▷ Not in the Senate nor in the House was there a murmur of protest.

Test the items the "nor" is attempting to connect to see whether they're clauses.

▷ (settle) nor (go into solution)

▷ (in the Senate) nor (in the House)

If they're not, rewrite:

> The mixture does not settle or go into solution.

or

> The mixture neither settles nor goes into solution.
>
> Neither in the Senate nor in the House was there a murmur of protest.

or

> Not in the Senate or in the House was there a murmur of protest.

Like all coordinating conjunctions, "neither . . . nor" must link grammatically parallel items.

▷ The staging was a success neither in 1728 nor 1750.

▷ (in 1728) nor (1750)

> The staging was a success neither in 1728 nor in 1750.

or

> The staging was a success in neither 1728 nor 1750.

# Paragraphing

Two points here:

The first is to notice that even after a very short introduction, parallel items require parallel paragraphs. You may introduce *A*, *B*, and *C* as parallel and treat all three together with an introduction. You may put the introduction in one paragraph and *A*, *B*, and *C* together in another. But if you give *B* and *C* their own paragraphs, *A* must have one too.

▷ I want to tell you about three things. The first one is this. Now I'll write something about the first one.

The second one is this. Now I'll write something about the second one.

The third one is this. Now I'll write something about the third one.

I want to tell you about three things.

The first one is this. Now I'll write something about the first one.

The second one is this. Now I'll write something about the second one.

The third one is this. Now I'll write something about the third one.

The second is a plea for paragraphing by eye. Scholars think big thoughts, and big thoughts make big paragraphs, but there's no excuse for the endless paragraph that goes on page after everlasting page. Give your reader a breather. Make it a rule never to let more than thirty lines go by without looking back to see whether you can't break them up. That means you must paragraph more frequently than usual for material to be printed in narrow columns— all to the good. Experiment with an occasional short paragraph for a change, even with a one-sentence paragraph.


# Passivity

I wish that scholars were the only ones who practiced the vice of passivity, but they are among the worst and should be chided for it. The passive voice ("*Y* is done by *X*," as opposed to the active, "*X* does *Y*") is a perfectly lovely voice, useful for placing emphasis correctly, for facilitating parallel construction, for ducking ambiguous or uninteresting agency, and for sheer variety. But it is not the normal working voice of English discourse. Passive after passive, one on top of the other, can dull the most sparkling ideas and turn golden work to dross.

The experimental sciences outdo everyone else on this score. You can read through paper after paper in which nobody ever does anything, nobody ever produces anything, nobody ever acts. Things are done, results are produced, actions are accomplished, as if by unseen hands. You get the feeling that our laboratories are staffed by disembodied spirits.

If you suffer from this addiction, look first for passives with "by." There you've already admitted the agency and can undertake the transformation from "was done by $X$" to "$X$ did" with little trauma. Steel yourself to the use of the indefinite pronouns. "Someone said" may at first sound strange compared to your old familiar "it has been said," but you can learn to like it. Eventually, if you have courage and determination, you can cure yourself of even the most insidious passives, the kind you use when you don't know, or don't want to say, who did what.

Here is a terrible example—terrible, but as anyone who reads scholarly prose will attest, not untypical:

> ▷ In what might be called the official Victorian world-view, a fairly clear-cut distinction was made between love and friendship. Friendship was conceived of as a relationship between members of the same sex based on shared interests and values; love was founded on the attraction of opposites, who were intended by their union to be bound in a complementarity of virtues and skills by which the basis for the foundation of a family could be laid.

Simple transformations from the passive to the active are impossible here. What the author must do is rethink, asking herself over and over "Who does what?" so that her answers will take that form.

The first passive, "might be called," is an attempt to wiggle out of responsibility. The author wants to use an expression but she doesn't want to own up to it. The second passive, "was made," further distances that same expression. The author must face squarely the question whether she likes the phrase "official Victorian world-view." If she likes it, she should use it straight out; if she doesn't, she should use something else.

> The official Victorian world-view made a fairly clear-cut distinction between love and friendship.

or

> The Victorians made a fairly clear-cut distinction between love and friendship.

The third passive, "was conceived of," seems to result from the author's fear that we have forgotten what she's talking about. Having started in the minds of the Victorians, we should be able to continue there for a sentence or two without nagging reminders.

> Friendship was a relationship between members of the same
> sex based on shared interests and values.

Now you should notice that there are two more passives here, "based" and "shared." Most past participles in English are passive. The wise writer will avoid other passives in sentences with past participles, to keep the passives from piling up. The wily writer will avoid past participles themselves when some other construction is more direct.

> In friendship, members of the same sex shared interests and
> values.

Passive #6, "was founded," is a knee-jerk passive; the author has no reason for it, she's just gotten so much in the passive habit that anything else sounds bare to her.

> Love was the attraction of opposites.

In the final portion of the sentence, we see the author being choked to death by her own passivity. "Were intended," "to be bound," "could be laid"—these are bad, but what's worse is that the twisted, backward construction has led the author to write nonsense. "Intended by their union to be bound in a complementarity" doesn't mean much, and "the basis for the foundation" is— what? The subsoil? There is no quick fix here. The only solution is to start again. What do you mean? What are you trying to say?

> Love was the attraction of opposites, whose complementary
> virtues and skills laid the foundation for a family.

I have a theory that passivity is tied up with personification. In strong personification, as you may recall, a non-human thing takes on human characteristics—the smiling sun, the sobbing wind, that sort of thing. Now look at a typical passive construction:

▷ The primary computation service has been provided by a large, central mainframe.

Why does the author write that instead of "a large, central mainframe facility has provided"? Aside from the automatic passivity that infests all scholars, she may feel that the active is too direct, too active. In the back of her mind there's the hazy idea that the mainframe didn't really provide the service, it just, well, it just somehow was provided. If my guess is correct, she feels the active as a mild personification. Then it must be said that mild personification is a good device, a worthy device, and one to use freely. Write without fear:

A large, central mainframe has provided the primary computation service.

No reader will imagine that the mainframe ran around with a towel over its arm, providing service, any more than she will think that the sun really smiles or the wind really sobs.


## Personal Fads

Most personal fads are not only harmless but tonic. Scholars spend their days and nights in intimate struggle with the language, and no one should go through that without developing a set of preferences and prejudices, even quirks. Readers prefer writing with some flavor, some tang—anything rather than bland, impersonal pablum. Personal peculiarities are harmful only when they get in your way, either by restricting your access to the whole range of the possibilities of the language or by obtruding themselves between your reader and your subject.

For restricting access, consider the case of "get." Many scholars seem to have something against the word. They go to great lengths to avoid it. Acquire, gain, obtain, derive, procure, earn, reap, gather, glean, collect, incur, be in receipt of, fall heir to—anything but "get." The word must be ten thousand times more frequent in normal speech than it is in scholarly writing, and it's a great loss because many of its substitutes are stiff.

▷ The family was unable to procure assistance and turned to crime.

The family was unable to get help and turned to crime.

"Get" is too protean a word to get along without.

For obtruding on your reader, repetition is what's usually at fault. Everyone has pet phrases and constructions that grow wearisome with reuse. I once read through a thirty-page paper in which the expression "the case that" occurred more than a hundred times (I counted): It is the case that so-and-so, it is not the case that so-and-so—there's nothing wrong with the expression, but after that many uses it began to sound like nonsense syllables. Catching such repetitions requires a high degree of self-awareness. In this as in many other instances, your best hope is to have a friend or a colleague read your work with a critical eye. You can earn the favor by reading hers.


# "Respective"

"Respective" and "respectively" are such complicated words that defining them is like a short excursion into the New Math. Their function is to link the members of two sets with identical cardinality in a one-to-one correspondence in the order of their enumeration. Got that? In other words, if you say that A, B, and C relate to X, Y, and Z respectively, you're saying that the two groups pair up A-X, B-Y, and C-Z. The times when that needs to be said are, to put it mildly, rare. Often it's understood without saying:

▷ The experimental animals were then returned to their respective cages.

Here is an author who does not trust her readers' common sense. If each animal were put in another animal's cage, that would require comment; but if, as we expect, each animal goes back to its own cage, we don't need "respective" to keep us on the track.

The experimental animals were then returned to their cages.

Even in the rare instance when you do need "respective" or "respectively," rewriting will usually do the job more neatly.

> Backhart, Miles, and Babbidge stood for Devon, East Anglia, and Wales respectively.

or

> Backhart stood for Devon, Miles for East Anglia, and Babbidge for Wales.

Both versions say the same thing, but the second makes easier reading. The first doesn't warn the reader that she is going to have to remember "Backhart, Miles, and Babbidge" in order; only when she hits "respectively" does she realize she has to backtrack in order to do the pairing.

# The Waffle

This is another case of hyperqualification, but at the level of sentences and paragraphs instead of words and phrases.

▷ We would like to have more information about the small-scale flow, but our model can account for all the information in laboratory experiments. Observations in nature are, however, all too few. The fact remains that under experimental conditions much of value can be learned. But the fieldwork will undoubtedly mean that we must correct many of our assumptions. In the meantime, nevertheless, the work in vitro will continue.

Any waffle this tightly woven is immediately apparent, and no one would veer back and forth this way in so short a space. But if the ideas are large ones, with a good deal of exposition, you do frequently see what amounts to "*A* but *B* but *A* but *B*."

Outlining is the best cure for waffles. I don't mean the kind of outlining done beforehand, because not one person in a hundred can work that way. But the outline you do afterward is a different story. Write a sentence of outline for each paragraph of text—a sentence rather than just a label, because what you're looking for are shifts signaled by words like "but" and "on the other hand," which won't show up with labels.

By the way, this kind of outlining is helpful for paragraphing too. A paragraph that can't be outlined in a single sentence should often be two paragraphs.

# "Which"-Hunting

I understand that if you tape a person who's carrying on a normal conversation, she follows the normal English pattern for relative pronouns: "that" for restrictive clauses, "which" for non-restrictive. She does, that is, unless you tell her that she's addressing an audience or dictating a formal letter or a paper. At that point, she starts substituting "which" for "that." This is another of those bending-over-backwards errors, the ones that result from affecting an unnatural, prissy diction in writing.

The first cure, then, is to listen to what you write. For many people listening will be sufficient.

▷ The novel which is emerging in the Third World does not fit our standard categories.

If you're lucky, that will sound awful to you, and you'll change it easily and automatically to:

The novel that is emerging in the Third World does not fit our standard categories.

Don't give up if you can't hear it right away. Your ear has undoubtedly been battered by all the bad prose you've had to read, but the damage is not permanent.

If you have a good grasp of comma punctuation, all you need to know is that which-clauses are set off by commas.

These regulations, which Elizabeth had no intention of following, went into effect the following summer.

No commas, no "which":

> ▷ He preferred the settlement which his sister had proposed.
>
> He preferred the settlement that his sister had proposed.

But if you're weak on both "which/that" and commas, you'll have to think about the grammar of restrictive and non-restrictive clauses. Restrictive clauses ("that" with no commas) are essential, defining, irremovable. Non-restrictive clauses ("which" with commas) are parenthetical, descriptive, detachable. The trouble comes in deciding what you mean to say. In most cases, you can't decide the sentence by itself; you need to look around at the context.

> The leaf _____ the grub has used for shelter now becomes its food.

"That" with no commas or "which" with commas? There's no way to tell by looking at the sentence in isolation. Check the context to see how the clause relates to the noun it's modifying. If "the leaf" is a fresh expression, not mentioned before, or not sufficient in itself for your reader to know what leaf you're talking about, the clause is restrictive.

> The leaf that the grub has used for shelter now becomes its food.

If you've already talked about the leaf, your reader knows full well what leaf you mean, and you're just reminding her, the clause is nonrestrictive.

> The leaf, which the grub has used for shelter, now becomes its food.

Another way of checking the same distinction is to try parentheses.

> Phoebus had a crow _____ he taught to speak.
>
> Phoebus had a crow (_____ he taught to speak).

If you can parenthesize the clause, it's "which" with commas:

> Phoebus had a crow, which he taught to speak.

If you can't, it's "that" with no commas:

> Phoebus had a crow that he taught to speak.

Only the context can tell you whether the parenthesizing makes sense or not.

And yet another way of checking the same distinction is to try out imaginary uprooting.

> The training _____ the Agency gives is free except for book and supplies.

"That" with no commas or "which" with commas? Again, only the context can answer the question. But try ripping out the clause and putting it after the sentence.

> The training is free except for books and supplies. The Agency gives the training.

If that makes sense in context, the clause is non-restrictive:

> The training, which the Agency gives, is free except for books and supplies.

But if the uprooted version is nonsense—if the reader must ask, "What training? What are you talking about?"—then the clause is restrictive. A restrictive clause uprooted would have to go before the sentence.

> The Agency gives training. The training is free except for books and supplies.

If this is the only version that makes sense in context, what you want is "that" with no commas:

The training that the Agency gives is free except for books and supplies.

As a desperate last measure, if you're completely at a loss, use "that" with no commas. It's the more common construction by maybe ten to one, so the odds will be with you.

# THE
# REFERENCE

To write a reference, you must have the work you're
referring to in front of you. Do not rely on your memory.
Do not rely on your memory. Just in case the idea ever
occurred to you, do not rely on your memory.

*do not rely on your memory*

The tidy, thorough scholar will take down a full reference on an index card or a laptop whenever she reads
anything worth mentioning, keep a file of these references, and construct her reference lists quickly and effortlessly from her file. If you are untidy and disor-
ganized, like most of us, you may find yourself throwing
together your reference list at the last minute. The temptation to write a reference without having the work before you will be powerful. Resist it. A vague recollection
is worthless; a vivid recollection is probably the product
of your imagination—ingenious, no doubt, but of little
use to your reader. Don't rely on your memory.

It is best to write out a reference when you first encounter a work you may later refer to. Now you can
remember how you found it. Later it will be part of your
mental furniture. You will no longer remember that you
once puzzled over its obscure publisher, its misleading
Library of Congress entry, its pseudonymous authorship. Now is the time to write a reference, to save your
reader from repeating your puzzlement.

If you failed to write out a reference you now need, get
hold of the source again. You will be surprised to see
that the incisive expression you remember is a misquota-
tion; the diagram you recollect shows something else;

the memorable anecdote illustrates another point; the book you can see as if it were before you doesn't exist. If you don't write references out at first encounter, you will waste many hours tracking them down in the library. Better you than your reader.

What should a reference say? As always, you can figure out the answer by putting yourself in your reader's place. Your text has captivated her. She wants to know more. It's your responsibility to help her. Of course you should make your references crisp and uniform whenever possible, because crisp, uniform reference lists are easier to read than muddy, jumbled ones. But you must never sacrifice information to form. If an informative reference must be messy and peculiar, it must—better that than a sleek and shiny one that lacks crucial data.

The objection is often made "But no one would be looking at my paper who doesn't know Brazzleton's work. No reader would be able to make out what I'm talking about without that background." Much scholarly writing is done at universities, in departments of like-minded people, all of whom correspond with like-minded people at other universities. The young scholar feels that she is writing for her thesis committee and her friends and that person at Toronto who's working along the same lines—a little world. She forgets that the written word is the instrument of a great world, a democracy of the mind. You may never reach the reader from that great world, the unexpected reader, the anonymous reader. But you must remember the possibility that she exists and by no action of yours exclude her. It is in writing references that the fellowship of scholars takes its most concrete, practical form. The careless or deliberate withholding of information about how to find sources is a betrayal of that fellowship. Writing references is an occasion for thoughtful generosity. I want to tell a story that illustrates two of these points.

The great mathematician G. H. Hardy was sitting one day in his study in Cambridge when he noticed in the afternoon's mail an odd letter. The letter covered many pages, and each page was different from the one before. Only two of the pieces of paper were new when the writer used them, one a piece of ordinary stationery, the other a piece of butcher's paper. All the rest of the pieces of paper were obviously recovered from wastebaskets, uncrumpled and smoothed out, the original contents effaced so that the writer could use the backs. The handwriting was the badly formed, childish scrawl of the nearly illiterate, written very small to conserve paper, and in smudged pencil to boot.

"Dear Sir," the letter said, "I am but a poor Indian sweeper boy, and you will think me foolish for even dreaming that I might be able to look at your splendid papers. Having done so, I have only demonstrated my unworthiness to attempt to understand your brilliant mind, because it seems to me that these papers are full of mistakes, and how could this be so? Let me show you what I have thought so that you can tell me the errors I am making and set me on the right path again."

Hardy read this with a tolerant smile. Prominent mathematicians get a steady trickle of mail from madmen and mathematical incompetents who believe that they have proved Fermat's Last Theorem or trisected the angle with a straightedge. Often the letters are amusing.

This one was not. As he read on, Hardy realized that he was seeing for the first time a fundamental error in his work. In a few badly written pages, the sweeper boy was demolishing several years of research. Hardy was astonished, embarrassed, and then (he really was a great man) delighted. Never before had he seen such insight, such unorthodox approaches, such delicious mathematical wit. He sent to India, but the boy would not come alone, so he went and fetched him. The Indian sweeper boy, whose name was S. A. Ramanujan, became Hardy's colleague and his best friend.

This story illustrates two points: It illustrates the possibility that your scholarly work may reach far beyond the little world you know. But it also illustrates the wisdom of writing down a reference on first encounter—because it is not correct. I didn't write the reference down when I first read it, and over the years I became confused.

Thanks to the kindness of my friends, I now have before me a copy of Hardy's essay about Ramanujan. My version of the story was wrong: Ramanujan was a clerk in the Port Trust Office at Madras, not a sweeper boy. His letter to Hardy contained new results, not corrections of Hardy's work. And Hardy didn't bring him back to England; Ramanujan's mother had a prophetic dream that convinced him to go.

So I repeat the story to support the second point as much as the first.

If you must not rely on your own memory, even less should you rely on someone else's. If your only access to a reference is through a secondary source, then you must refer to the secondary source as well as the primary one. <u>The principle of secondary reference is not just scholarly etiquette, it's scholarly ethics</u>.

To invent an extreme case, let's say that I'm trying to recall where Paul speaks of himself as a citizen of no mean city in order to refer to it in a paper I'm writing on Roman law. I flip through the Epistles with no luck. I don't have a concordance at home, and the library's shut. Stumped. Suddenly I remember that I once read something about that line in an essay on Luther's Pauline commentaries. I search out the essay, leaf through it, and there it is: Such-and-such, so-and-so, citizen of no mean city, Acts 12:39. May I then write my reference to Acts 12:39?

No.

Secondhand information must be presented as secondhand. To treat it as if it came from the horse's mouth is dishonest. Unless I confirm the reference, I must give it as

> 4] Acts 12:39.
>     Cited in S. Pilov, Luther's commentaries on Law and Gos-
>     pel in Paul. *A Light to Lighten the Gentiles*, page 341.
>     J. A. Allen, London, England, 1979.

Since the Bible is sitting right there in front of me, I can use the only permissible device for avoiding a secondary reference by writing my reference straight from the primary source.

<u>As you will see if you look at Acts 12:39, treating a secondary reference as if it were primary is not only dishonest but dangerous.</u> There is no verse 39; chapter 12 ends with verse 25. What happened to Pilov? Maybe she dozed off as she was checking that item on her reference list; maybe (perish the thought) she was relying on her memory. Whatever the reason, unless I give the reference as secondary, the responsibility for the error in my paper is mine. I make enough mistakes on my own without taking the blame for other people's too. <u>So if you cannot confirm a reference in its primary source, give it in secondary form for your own sake as much as for your reader's</u>.

To bring this little fable to a happy conclusion, let's say that after only five more minutes of searching I find the primary source, write my reference to Acts 21:39, and sigh with relief.

# Panorama

The next sections cover in great detail the construction of a reference and the compilation of a reference list. But first, here is a sample list (on the right) with labels (on the left).

The purpose of the right-hand side is to give you something to look forward to as you work on your references. Some of the decisions you must make about setting up an individual reference depend on visualizing your final list and where you want the reference to fall in that list. So this is what the end of the process typically looks like, a numbered alphabetical listing with some cross-references from one item to another.

The purpose of the left-hand side is to serve as a quick review of the most common components of a reference list. The labels are in alphabetical order, and the examples are of the simplest cases, not of the tricky and unusual ones. When you have a hard case or need an explanation, go to the index. But when all you need is to jog your memory, here are some short reminders.

Since the pattern of your research may lead you to make frequent use of a kind of reference the rest of the world would call uncommon, some space is left at the end of the list for additional entries.

| | |
|---|---|
| Author's name as she gives it | 1] M. Atamer. |
| Book title | *Prehispanic Art in Mexico,* page 279. |
| | Pennsylvania State University Press, 1958. |
| | J. Blount. |
| | *The Modern Temperament.* |
| | Schocken, 1971. |

|                              | 2] Pages 49–61. |
| Compound reference           | 3] Page 134. |
|                              | 4] Pages 197–203. |
| Corporate author             | 5] The Brighton Conservatory. Catalog of primitive instrument collection. Oxton House Press, Brighton, England, 1979. |
| Cross-reference              | Kathleen Chaudry, see Slater [25]. |
|                              | 6] N. L. Dahlgard. *Formability in Sheet Metal.* University of Newfoundland |
| Date of publication          | Press, 1974. |
|                              | 7] P. G. Enriquez, editor. *Infant Development.* |
| Edition after the first      | Macmillan, third edition 1984. |
| Editor-compiler              | 8] Raymond Fukada, editor. *Teaching Machines.* University Press of Virginia, 1979. |
|                              | 9] Oliver Goldsmith (1730–74). *The Complete Plays.* |
| Editor-preparer              | Edited by A. Broder. Cambridge University Press, 1970. |
|                              | 10] J. A. Hein. My turn: The dwindling supply of sunshine. |
| Extended date                | *Newsweek* XXXII (17):39, 21 July 1983. |
|                              | 11] L. Insdorf. *The French Fable*, pages 206–220. |
| First edition (no mention)   | Dutton, 1971. |
|                              | 12] H. O. Jarvin. *Los Entremesos.* (The Snacks.) Calledoros, Maracaibo, Venezuela, 1985. |
|                              | 13] M. Klingfield, B. C. Mangino, |
| Joint authors                | and J. A. Betts. Foci of cortical degeneration. |

| | |
|---|---|
| Journal article | *Cerebrum* XIV (2):134–191, 1974. |
| | 14] M-A. Lepesant. *Kafka's Dreams.* |
| Major publisher (no address) | Cornell University Press, 1959. |
| | 15] Herman Matthews, editor. *The Death of the Frontier.* |
| Multivolume work | Four volumes. Random House, 1973–75. |
| | 16] F. J. Narendra. Counterforce attacks: A |
| Non-book title | strategy for limiting nuclear warfare. *Foreign Affairs Quarterly* IX (1):34–39, 1980. |
| | 17] Eleanor Ortel. *Pitching Pennies.* |
| Obscure publisher | The Wheelwright Press, 1348 Milburne Street, Springton, Ohio 40873. 1957. |
| | 18] A. J. Pantini. *The Road West,* pages 59–82. |
| One volume of multivolume work (cross-reference) | Volume II in Matthews [15], 1978. |
| | 19] R. D. Quinn. *Drama in Britain.* |
| One volume of multivolume work (no cross-reference) | Volume IV in M. Burrows, editor, *Modern Drama.* Viking, 1977. |
| | 20] Jill Rawlick. *Shakespeare on Film.* |
| PhD thesis | PhD thesis, City University of New York, 1979. |
| | 21] V. Rowlins. *Quarks and Hadrons,* pages 47–59. |
| Pinpointing after title | Harcourt Brace Jovanovich, 1986. |
| | 22] Siegfried Sassoon. *Memoirs of a Fox-Hunting Man,* |

| | |
|---|---|
| Pinpointing without pages (for works in many editions) | chapter 9.<br>St. Martin's Press edition, 1981. |
| | 23] A. Scalia.<br>Motor skills at fourteen months. |
| Portion of a compilation (cross-reference) | In Enriquez [7], pages 300–342. |
| | 24] Peter Seever.<br>The salvation of Lake Huron. |
| Portion of a compilation (no cross-reference) | In Carla S. Braceland, editor, *The Biology of the Great Lakes,* pages 79–142. Doubleday, 1980. |
| Pseudonym | 25] Anne Slater (pseudonym of Kathleen Chaudry).<br>*Sail a Tall Ship.*<br>Grove Press, 1977. |
| Review | 26] R. L. Snowden, Jr.<br>Review of Mark Heidmann, *The Melville Knot.*<br>*The New Republic* XLI (31):34, 1981. Cited in Lepesant |
| Secondary reference | [14], page 433. |
| Translation | 27] Claude Trussé.<br>*A Stroll in the Lobby.* (Un Tour au Foyer.) |
| Translator | Translated by S. Griman.<br>University of Toronto Press, 1971. |

I find it entertaining to try to construct the article for which this would be the reference list.

# Reference Format

Here come a lot of rules. The purpose of the rules is to save you from having to make a large number of petty, nearly arbitrary choices about form. If you either follow them or break them uniformly, you will also save your reader from having to guess whether any significance attaches to differences in form between one of your references and another.

## Style

### The Three Basic Blocks

Easy references fall into three blocks:

> I. Author.
> II. Title
> III. Bibliographic information.

For instance, the two most common references are to books and journal articles:

> author → Sharon Fiedler.
> title → *Small-Scale Aquaculture*.
> bibliographic → Princeton University Press, 1978.
> information

> author → Clement Simms.
> title → Elements of pattern in Matisse.

bibliographic → *Art Notes* XII(2):47–81, 1981.
    information

All of the references in the panorama are easy references; they fit the three-block format naturally.

## The Two Optional Blocks

To help your reader, you will sometimes add one or both of the two optional blocks:

> IV. More bibliographic information.
> V. Annotation.

The bibliographic information in block III describes the work you have before you; the bibliographic information in block IV describes some other version of the work that you happen to know about and that your reader may find more accessible than the one you're using. For instance:

author → C. L. Granger.
    title → Courtship among the Duhbir.
bibliographic → In Frances Rounds, editor, *Marriage*
    information     *and Family Structure*, pages 38–96.
                  Harper & Row, 1981.
    more → Originally in *Anthropos* XI(1):211–
bibliographic     296, 1978.
    information

In other words, you're working with the version that appears in the compilation edited by Rounds, but your reader might more easily put her hands on the original publication in the journal.

For the sake of convenience, I will call a block of annotation that's not bibliographic block V even when there's no block IV. Annotation might be special information on the author, a comment on the work, or a cross-reference to a related work—anything that your reader might find useful.

References with all five blocks are rare. For the sake of illustration, here are two examples:

author → M. H. Schultz and R. S. Varga.
title → L-splines.
bibliographic → *Numerische Mathematik* 10(2):345–
information      369, 1977.
more → Also published as Stanford Technical
bibliographic      Memorandum on Splines
information      #334207-Bromo-002, September
              1977.
annotation → Chapter 2 of Schultz [3] gives a
              smoother presentation of these
              results.

author → V. Nabokov.
title → The nearctic members of the genus
              *Lycaeides* Hübner.
bibliographic → *Bulletin of the Museum of*
information      *Comparative Zoology,* Harvard
              University, 101(4):1–149, 1949.
more → Collected in A. C. Simon, *Color and*
bibliographic      *Camouflage.* Ohio State University
information      Press, 1954.
annotation → The author is the Nabokov better
              known outside lepidopterist circles
              for *Lolita* and *Ada.*

## Bite-sized Chunks

Each block starts with a capital letter and ends with a period. One
or more phrases within a block may also end with periods; break
the information up to make it as readable as you can. For instance,
block III of a book reference usually has the publisher and the date
of publication separated by a comma:

▷ Hopkinson and Blake, 1979.

But that format doesn't work when you're listing the address of an
obscure publisher:

▷ The Press in the Barn, RFD Route 7, Miller's Falls, Oregon
94883, 1972.

Use a period to separate the zip code from the date in this case:

✳ The Press in the Barn, RFD Route 7, Miller's Falls, Oregon
94883. 1972.

Or again, block III of a reference to a portion of a compilation usually has a comma between the word "editor" and the title of the compilation:

In F. N. Osman, editor, *The Quest for Rectitude*, pages 230–251. Scribner's, 1942.

But when the compilation has a very long title, then editor, title, and pages are too much to swallow all at once:

▷ In Simon Ashe, editor, *A Vision of the Future: Psychology, Sociology, and the Overthrow of Theology in Hawthorne*, pages 160–184. Louisiana State University Press, 1981.

A period after "editor" is a help in this case:

In Simon Ashe, editor. *A Vision of the Future: Psychology, Sociology, and the Overthrow of Theology in Hawthorne*, pages 160–184. Louisiana State University Press, 1981.

## Open versus Compressed Format

In the open format, each block starts a fresh line:

13] Evan Graham.
18th century keyboard fingering.
*Musica* XII(3):41–102, 1975.

---

Bad examples are marked with an arrowhead (▷).

When a block runs over one line long, the second and following lines are indented:

> 29] E. D. Hiatt, editor.
> *The Speculative Tradition in the Middle Ages.* Volume
> II: *Technological Innovation in Medieval Agriculture
> and Weaponry.*
> Pergamon, 1956.

The indentation should be neither puny nor gross:

▷ *The Speculative Tradition in the Middle Ages.* Volume II: *Technological Innovation in Medieval Agriculture and Weaponry.*

▷ *The Speculative Tradition in the Middle Ages.* Volume II: *Technological Innovation in Medieval Agriculture and Weaponry.*

In the compressed format, the blocks are run together with no indentation:

> 4] Michael Dewer. A raving maniac. *The New York Review of Books* XIX(4):5–9, 18 May 1981.

Because it's easier to read, most of the examples in this book are in the open format. The compressed format is usually just as suitable unless your references are exceptionally complicated and messy. ←

### Numbered Examples

At the time when you construct your references (on first encounter with the works, naturally) they won't be numbered. Most of the examples that follow are numbered, as if they were taken from a finished reference list, to get you accustomed to the system and to demonstrate the uses of cross-reference.

### One Bracket

Because the bracketed number is always at the left margin of your reference list, you may if you like use only the right bracket:

51] L. E. Vanderhaben.
Scott Fitzgerald and the will to tragedy.
*Perspectives* VIII(3):47–58, 1973.

That's the style I've followed in this book because I like its sleekness. But if you prefer, you may use both brackets:

[51] L. E. Vanderhaben.
Scott Fitzgerald and the will to tragedy.
*Perspectives* VIII(3):47–58, 1973.

In your text, the numbers always need both brackets even if they chance to fall at the left margin now and then.

# I. Authors

## Normal Order

List authors' names in normal order, not in reverse order.

▷ Perkins, Edward.
Edward Perkins.

Reverse order doesn't do much harm to simple names and may even be some help in alphabetizing, but it makes hash of joint authors:

▷ Sewell, E. R., Pastern, B. L., and Cooper, D. G.
▷ Sewell, E. R., B. L. Pastern, and D. G. Cooper.
E. R. Sewell, B. L. Pastern, and D. G. Cooper.

## Initials

This is a small point even for a book that deals with little other than small points, but people's initials are spaced out:

▷ M.J.Bruner.
▷ M.J. Bruner.
M. J. Bruner.

## What Name?

It is an elementary courtesy to an author to give her name as it appears on her work. For a book, the title page is the thing to follow, not the spine or the dust jacket or the library catalog entry. For a journal article, the name at the head or the foot of the article is the thing to follow, not the table of contents or the running head at the top of the page or the annual index.

In theory, this rule applies to your own work as well as other people's. Suppose, for instance, that an author who usually calls herself "Rosamund Moon" gets an article published and finds to her surprise that her name has been rendered "R. Moon." How should she list herself in a reference to her own article? By strict and narrow propriety, the answer is "R. Moon." But since it was an impropriety that worked the alteration to start with, it's forgivable for her to restore her name to the version she prefers, and she needn't even use brackets for her restorations.

## Adding Information

You have no obligation to search out the parts of an author's name hidden by initials. Even when you know this information, you have no obligation to give it unless you think it will be helpful to your reader. When you do add information, use brackets around your contributions. Suppose you're referring to an article on which the author's name appears as "W. B. Clark." Your entry may follow the original:

W. B. Clark.

Or you may plump it out:

W[illa] B[aines] Clark.

## Joint Authors

The names of joint authors appear in block I as they do on the original, but with the following exceptions. Regardless of the style of the original, write out "and" before the final name:

▷ Michael I. Shamos, Daniel P. Hoey.

▷ Michael I. Shamos & Daniel P. Hoey.

Michael I. Shamos and Daniel P. Hoey.

Regardless of the style of the original, if there are three or more authors use a comma after every one but the last:

▷ W. Lehnert, J. Meehan and R. Schank.

W. Lehnert, J. Meehan, and R. Schank.

Joint authors with the same last name should have listed themselves on the original:

Bergan Evans and Cornelia Evans.

If they didn't, fix the entry up:

Ruth [Wallerstein] and Margaret Wallerstein.

## Pseudonymity

The reference to a work published under a pseudonym uses the pseudonym as block I. (This is just an extension of the rule about giving an author's name as she prefers it.) Enclose whatever additional information you have to contribute in parentheses— parentheses rather than brackets because you may want to include a cross-reference, and brackets within brackets look awful.

▷ Samuel Clemens.

▷ Samuel Clemens (Mark Twain, pseudonym).

Mark Twain.

or

Mark Twain (pseudonym of Samuel Clemens).

When you have entries for one author under more than one name, use cross-references to help your reader see the connection:

5] John Canaday. See also Head [19].
Kitchen implements of the Neargos.
In J. L. Mattison, editor, *Tools and Totems of the Congo People*, pages 18–22. T. Y. Crowell, 1973.

. . .

19] Matthew Head (pseudonym of John Canaday [5]).
*Congo Venus*.
Dutton, 1949.

Sometimes you may not know who stands behind a pseudonym:

Pauline Réage (pseudonym).

## Anonymity

Block I for a work of unknown or unacknowledged authorship reads:

Anonymous.

Use the last block to give further information:

3] Anonymous.
The running dogs of intellectual imperialism.
*The Old Mole*, 9 February 1979.
Attributed to Michael Ansarra.

You needn't try to keep a secret once the cat's out of the bag:

▷ 3] Anonymous.
Against prelacy.
London, 1641.
Known to be the work of John Milton.

26] John Milton.
Against prelacy.
London, 1641.
The pamphlet was unsigned.

Do not confuse corporate authorship with anonymity:

▷   1]  Anonymous.
        Final report of the President's Committee on Expansion.
        St. Louis University, 1935.

    26]  St. Louis University, President's Committee on Expan-
         sion.
         Final report, 1935.


## Honorifics

Titles of education, occupation, and honor do not ordinarily appear
in block I. (For that matter, they should never have appeared in the
original works. An author who feels compelled to list herself as
"PhD" or "Professor of Entomology" or "Member of the American
Academy of Arts and Sciences" has the scent of snake oil about her,
no matter how respectable the designation she lays claim to. Of
course, the fault may be not hers but her publisher's. Few publishers
realize the strength of the academic bias against honorifics, and
many an innocent author has been made to look braggardly against
her will.)
     You may sometimes want to mention an author's special qualifi-
cations in the last block:

    9]  N. J. Froissart.
        Notes on cheilostomatoplasty aftermath.
        *Proceedings of the 17th Annual AASP Convention,*
            American Association of Surgical Practitioners, 1984.
        The author is the head of surgery at Mount Zion Hospi-
            tal in Kansas City, Missouri, where Stamitz and Benton
            [18,19,22] developed the procedure.


     The main entry for a noble or a royal should follow the style you
adopt in your text. If you call the poet "Rochester" or "Lord
Rochester," alphabetize the item under *R:*

    38]  S. A. Richards.
         Review of Graham Greene, *Lord Rochester's Monkey.*
         *Tarnation* 11(7):57–61, 1985.

→   39]   John Wilmot, second earl of Rochester.
            Revile this hand.
            In C. L. Bel Geddes, editor, *The Complete Poems*, page
            20?.. Aquila Publishing, Isle of Skye, Scotland, 1981.

    40]   Friedlind Rumsfeld.
            *A History of Wadham College*, pages 278–291.
            Oxford University Press, 1922.

On a long list, a cross-reference under W would not be amiss.
Notice that a cross-reference standing alone needs no number:

    58]   Pamela Wilkins.
            Banishment and disgrace: Lord Rochester at court.
            *The Restoration Quarterly* VII(3):102–164, 1979.

→         John Wilmot, see Rochester [39].

    59]   E. N. Worthy.
            New light on the kidnaping affair.
            *The Journal of the Rochester Society* XXI(3):41–60,
            1981.

If you call him "Wilmot," the main entry goes under W and the
cross-reference under R.


## Corporate Authors

Some flexibility is desirable in describing corporate authors. Suppose for instance that you're referring to a pamphlet put out by the
Leeds branch of the Royal Society for the Prevention of Cruelty to
Animals. If your article is about Leeds, you might want to do the
entry for the pamphlet as:

    Royal Society for the Prevention of Cruelty to Animals,
    Leeds Branch.

If your article is about RSPCA, you might want to do the entry as:

    Leeds Branch, Royal Society for the Prevention of Cruelty to
    Animals.

It's not a matter of major importance as long as you get the information across.


## Editors and Translators

There are two kinds of editors, the kind who compiles the work of several authors and the kind who prepares the work of a single author. The first may sometimes be called a compiler or an anthologist; the second is almost always called an editor.

The compiler-editor is listed in block I if you are referring to the whole compilation:

> 15] A. Rolinson, editor.
> *The Language of Labor: An Anthology.*
> Smith David & Company, Atlanta, Georgia, 1977.

She gets listed in block III if you are referring to part of it:

> 6] R. Winston Hyat.
> The lingo of high steel, with a few notes on the Plains Dakota.
> In A. Rolinson, editor, *The Language of Labor: An Anthology,* pages 46–87. Smith David & Company, Atlanta, Georgia, 1977.

If you refer to both the whole compilation and a part of it in the same list, use a cross-reference in block III of the reference to the part.

> 11] E. D. Klemke, editor.
> *Essays on Wittgenstein.*
> University of Illinois Press, 1982.
>
> . . .
>
> 24] S. A. Rownia.
> Patterns of influence in the later years.
> In Klemke [11], pages 42–57.

The preparer-editor usually appears in block III:

114] Robert Wood.
    *Ruins of Palmyra.*
    Edited by M. H. Chevale. Boston University Press,
    1968.
    Originally published in London, 1753.

Occasionally you may want to compare two or more editions of one author's work. Then your reference list may be easier to read if you put the preparer-editors in block I. Suppose you are comparing two editions of Washington Irving. Your reference list might read:

3] Saxe Commins, editor.
    *Selected Works of Washington Irving.*
    Random House, 1945.

4] Amos Dodd, editor.
    *Washington Irving: The Complete Works.*
    New York, 1863–66.

But there is nothing wrong with using the alternative form:

10] Washington Irving.
    *The Complete Works.*
    Edited by Amos Dodd. New York, 1863–66.

11] Washington Irving.
    *Selected Works.*
    Edited by Saxe Commins. Random House, 1945.

Just be sure to treat both editors the same way.
Translators, like preparer-editors, usually appear in block III:

4] Theodore Blatch.
    *Thomas Erastus and Ecclesiastical Discipline.*
    Translated from the French by Sylvia Schauerbach. University of South Dakota Press, 1977.

But again, if you are comparing two or more translations you may want to list the translators in block I. Suppose you are comparing the first translation of Euclid into English with the first translation into French. Your reference list might read:

2] H. Billingsley, translator.
*The Elements of Geometry of the Most Ancient Philosopher Euclide of Mégara.*
London, 1570.
Facsimile edition published by the Society for Historical Mathematics, Norton Road, Masham, Yorkshire, 1912.

. . .

13] D. Henrion, translator.
*Les Quinze Livres des Elements d'Euclide.*
Paris, second edition 1623.
Originally published in 1615. There are about twenty copies extant, one of them in the Archives Nationales in Paris.

But the alternative form, with Euclid in block I and the translators in block III, is equally good.

If it's not apparent, let your reader know what language the translation is from:

21] K. J. Lindskog.
*Dreams of Flight.*
Translated from the Swedish by A. Richards. Sussex University Press, 1985.

Writing some notes and front matter is a regular part of the job of editing or translating and requires no special mention in your reference.

▷ 4] R. L. Chee, editor and author of an introduction, an appendix, and explanatory notes.
*Biological Controls.*
University of Texas Press, 1985.

4] R. L. Chee, editor.
*Biological Controls.*
University of Texas Press, 1985.

But sometimes your reference is to the annotative material. This is how it might look for an editor-preparer:

9]  Rolf Eberle.
    Foreword to Turbayne [43], pages x–xxviii.

    . . .

43]  Colin Murray Turbayne.
     *The Complete Poems.*
     Edited by Rolf Eberle. University Press of New England,
       1979.

For an editor-compiler:

14]  D. M. Julianelle.
     Introduction to D. M. Julianelle, editor, *Ethnic Geogra-
       phy,* pages i–xxxii.
     Harper & Row, 1958.

And for a translator:

18]  Rosario Sawyer.
     *Moorish Influences in the Cathedral Architecture of
       Mexico.*
     Translated from the Spanish by F. A. Wright. Scribner's,
       1978.

     . . .

44]  F. A. Wright.
     Appendix to Sawyer [18], pages 689–714.

Even if you make no other mention of the main work, it's sometimes worthwhile to write a reference to it for the sake of cross-
reference. If the reference looks tidy without the cross-reference,
keep it self-contained:

83]  S. Glassman.
     Introduction to L. Glassman, *The Naomi Poems,* edited
       by S. Glassman.
     The University of Chicago Press, 1990.

But if it gets too complicated, give the main work separately and use
cross-reference:

▷ 15] J. R. Ellis, translator.
      Footnote, page 212.
      In M. Van Lasserty, *Omelette, Das Ist Die Pop-Pop*
          *Spook* [Hamlet, It Is Thy Father's Ghost], translated
          from Afrikaans Pidgin by Ellis. University of Loui-
          siana Press, 1982.

  15] J. R. Ellis, translator.
      Footnote to Van Lasserty [31], page 212.

      . . .

  31] M. Van Lasserty.
      *Omelette, Das Ist Die Pop-Pop Spook* [Hamlet, It Is
          Thy Father's Ghost].
      Translated from Afrikaans Pidgin by J. R. Ellis. Univer-
          sity of Louisiana Press, 1982.

# II. Titles

Block II of an easy reference is the title of the work; in references to
journal articles, portions of compilations, and volumes of multivolume works there are titles in block III as well.

### What Is a Book?

Since the punctuation of a title depends on whether the work is a
book or a non-book, it is necessary to ask what a book is.

A book is a fat thing bound by itself or the equivalent in some
other medium of a fat thing bound by itself. A non-book is a thin
thing or a thing that's part of something else, or the equivalent in
some other medium of a thin thing or a thing that's part of something else.

A book is a book. One volume of a multivolume work is a book,
and so is the whole multivolume work.

Anything that contains articles by different people is a book, even
if it's thin. A journal is a book. A magazine is a book, and so is a
newspaper. A conference proceedings is a book.

An article in a journal or a magazine is a non-book, even if it takes up one whole issue. What if it's later published as a book? Then the book is a book, but the article remains a non-book.

Is a PhD thesis a book? Yes, but a Master's thesis is not, and neither is any other homework assignment before the PhD. What if a Master's thesis is later published as a book? Again, the book is a book, but the thesis remains a non-book.

A short novel is a book; a long novella is not. A short story is not a book. A poem is not a book unless it's book-length and bound by itself. Chapters of books are not books.

A pamphlet, leaflet, brochure, or booklet is not a book. A report is usually a non-book, although if it's very long and bound by itself you may want to call it a book.

Letters, memos, and notes are not books. Recipes, formulas, equations, and theorems are not books. Laws are not books, although they do tend to go on.

An opera is a book; an aria is a non-book. A musical is a book; a song is a non-book. A record album is a book; a band, a side, or a cut is not. No sketch, print, or painting is a book. A sculpture is not a book.

In both religious and classical studies there are any number of works that were never titled. We call them by conventional names, and these names, being proper nouns, are capitalized. But they're not titles, and they're not underlined or italicized. The Bible and the books of the Bible, the Socratic dialogues, the Koran, the Rig-Veda, and many other works are named but not titled. The Fleta and the Britton, from the reign of Edward I of England, follow this pattern; so does the Penal Code.

When you have a choice, your bias should be toward classing works as non-books; the less punctuation in your reference list, the easier it is to read. Make a decision and stick to it—don't punctuate a borderline case as a book in your text and a non-book in your reference list.

## Book Titles

In both your text and your reference list, book titles get uppers-and-lowers capitalization (capitalize the first word, the first word after a colon, and all other words except articles and unstressed conjunctions and prepositions). Book titles also get underlined or italicized. Underline straight through:

▷ <u>Oxford Reformers</u>.

    <u>Oxford Reformers</u>.

Do not underline the period at the end of the block:

▷ <u>Citizen Involvement.</u>

    <u>Citizen Involvement</u>.

If your reference list is fairly simple and you're using the open format, you may omit the underline or italics from book titles; the uppers-and-lowers punctuation alone will be enough to do the job.

> 22] Jane Henry.
>      A Systematic Study of the Marine Algae of the American
>        East Coast.
>      Dodd, Mead, 1981.

Never omit the underline or italics in the compressed format or in your text.

In uppers-and-lowers capitalization you encounter the problem of how to capitalize hyphenated words. Choose a policy and stick to it:

▷ *An Affair of Far-reaching Consequences.*

*The Angle-Bracket Convention.*

*Arrière-pensée and Other Reservations.*

*An Affair of Far-Reaching Consequences.*

*The Angle-Bracket Convention.*

*Arrière-Pensée and Other Reservations.*

or

*An Affair of Far-reaching Consequences.*

*The Angle-bracket Convention.*

*Arrière-pensée and Other Reservations.*

## Non-book Titles

In your text, non-book titles are punctuated with uppers-and-lowers and surrounded by quotation marks. In your reference list, neither the uppers-and-lowers nor the quotation marks are necessary. Use sentence capitalization (capitalize the first word, the first word after a colon, and no other words except proper nouns and proper adjectives). Omit the quotation marks.

> The Chinese brush: A critical study of the period 1848–1910.
> Even data bases that lie can be compromised.
> Sources for a survey of English porcelain.

## Titles Within Titles

Critical works give rise to titles within titles. Here are the possible combinations and how to handle them. If you have no italics, use this chart:

| Inner Title | Outer Title | Inner Style | Outer Style |
| --- | --- | --- | --- |
| non–book | non–book | "Uppers and Lowers" | Unquoted sentence capitalization. |
| book | non–book | Unquoted Uppers and Lowers | Unquoted sentence capitalization. |
| non–book | book | "Uppers and Lowers" | Unquoted Uppers and Lowers. |
| book | book | "Uppers and Lowers" | Unquoted Uppers and Lowers. |

If you have italics, use this chart:

| Inner Title | Outer Title | Inner Style | Outer Style |
|---|---|---|---|
| non-book | non-book | "Uppers and Lowers" | Unquoted sentence capitaliza-tion. |
| book | non-book | *Unquoted Uppers and Lowers* | Unquoted sentence capitaliza-tion. |
| non-book | book | "Uppers and Lowers" | *Unquoted Uppers and Lowers* |
| book | book | "Uppers and Lowers" | *Unquoted Uppers and Lowers* |

Non-book within non-book looks the same whether you have italics or not:

An addendum to Marinovski's "Motions in Log Space."

Book within non-book varies:

Citizen Kane, The Great Gatsby, and some con-ventions of American narrative.

*Citizen Kane, The Great Gatsby*, and some conventions of American narrative.

Without italics, both non-book and book within book look the same:

Collected Essays on Yeats's "A Prayer for My Son."

Lawrence, Sartre, and "Women in Love."

With italics, non-book within book looks like this:

*Collected Essays on Yeats's "A Prayer for My Son."*

And book within book looks like this:

*Lawrence, Sartre, and* Women in Love.

## Odd Originals

A number of important works of the twentieth century deliberately violate typographical conventions. If you follow the style of the original, your reference looks odd; if you don't, it looks prissy.

> *i: six nonlectures.*
> *I: Six Nonlectures.*

The joke would cease to be a joke if it ceased causing us discomfort.

When odd typography is a convention rather than a flouting of convention, ignore it. Some journals, for instance, style themselves and all the articles in them in full caps. Convert such titles to the usual pattern.

▷ 2] S. P. Bower.
   AFFERENT IMPULSES TO THE CEREBELLAR HEMISPHERES.
   *THE JOURNAL OF NEUROPHYSIOLOGY* 130(1): 55–75, 1957.

2] S. P. Bower.
   Afferent Impulses to the Cerebellar Hemispheres.
   *The Journal of Neurophysiology* 130(1):55–75, 1957.

## Short Titles

Shortened versions of titles should never appear on your reference list. The chapter on special schemes gives some uses for short names in your text, in your footnotes, and in a special section between your text and your reference list. But on the reference list itself, a title should appear in its entirety.

> ▷ *The Sublime and Beautiful.*
>   *Philosophical Inquiry into the Origin of Our Ideas on the Sublime and Beautiful.*

The only reason ever to eliminate part of a title is to avoid uninformative reception.

> ▷ W. B. Yeats.
>   *The Collected Poems of W. B. Yeats.*
>
>   W. B. Yeats.
>   *The Collected Poems.*

## Title-Colon-Subtitle

Regardless of the style of the original, add a colon if it's needed to separate title from subtitle.

> ▷ *Public Electricity Supply and Demand.*
>   *Public Electricity: Supply and Demand.*
> ▷ Ancient Egyptian language and writing techniques for translation.
>   Ancient Egyptian language and writing: Techniques for translation.

Regardless of the style of the original, subtract an awkward comma or colon separating title from subtitle (or sub-subtitle, as in the third example):

> ▷ Security considerations: IV.
>   Security considerations IV.
> ▷ Lectures in obstetrics, 7.
>   Lectures in obstetrics 7.

▷ *Welles and Salisbury: 1818–1826: The Quiet Years.*

  *Welles and Salisbury 1818–1826: The Quiet Years.*

If the original uses a dash to separate title from subtitle, you may change it to a colon.

## The Trumpeting Subtitle

It is the custom in some scholarly circles to draw a discreet veil over any subtitle that seems crude or hucksterish—the custom, but a bad one. Give your reader the title whole, not a bowdlerized version.

▷ The whore of Babylon.

    The whore of Babylon: Being an inquiry into the iniquities of the pope of Rome, the beast with seven heads, most assiduously compiled and brought together with great care and its author hopes some purpose.

▷ *Wires and Wiring.*

    *Wires and Wiring: An Indispensable Guide for Every Engineer and Student.*

Even less is there any excuse for suppressing an informative subtitle:

▷ *The Nuer.*

    *The Nuer: A Description of the Modes of Livelihood and the Political Institutions of a Nilotic People.*

With subtitles as with main titles, the only reason to eliminate part of the original is to avoid useless repetition:

▷ Louise d'Epinay.
  *From la Chevrette to La Briche: The Collected Correspondence of Louise d'Epinay.*

  Louise d'Epinay.
  *From la Chevrette to La Briche: The Collected Correspondence.*

## Changes in Titles

In order to bring titles into conformity with your reference style, you may change uppercase letters to lowercase and vice versa; you may add and subtract underlines or italics; you may add and subtract colons. You may shorten a title to avoid repeating information given in another block of the reference.

Otherwise, change nothing. Do not correct punctuation. Do not correct or Americanize or modernize spelling. Do not feel that you need to make the titles on a reference list uniform. The young scholar is sometimes upset at the sight of an inconsistent reference list:

6] Martin Bennett.
The arithmetical limits of logspace.

7] Rosemary Browne.
The arithmetic limits of log-space.

Consistency is a virtue in many places, but not here. Bennett is entitled to his preferences, Browne to hers.

The slighter the variation, the harder your task in copying it exactly: judgment/judgement, catalog/catalogue, traveled/travelled. Be scrupulous. Check and double-check.

## What Title?

What do you do if the title of the work appears in more than one form? For a book, follow the title page; for a journal article, follow the title at the head or the foot of the article.

## Foreign Titles

Foreign book titles are underlined or italicized because they're book titles, not because they're foreign. Foreign nonbook titles are not underlined or italicized.

Unless a foreign title is so highly cognate with English that its meaning is immediately apparent, it's a courtesy to provide a translation for your monolingual readers:

Sylvie Blanchette.
L'agrandissement. [The blowup.]

In J.-P. Lache, editor, *Six Contes Modernes* [Six Modern Tales], pages 293–370. Flammarion, 1981.

If you are referring to a translation, giving the original title is helpful when your reader is likely to have heard of it.

Karl Marx.
*Pre-capitalist Economic Formations.* [*Formen die der Kapitalistischen Produktion Vorhergehen.*]

Since this work is generally called the *Formen,* your reader will want to connect the nickname with your reference.

Every language has its own rules about capitalizing words in book titles. Following the rule of the mother tongue requires uniformity; it would be rude to capitalize Spanish titles by Spanish rules and Portuguese titles by English rules. A further difficulty is that many title pages are printed in full caps, so that you can't tell what the native punctuation would be in uppers and lowers. If you prefer nonetheless to follow foreign conventions for foreign titles, you must be both erudite and dogged. But if you're afraid that your performance may not live up to your ambition, impose English rules on all titles regardless of origin.

## Untitled Works

If a work has no title, describe it in block II.

▷ 48] Thomas R. MacMahon.
   *Frontiers in Psychometrics* LIV(2):24, 1985.

48] Thomas R. MacMahon.
   Letter to the editor.
   *Frontiers in Psychometrics* LIV(2):24, 1985.

Only as a last resort, when you can't figure out any sensible description for a work, should you write:

19] E. T. Heald.
   Untitled.
   In Evelyn Zeller, editor, *A Celebration,* pages 16–18.
   University of Oklahoma Press, 1978.

# III. Bibliographic Information

A brief note here, just so you won't be confused about what comes between blocks II and IV: Block III is the workhorse of the reference. Having said who wrote the work you're referring to and what it's called, you must now give your reader the information she needs to get the source for herself. That information varies tremendously from one kind of source to another, and there's no such thing as a Platonic ideal of block III, just a practical answer to the practical question "How do I find this?" The chapter on easy references describes the many answers you can give to that question.

# IV. More Bibliographic Information

If you work in a field where most of the sources are current, published, and easily available, you may never need to use block IV to add bibliographic information to a reference. But if your field and your tastes incline you to sources that are difficult to come by, you may frequently be in a position to help your reader out.

Are you referring to a rare work? Your inexperienced reader will want to know how to get hold of another copy. Are you referring to an expensive hardcover? Your impoverished reader will bless you for mentioning the cheap paperback as well. Are you referring to a pirated Taiwan edition? Your reader of tender conscience will appreciate knowing about a version on the up-and-up. Are you referring to an early edition? Your young reader will want to know about current versions. Are you referring to an archival source? Your homebound reader will be grateful to you for telling her about any published materials on the subject.

One of the kindest uses you can make of block IV is to suggest a translation for monolingual readers:

> 15] Rudolf K. Goldschmit-Jentner.
> *Die Begegnung mit dem Genius.*
> Fischer Bücherei, Frankfurt and Hamburg, Germany, 1964.
> Translated as *Brilliant Encounters* by Edward Miel. Bantam, 1982.

You have no obligation to exhaust yourself chasing down information for block IV. When you know something that your reader
may find useful, tell her:

> 38]  Michele Wexler.
>        The vanity racket.
>        *Partisan Review* XLII(5):39–54, 1979.
>        Also in *Women at War*, Dell, 1983, in a longer version.

If what you know is too vague to be of any use, don't abuse your
reader's interest by being airy:

> ▷  14]  S. A. Shepard.
>        The lives of the Massachuset Indians.
>        *Readings in Anthropology* 12(3):113–168, 1974.
>        Later collected.

# V. Annotation

The occasions for using the last block are rare, but sometimes, for
instance, you would like to warn your reader about a flawed source:

> 13]  H. Mendes-Citié.
>        *Orthogenesis in the Trans-Jordan Flora.*
>        University of Illinois Press, 1921.
>        The author's evolutionary beliefs have been totally dis-
>           credited, but his drawings remain valuable illustra-
>           tions of the region's plants and flowers.

Sometimes you would like to connect two sources with a cross-
reference:

> 22]  Juan Fernandez.
>        A constructive proof of Fowker's theorem.
>        *The Amateur Mathematician* VII(8):47–48, 1972.
>        This is the most elegant proof, but not the first one [16].

Sometimes you may know some special information about a source
too fascinating to keep to yourself. Play this tune with a light hand:

14] Benjamin Hardan Howett.
   *Memoirs.*
   Cassell, London, 1862.
   The E. M. of the dedication is probably Edward Morris.

And sometimes you may want to commend a source to your reader for some special reason. Since every reference constitutes a recommendation, use block V this way only when you have something unusual to pass on. If you were to attempt to summarize the virtues of every source, your reference list would begin to look like *TV Guide*.

# Pinpointing

To pinpoint a reference is to describe exactly what pages, verses, figures, lines, and so on you're discussing—usually what pages.

### Simple Versus Compound

In a simple reference, the page numbers to which you're pointing go where they fit most neatly, either in block II or in block III:

38] N. K. Prosnitz.
   *Sequences of Evolutionary Branching,* pages 247–283.
   W. H. Freeman, 1976.

5] Dorothy Beale.
   A small adventure.
   In *The Collected Stories,* pages 41–65. Viking, 1981.

In a compound reference, the page numbers go after the main entry:

P. T. Alonzo.
*Minority Voting Rights.*
Basic Books, 1981.
   [4] Pages 39–51.
   [5] Pages 106–130.
   [6] Page 271.

Sometimes a young scholar will try to get around writing a compound reference by putting part of the information in her text and the other part in the reference list:

▷ While the Chinese in San Francisco were organizing themselves into Irish-style voting blocs, the Chinese in the Sacramento Valley had no interest in remaining in America and formed organizations only for burial insurance [4, pages 106–130; 19, page 331].

Be sure that any computer system you intend to use for word processing or type-setting can handle compound references correctly.

## Be Reasonable

No task in writing a reference requires more taste and judgment than pinpointing. At one extreme there's the author who has used only four pages from a thousand-page book but won't tell her reader what the four pages are. At the other extreme there's the author who pinpoints every second or third page of her source, cluttering up her reference list to no advantage. Steer clear of both extremes.

The page numbers that you give should reflect accurately the use you've made of your source. If you summarize the central argument of a whole book or article or pamphlet or build on its central thesis, the most accurate reference you can write is to the whole work, with no pinpointing:

41] M. G. Souther.
 *Eugene O'Neill and the Lace-curtain Irish.*
 Miami University Press, 1984.

If you use a hunk of material, identify the beginning point and the end point. Do not construct a compound reference of rags and tatters.

▷ G. S. Jestin
 *Work-to-Rule as a Tactic in the Early Labour Movement.*
 Longmans, 1955.

[18] Page 41.          [21] Pages 50–52.
[19] Page 43.          [22] Pages 54–55.
[20] Pages 45–48.      [23] Pages 56.

Draw this together into one coherent mass:

18] G. S. Jestin.
   *Work-to-Rule as a Tactic in the Early Labour Move-*
      *ment*, pages 41–56.
   Longmans, 1955.

To some extent, the way that you pinpoint depends on how much work your source has done for you. Suppose, for instance, that you've talked about two poems. One appears in a collection that has a table of contents; the reference to it may have a page number or not, as you prefer.

12] C. J. Danehauer.
   Frost-heaves.
   In *November and Other Poems,* page 6. Yellow Gate
      Press, Pickering, Rhode Island, 1978.

or

12] C. J. Danehauer.
   Frost-heaves.
   In *November and Other Poems.* Yellow Gate Press,
      Pickering, Rhode Island, 1978.

The other appears in a collection that has no table of contents; the reference to that poem needs a page number:

18] Aaron Higgins.
   Safety shoes.
   In W. M. Cooperman, editor, *The Industrial Revolution*
      *in Poetry,* page 139. Penguin, 1969.

## Pinpointing Without Pages

In referring to a work that has appeared in many editions, pinpointing by chapter or section is preferable to pinpointing by page.

▷  3] Jane Austen.
       *Mansfield Park,* pages 40–46.
       D. C. Heath edition, 1958.

   3] Jane Austen.
       *Mansfield Park,* chapter 3.
       D. C. Heath edition, 1958.

The two versions are not identical; chapter 3 extends from page 39
to 51. But the chapter reference is more useful, since in your reader's
edition pages 40–46 may fall in chapter 2 or chapter 4.


## Pinpointing Quotations

There are two schools of thought about pinpointing quotations.
The first holds that every quotation must have an exact page reference. This has much to recommend it, if for no other reason than
that it curbs excessive quotation. The second school (which I incline
to) relaxes this rule for the sake of brevity. The difference shows up
when you're using a portion of material from a source and quoting
from the middle of it. School #1 says that you must write a compound reference:

    E. L. Grannis.
    Simulated navigational geometries.
    *The Journal of Applied Mathematics* XI(4):201–330, 1986.
       [15] Pages 235–248.
       [16] Page 239.

School #2 permits a simple reference in this case:

    [15] E. L. Grannis.
         Simulated navigational geometries, pages 235–248.
         *The Journal of Applied Mathematics* XI(4):201–330,
         1986.

You must decide for yourself what method you prefer in what circumstances.

## Other Kinds of Pinpointing

Your points of reference are usually page numbers, but they might just as easily be something else:

> Ralph Batriban.
> Chemical gasification of solids and liquids.
> *Journal of the American Engineering Association* XXXIV(2): 1248–1267, 1975.
> [8] Figure 3.
> [9] Figure 14.

## Shorthand

There's no way to make a reference list an easy read, but you can keep it from being any more forbidding than it has to be. An important consideration is that hyperpunctuated material is much harder to read than ordinary text, and the reference list is the very exemplar of hyperpunctuation.

For that reason I strongly recommend that you do not abbreviate "p." for "page," "ch." for "chapter," "fig." for "figure," let alone "fasc." for "fascicle." Even over the course of a very long list, these abbreviations will save you only a line or two because of the way that references are set up. Typically the unabbreviated version works out to be no longer than the abbreviated one:

> ▷ 21] Carol Kulakowski.
>    *Marxist Views on the Oil Economy*, pp. 304–329.
>    University of Missouri Press, 1983.
>
>    21] Carol Kulakowski.
>    *Marxist Views on the Oil Economy*, pages 304–329.
>        University of Missouri Press, 1983.

This is true in the compressed format too:

> ▷ 7] L. C. Loke. *Hervey at Court,* pp. 237–280. Leslie Frewin Publishers, 1979.
>
>    7] L. C. Loke. *Hervey at Court,* pages 237–280. Leslie Frewin Publishers, 1979.

Abbreviation is usually a false economy. It saves little or nothing in space and costs your reader extra effort in looking at it.

Should you write "pages 113–28" or "pages 113–128"? The one-character saving is not worth even the very slight increase in difficulty in reading the shorter version.

"Pages 35 f." means pages 35–36; write it out. "Pages 119 ff." gives your reader no idea when to stop; write out the end point as well as the beginning, "pages 119–133."

"Passim" means here and there, as in "pages 209–240 passim." Since no one thinks that you're referring to every word or every sentence in that portion of your source, the expression is usually silly.

# Needless Information

If you were a publisher or a bookseller, you might wish to indicate how long an item is, by what process and in what profusion it is illustrated, how many informative tables, glossaries, and indexes it contains—all in order to justify the price you intend to ask. But if you're writing a reference, you can forget about all this information unless it is so unusual as to require mention in block V.

▷ 88] Basil Willey.
*Nineteenth-Century Studies: Coleridge to Matthew Arnold.*
Introduction by Philippa Ashby. 293 pages, 16 pages of illustrations, 4 in color. With a chronology of English letters, 1800–1888. Columbia University Press, 1981.

88] Basil Willey.
*Nineteenth-Century Studies: Coleridge to Matthew Arnold.*
Columbia University Press, 1981.

# Easy References

Easy references fit the three-block reference format smoothly and naturally:

> I. Author.
> II. Title.
> III. Bibliographic information.

## Books

In the best of all possible worlds, you would refer only to first editions of English-language books put out by major American and English publishers, and your book references would all look like these:

> 5] R. Dudley Edwards.
> *A New History of Ireland.*
> University of Maryland Press, 1983.

> 32] W. D. Routt.
> *Eratosthenes of Alexandria: The Sun, the Moon, and the Numbers.*
> Random House, 1972.

> 18] Deirdre Liam.
> *Excesses of Etiquette: The European Courts of the 17th Century.*
> Chatto & Windus, 1959.

Every book reference is an elaboration on this simple format.

## Publishers

It seems a sensible rule to follow the publishers' own style in describing them. Unfortunately, many publishers are as fickle as thirteen-year-olds about how to style themselves. The book in front of me was published by Hill and Wang; or by Hill & Wang; or by Hill and Wang, Inc. All three forms appear on the one book. So common is this multiplicity of designations that a better rule is: Follow the title page, but not slavishly. Since you are describing rather than filing suit, you may leave off legal bumph like Inc., Ltd., and Cie. And no harm will result from calling the publishers T. Y. Crowell instead of Thomas Y. Crowell Company, so long as you avoid shorthand your reader will not recognize. Just be sure to give any one name in the same form through any one list—not "Scribner's" in item [12] and "Charles Scribner's Sons" in item [37]. Choose one or the other and be faithful to it.

Old-fashioned references gave a city for every publishing house, which was always either too much information or not enough. "Random, New York" is silly in one direction; "The Bandersnatch Press, New York" is silly in the other. Give as complete an address as you can for an obscure publisher:

2] A. K. Amady.
*Songs and Tunes of the Wetheheld Hills.*
Kammen & Condry, Mason City, Iowa, 1957.

54] B. K. Liapunov, editor.
*Exploring local parks.*
The Angleworm Press, 42 Vernon Street, New Haven,
Connecticut 06511. 1984.

Give no address for a major publisher:
9] Lawrence Johns.
*Assemblage and Collage.*
Simon & Schuster, 1978.

Between dark obscurity and bright fame there is a great middle ground where you must let your knowledge of the patterns of publication in your field guide you. When you think that an address will help your reader, give it to her.

For foreign publishers, city and country should be in the English version:

▷ Bellini, Firenze, Italia, 1972.

  Bellini, Florence, Italy, 1972.

▷ Stammenverlag, Hollerstrasse 143, Köln, Deutschland, 1934.

  Stammenverlag, Hollerstrasse 143, Cologne, Germany, 1934.

Multilingual people should communicate in one language at a time; unilingual people should not pretend to be multilingual.

## No Publisher

When a place of publication is listed with no publisher, tell your reader what you know:

    31] R. Colt Hoare.
        *A Tour through the Island of Elba.*
        London, 1814.

When there is no information about publication, say so;

    42] S. D. Gaites.
        *The Foundations of German Nationalism.*
        No publisher, 1917.

Often you will want to annotate such a reference:

    34] M. R. Helder.
        *The History of the Helder Family.*
        No publisher, approximately 1875.
        Mattie Helder's will lists a printing press among her possessions, on which she probably produced this volume. The only known copy is in the Wisconsin State Archive.

Until quite recently, of course, publication was a haphazard phenomenon, and even today there are many books published off the

---

Bad examples are marked with an arrowhead (▷).

beaten track. The fine points of bibliographic provenance are interesting, but your main object in writing a reference is to help your reader get her hands on your sources. Keep that in mind when you deal with works that, although published, are for all practical purposes archival.

Books that list no publisher because they are still in manuscript present one last possibility; see the section on works not yet published.

## Series and Imprints

Publishing books in series and under special imprints appears to be resolute and diligent, so there are many series and imprints, some genuine, some spurious or at least short-lived. You may therefore decide for yourself, based on your preference and knowledge of the source, whether to include such information in block III. Avoid repeating the publisher's name in the series or imprint name.

> ▷ 8] Priscilla Braids, editor.
>    *Views of the Baroque.*
>    An Iowa History of Arts and Letters Book. Iowa State University Press, 1978.

> 8] Priscilla Braids, editor.
>    *Views of the Baroque.*
>    A History of Arts and Letters Book. Iowa State University Press, 1978.

or

> 8] Priscilla Braids, editor.
>    *Views of the Baroque.*
>    Iowa State University Press, 1978.

## Dates, Editions, and Reprints

If a date appears on the title page of a book, give that as the date in your reference and thank your lucky stars. If there is no date on the title page, you may have a difficult task before you. What you are aiming for is the date of publication; if the work you are referring to has been published more than once, you would like to give dates for both the current and the original publication.

Let's consider first a modern work that is not a reprint. On the page behind the title page, copyright and printing history are usually given. Look first for a copyright date; if there's only one, use it in your reference. If there are several copyright dates, use the latest one unless it's a renewal.

© 1937, 1955, 1977, 1983.

Copyright 1927, copyright renewed 1954.

The date to use in the first case is 1983, in the second 1927. Lacking a copyright date, use the first printing date of the latest edition.

First published 1906. Second edition 1907, reprinted 1908, 1910, 1911, 1914, 1916, 1918, 1919, 1922, 1923, 1925, 1927. Third edition 1931, reprinted 1934, 1936, 1938, 1940, 1947, 1949, 1951, 1954, 1958.

(This publisher seems short on warehousing.) Here the date to use is 1931. Always mention along with the date any edition other than the first:

8] H. W. Fowler and F. G. Fowler.
    *The King's English.*
    Oxford University Press, third edition 1931.

A reprint of a modern work—and that includes most paperbacks—will usually present more difficulties. Blessings on the paperback publisher who makes it possible for you to write a sensible, informative reference:

36] B. H. Wardmoore.
    *The Nightingale and the Lark.*
    Vintage, 1983.
    Originally published as *Dualities in Keats and Shelley,*
       University of Tennessee Press, 1948.

All too often one or another of these pieces of information is missing. Fill in as much as you can.

Worse still are reprints of works from previous centuries. Copyright dates on these are useless—the copyright refers only to the front matter, not to the work. Relying on the information the reprint publisher provides would often produce such anomalous references as:

▷  15]  Charles Dickens.
         *Great Expectations.*
         Ehrlich & Murphy, 1954.

You will probably want to plump out this scanty information for your own sake, to keep from feeling foolish, as well as for the sake of your naive reader, who might picture Charles Dickens as a figure from the time of Eisenhower's administration. At the least, insert the word "edition" into block III to give your reader a clue about what's going on:

   15]  Charles Dickens.
        *Great Expectations.*
        Ehrlich & Murphy edition, 1954.

Better yet, supply the author's dates:

   15]  Charles Dickens (1812–70).
        *Great Expectations.*
        Ehrlich & Murphy edition, 1954.

   Never let a reference go without a date. Here is how to indicate an exact date established from external evidence:

   18]  Elizabeth (pseudonym).
        *The Tale of a Girl.*
        Birmingham, England [1833].

Here is how to indicate a good guess:

    9]  R. V. Hailor.
        *The Hygienic Instructor.*
        William Manor & Sons, Boston, approximately 1910.

("Ca." is OK here in place of "approximately" if you prefer.)

6]  Albert Edwardi.
    *The Universal Parent.*
    Edinburgh, early nineteenth century.

Use your knowledge of the source to date it as best you can.

### Library of Congress

Many books published recently in the United States have Library of
Congress cataloging information on the page behind the title page;
some reproduce the whole cataloging-in-publication card. You can
use it to verify information you've gathered elsewhere, like the author's name and the publication date.

### ISBN Number

If you work in a field where your reader is likely to want to purchase
the book to which you're referring, by all means tell her its ISBN
number.

# Compilations

By "compilation" I mean the work of several authors gathered together by an editor into a book. In a reference to the whole compilation, the editor takes block I and the authors are not mentioned:

13]  N. C. Grafton, editor.
     *Recent Results in Analysis.*
     Addison-Wesley, 1978.

In a reference to one of the articles or stories or poems in the
compilation, the author takes block I:

29]  C. I. Varick-Weiss.
     Slow patching routines with very small error bounds.
     In N. C. Grafton, editor, *Recent Results in Analysis,*
         pages 40–49. Addison-Wesley, 1978.

If you're referring to more than one piece from the compilation, you'll certainly want to mention the whole work as well in order to make cross-reference possible:

> 4] G. N. Fontana.
> Needlepoint and bargello.
> In McNeill [16], pages 320–342.
>
> . . .
>
> 16] A. R. McNeill, editor.
> *Renaissance Handiwork.*
> Thames & Hudson, 1959.
>
> . . .
>
> 24] F. S. Sibbett, Jr.
> Secular gold.
> In McNeill [16], pages 41–63.

## Collections

By "collection" I mean the work of one author gathered into a book. (I'm distinguishing the words "compilation" and "collection" artificially, for the sake of convenience.) The reference to a whole collection looks like any other book reference:

> 8] Glenda Batson.
> *Thoughts and Afterthoughts.*
> Crown, 1981.

If you're referring to only one piece from a collection, the whole work gets no separate entry; push it down to block III:

> 8] Glenda Batson.
> Castro at fifty.
> In *Thoughts and Afterthoughts,* pages 288–320. Crown, 1981.

If you're referring to several pieces from the gathered work of one author, do not use cross-reference. It looks quite strange, and there's no advantage to it:

▷ 27] C. R. Ridgeway.
 *Currents in Criminal Law.*
 Eerdmans, 1976.

28] C. R. Ridgeway.
 The Miranda decision.
 In Ridgeway [27], pages 13–40.

29] C. R. Ridgeway.
 Preventive detention.
 In Ridgeway [27], pages 239–248.

Construct a compound reference instead:

C. R. Ridgeway.
*Currents in Criminal Law.*
Eerdmans, 1976.
[27] The Miranda decision, pages 13–40.
[28] Preventive detention, pages 239–248.

# Editions with Editors

Sometimes an author does a substantial revision of her own work; the new version is called a new edition:

22] D. F. Stockham.
 *Land Values in Parma, 1400–1700.*
 Louisiana State University Press, second edition 1958.

Sometimes a publisher reprints work that's no longer under copyright with no editing or none to speak of; that too is called an edition:

17] John Ruskin (1819–1900).
 *The Seven Lamps of Architecture.*
 The Ridge Press edition, 1978.
 Originally published in 1849.

But in the sort of edition that this section is about, an editor prepares the work of an author for publication, and the editor's contribution is acknowledged. Except in comparing two or more editions of one author, the editor takes block III:

11] K. M. Hofmann.
    *The Collected Correspondence.*
    Edited by G. V. Larch. Random House, 19–58.

These things pile up. Suppose a book is both a collection (several pieces by one author) and an edition (with an editor), and suppose you want to refer to a piece of the work. Block III gets a little crowded, and the editor's name must follow the name of the whole collection:

39] Chaim Muybridge.
    Uncontrolled chain reactions.
    In *The Posthumous Papers,* pages 560–596. Edited by
        Kevin Costabel. Cambridge University Press, 1979.

In referring to several pieces from one collection-edition, construct a compound reference.

# Translations

Here again, the work you're referring to has a midwife. Except in comparing two or more translations, the translator of a single author takes block III:

29] Cosimo Varda.
    *A New Classification System for the Succulents.*
    Translated from the Italian by R. Wyllie. New Horizon
        Press, 1985.

The translator of a single author's work may also edit it:

14] J-M. Gaudel.
    *The Vest-pocket Park.* [*Un Coin de Verdure.*]
    Edited and translated by H. L. Prior. Schenkman, 1981.

What with translated collections and translated compilations and translated multivolume works and translated articles, there are hundreds of kinds of references in which the name of a translator might appear. When you encounter one of these situations, you must combine the format for the work with the format for the translation. A compilation-translation, for instance, would look like this:

28]  H. E. Harton, editor and translator.
       *Readings from Modern Arabic.*
       University of Georgia Press, 1980.

Just be sure that no information gets lost in the combination.


# Multivolume Works

A multivolume work, unlike a series, contains a definite number of volumes. One author may write a work of several volumes, or several authors may write a volume or two apiece under the guidance of an editor.

The key to writing good references to multivolume works is never to mention the name of more than one volume in any one reference. In referring to a multivolume work by a single author, the names of the individual volumes are suppressed:

▷   4]  Georges Branaque.
         *The Decline of Manners.* Volume I: *The Jacksonian Age.*
            Volume II: *The Plutocrats.* Volume III: *The Modern
            Barbarians.*
         Schocken, 1971, 1974, and 1979.

     4]  Georges Branaque.
         *The Decline of Manners.*
         Three volumes. Schocken, 1971–79.

Notice that only the first and last dates are mentioned in the correct version. In referring to a multivolume work by several authors, both the names of the individual volumes and the names of the authors are suppressed:

▷  56] Alma MacRae, editor.
       *Natural-language Processing.* Volume I: *Machine Trans-
       lation,* by R. Wilensky. Volume II: *Artificial Intelli-
       gence,* by J. R. Meehan.
       Yale University Press, 1974–75.

    56] Alma MacRae, editor.
        *Natural-language Processing.*
        Two volumes. Yale University Press, 1974–75.

That's how you would refer to a multivolume set as a whole. But
such references are uncommon; usually you want to refer to the
individual volumes. For a work by a single author, drop the reference to the whole set:

     4] Georges Branaque.
        *The Decline of Manners.* Volume I: *The Jacksonian Age.*
        Schocken, 1971.

For a work by several authors, retain the reference to the whole set
to make cross-reference possible:

    15] Alma MacRae, editor.
        *Natural-language Processing.*
        Two volumes. Yale University Press, 1974–75.

        . . .

    38] R. Wilensky.
        *Machine Translation.*
        Volume I in MacRae [15], 1974.

If you refer to several volumes in a set by several authors, the
references will be scattered around your list in alphabetical order. If
you refer to several volumes in a set by a single author, ignore
alphabetical order for those references and put them in volume
order instead.

     4] Georges Branaque.
        *The Decline of Manners.* Volume I. *The Jacksonian Age.*
        Schocken, 1971.

5] Georges Branaque.
   *The Decline of Manners.* Volume II: *The Plutocrats.*
   Schocken, 1974.

6] Georges Branaque.
   *The Decline of Manners.* Volume III: *The Modern Barbarians.*
   Schocken, 1979.

Volume order, I, II, III, not alphabetical order, Jacksonian, Modern, Plutocrats. It is not reasonable to ask authors to name their works in alphabetical sequence just for the sake of reference lists.

It is important to get the pattern straight at the start, because multivolume works are subject to many a change between conception and completion. They can be unfinished:

39] D. N. B. Preston.
   *Paths to Socialism.*
   Six volumes planned. Volumes 1–4, Scribner's, 1963–74.

Editors can quit or die:

13] E. van der Leigh, editor.
   *Economics, Armament, and Foreign Policy.* Volumes II–VI.
   University of Wisconsin Press, 1957–64.
   Eight volumes in all. Martin Handsore edited volume I [6]; Catherine Shotte edited volumes VII and VIII, 1966–67.

Publishers can change:

29] Diane Halas, general editor.
   *The Medieval Town.*
   Four volumes. Volumes 1 and 2, Princeton University Press, 1956–58. Volumes 3 and 4, Simon & Schuster, 1960–64.

Projects can be abandoned:

8] J. Sachs, editor.
   *Vernacular Gothic.*
   Four volumes. Livermore, London, 1922–28.
   Of the fifteen volumes originally planned, only those on
      Northumberland, Durham, Lincoln, and Chester were
      completed.

In numbering volumes, follow the style of the original unless the
original uses a mixture of Arabic and Roman numerals, which happens surprisingly often; use all Roman if there is a mixture.

## Span Dates

I tend to give span dates in elided form (1750–82) although I write
span pages out in full (pages 1750–1782). My reasoning is that
dates have come in fours for almost a thousand years now and will
continue to do so for another eight thousand. For years, we automatically supply the missing 17 in the elided form "-82." Page
numbers, on the other hand, have no automatic shape; they come in
a jumble of ones, twos, threes, and fours. It takes only a fraction of
the reader's time to think, "Pages 175–82, must be 175–182," but I
see no point in troubling her at all. If this rationale seems specious
to you (and I admit that it's not watertight), give both dates and
pages in full. You must not, of course, impose your preference on
someone else. If the author calls her book *Vienna 1858–1861,* you
may not change it to *Vienna 1858–61* to suit your style.

# Journal Articles

In the best of all possible worlds, you would refer only to English-
language pieces in thriving major publications, and all your journal
references would look like these:

112] Richard P. Schaedel.
     The native ethic of Latin American cities: Hope or
        illusion?
     *Journal of Urban Studies* LV(7):246–287, 1978.

7] Cynthia Benton.
Upper and lower bounds on the solution to Bay's problem.
*Readings in Analysis and Theory* 19(3):146–151, 1954.

19] Simon Hamish.
Collective psychology in the "era of crowds."
*The Positivist* XXXIV(12):9–58, 1982.

Here is what the parts of block III stand for:

Every journal reference is an elaboration of this simple format.

## Abbreviations

Old-fashioned references to journal articles were marvels of abbreviation, harder to crack than the Purple Code. Having eliminated bibliographic footnotes and all the duplication they entailed, we can spend a little of that space on avoiding abbreviations.

▷ *J. Amer. Ass. Mech. Eng.*
*The Journal of the American Association of Mechanical Engineers.*

▷ *Q. Soc. Res. Psych. Psych.*
*Quarterly of the Society for Research in Psychology and Psychiatry.*

If the name of a journal incorporates an abbreviation your reader may not recognize, spell it out for her in block V:

▷ *ASGG Journal of Biogeological Results* XVII(8):212–214, 1978.

*ASGG Journal of Biogeological Results* XVII(8):212–214, 1978.

ASGG is the American Society of Geologists and Geophysi-
cists.

## Missing Elements and Extended Dates

Some journals number their issues but do not collect them into
volumes:

*Civil Disobedience Newsletter* 43:18–26, 1982.

Some number the volumes and call the numbers by months or
seasons:

*Journal of East Asian Studies* IX:349–362, Autumn 1936.

*The American Anthropologist* 46:321–235, February 1971.

Some number both volumes and issues but are easier to identify by
date:

*Vogue* XXXIII(7):47, April 1923.

*Newsweek* XXIX(35):19–21, 17 March 1978.

Some carry only a date:

*The Pathfinder* 36–51, July 1947.

Dates are among the elements you regularize in writing your
reference. Regardless of the style of the original, write the dates for a
periodical:

month (no comma) year

or

day (no comma) month (no comma) year.

Write out the name of the month; if you were to represent it numerically, it would be difficult to read and subject to ambiguity.

▷ 9/11/1979.

9 November 1979.

## Whole Number

Sometimes an entire issue of a journal is devoted to one article. It makes no difference; it's still an article:

> 12]  M. Clemens.
>       Datives of purpose and intent.
>       *The Classical Philologist* CIII(3):1–128, 1981.

If you feel that you must stress the importance given the article by devoting a whole number to it, here is how you show it:

> 9]  A. L. Heppel.
>       The census in Massachusetts 1880–1920.
>       *Social History Quarterly* XIV(whole number 2):156–213, 1985.

I am unable to think of an occasion that requires this form.


## New Series

Have you ever seen a journal issue marked something like "Volume 2 n.s., number 3"? "N.s." means new series, and the story behind it is usually that the old volume and number system got so mixed up and behindhand that the editor gave up on it and started over. There is no need to indicate the new series in your reference to such an issue; the date will serve to distinguish the new 2(3) from the old one.


## Combined Numbers

Have you ever seen a journal issue marked something like "Volume XXXI, combined numbers 5 and 6"? Here again, the journal has fallen further and further behind its publication schedule and the editor has decided to catch up by a piece of legerdemain, numbering one issue as two. Follow her lead with bland acceptance in your reference—XXXI(5–6)—and with compassion in your heart. Most journals are understaffed and underfunded, and any little tricks their editors need to use should be forgiven them.

## Broken Pagination

Rarely in scholarly journals but frequently in magazines, articles are split into small pieces and strewn through an issue to fit layout and advertising requirements. Use the first page number and a plus sign (+) to indicate broken pagination.

▷ 71] Garry Wills.
    A primer of state and local politics.
    *The Atlantic Monthly* CVII(8):186–188, 191, 194, 200–214, 228–230, August 1978.

71] Garry Wills.
    A primer of state and local politics.
    *The Atlantic Monthly* CVII(8):186+, August 1978.

## Serial Publication

Sometimes an article is split into several parts and published in several issues. Compress this information as neatly as you can.

▷ 53] R. Proffer.
    Requirements in translation.
    Part 1, *Russian Literature Triquarterly* VIII(2):238–65, 1977. Part 2, *Russian Literature Triquarterly* VIII(3):12–55, 1977. Part 3, *Russian Literature Triquarterly* IX(1):31–60, 1978.

53] R. Proffer.
    Requirements in translation.
    Three parts. *Russian Literature Triquarterly* VIII(2):38–65, 1977; VIII(3):12–55, 1977; IX(1):31–60, 1978.

## Obscure and Ephemeral Journals

Periodical publication is so precarious an enterprise that it makes dowsing for water look secure by comparison. Share with your reader whatever information you have about sources that are hard to find:

12]  S. L. Mouli.
    Aspects of Wagner's harmonies.
    *Agrippa* III(2):49–61, 1956.
    The library at the Boston Conservatory of Music has a
    complete set of this journal.

25]  Martine l'Hereux.
    Downward-sloping demand curves and Markham's ob-
    servation.
    *The Economists' Monthly,* Paxmore House, Raile Place,
    Cambridge, England. XXI(4):27–38, 1982.

# Reviews

If the title of a review does not indicate what work is under consideration, supply the information:

29]  R. A. Russo.
    Plaything of the gods. Review of Anatos Teriekes, *The*
    *Forgotten Prophet.*
    *The Literary Review* VIII(4):28–31, 1957.

Use cross-reference when you can:

12]  Daniel Gomez.
    Review of Trenton [26].
    *Pharmacology Notes and Abstracts* 15(6):95, 1981.

In a reference to an omnibus review, you may mention all the works
reviewed or just the ones you're interested in.

# Pamphlets

Pamphlet, report, memorandum, broadside, leaflet, brochure, tract,
folder, booklet—something thin, bound by itself. Block II of the
reference to a pamphlet is punctuated as a non-book:

29] Frank Tergon.
    Handlist of Negro playwrights in the American theater.
    English Department, Tulane University, 1972.

Pamphlets are often published in series, and the number in the series may be an important piece of identification:

52] M. L. Zabibian.
    The gittern (with notes on the guitar, cithara, and cither).
    Juilliard Stringed Instruments Series #74–23, 1984.

Pamphlets are seldom issued by the standard publishing houses, and describing nonstandard publishers requires some thought. The middle road is the one to seek, neither so little information that your reader will have trouble finding the source nor so much that your reference will be a cluttered mess.

▷ 17] Michael A. Harrison.
    Miosinic coagulation in rigor mortis.
    Washington University, 1958.

▷ 17] Michael A. Harrison.
    Miosinic coagulation in rigor mortis.
    Department of Pathology, Room 404-B Thalier Memorial Building, Washington University Medical School, 2382 Flora Ave, St. Louis, Missouri 67228. 1958.

17] Michael A. Harrison.
    Miosinic coagulation in rigor mortis.
    Department of Pathology, Washington University Medical School, St. Louis, 1958.

# Works Not Yet Published

In most fields, scholars know about each other's work before it is published. If you refer to such a piece of work, it will be because you know the author; check with her at the latest possible moment to see what state her work is in. It may have been accepted by a journal and assigned to an upcoming issue but not yet paginated:

30] Leonard H. Gordon.
Effectiveness under stress: The Chinese Communist army in Korea.
To appear in the *Washington Newsletter* XXII(8), 2 March 1992.

It may have been accepted but not yet assigned a publication date:

12] Janet F. O. Moyle.
High-speed printers in grades K–4.
To appear in *The Journal of the Association for Classroom Computing.*

5] A. T. Embree, editor.
*Muslim Civilization in India.*
To be published by E. P. Dutton.

If it hasn't yet found a publisher, give the author's work address:

18] J. E. B. Linkman, Department of Chemistry, State University of New York at Binghamton.
Linoleic acid treatment of oil paints with vegetable pigments.
In preparation, May 1986.

"In preparation" may be a bit of a fiction, and you may have to invent your own name for an article the author seems disinclined to finish. Many a scholar finally settles down to work only because so many references have been made to an article she's talked about that she finally feels obliged to write it. If all you have to go on is a letter, a memo, a telephone call, or a conversation over coffee, you may have to write your reference:

38] Martin Henner, the Wellcombe Unit, Cambridge University.
Private communication, 15 June 1985.

Reserve this form for results that will probably never be published independently because they are too small.

# Theses and Dissertations

More confusion surrounds writing a reference to a thesis than any other common scholarly reference; what follows is arbitrary, but not capricious.

Let us say that a PhD thesis is a book and any paper short of a PhD thesis is an article:

92] Onora Nell.
*Acting on Principle: The Application of Kantian Ethics to Real-life Choice.*
PhD thesis, Marquette University, 1951.

8] J. N. Munson.
Envelope solutions to sparse matrices.
Master's thesis, University of Nebraska, 1974.

Degrees are granted by universities, not departments:

▷ 41] G. H. von Wright.
*Parsee Refugees of the 7th and 8th Centuries.*
PhD dissertation, Department of Oriental Studies, University of Oklahoma, 1978.

41] G. H. von Wright.
*Parsee Refugees of the 7th and 8th Centuries.*
PhD dissertation, University of Oklahoma, 1978.

If you're writing a reference to a thesis that you know was subsequently published, share whatever information you have with your reader:

42] Christine Tyler.
The audience as author.
Master's thesis, Sudbury University, 1979.
Published under the same title by Little, Brown, 1981.

"Thesis" applies to papers at all levels, "dissertation" only to the doctorate. You may follow the style of each original scrupulously or call everything a thesis so as not to worry about the nomenclature.

# Secondary Reference

*A* writes a reference to *B*. You learn about *B* by reading *A*. May you copy *A*'s reference? Not without adding the information that it comes from *A:*

> 17] Kenneth Hudson.
>     The role of the museum in the urban cultural center.
>     *American Architect* LIII(3):138, 1973. Cited in Marshall Hohenburg, Toward a more realistic renewal.
>     *Dimensions in Planning* XXIX(9):14–28, 1981.

Only if you have the original Hudson article before you may you write:

> 17] Kenneth Hudson.
>     The role of the museum in the urban cultural center.
>     *American Architect* LIII(3):138, 1973.

Once it's in front of you, it makes no difference how you found out about it.

I've said it before, but it can't be overstressed: The principle of secondary reference is crucial to sound scholarship. Treating a secondary reference as if it were primary is a highly refined way of talking through your hat.

# Hard References

Hard references (you may have wondered what was so easy about the easy ones) do not fall neatly into three blocks for author, title, and bibliographic information. Some can be squeezed and squashed into a fair approximation of the usual format; some resist.

## Archival Sources

Sight unseen, you can predict a few things about almost any archive in the world. It's short on money, short on space, short on time, and short on personnel. It probably once started in on a system of classification that, although not yet complete, has proved inadequate, so that another system (and sometimes even a third) is also under way. You're safe in assuming that the physical size and shape and condition of the holdings have had an astounding influence on the way they're organized.

Aside from that, there's little that can be said about archives in general. Every archive is unique; no archive arranges, describes, and manages its holdings like any other archive. Before you start on a project of archival research, you might want to read

T. R. Schellenberg.
*The Management of Archives.*
Columbia University Press, 1965.

You can be more sensible and more appreciative if you have some idea what archivists are up against.

Write your references while the material is before you—and while the archivist is by your side. She has a vested interest in helping you, since she's the one who will have to suffer the weird, unintelligible queries from your readers if you write your references badly. Even if you understand the organization of your archive thoroughly, double-check with the archivist. Only she can predict the future of the holdings; that item you've come to think of as "Gathering 27-J" may be reclassified "19 Record Series 212" before the year is out.

The archival reference is no place for false dignity. Some small archives are very informally arranged. If your source is in the big red folder, you're going to have to designate it "Big red folder"; if it's in the green cardboard box, you're going to have to write out "Green cardboard box." I once knew a small private archive where the file drawers were called by saints' names as a pious gesture, having nothing to do with their contents. References to small archives make up in charm whatever they lack in formality.

If you have a group of references to one archive, you will probably want to give them a section of their own in your reference list and preface the section with a note about how they're arranged and how you're describing them. The address of the archive and the name of the archivist belong in this preface, along with any other information your reader will find useful. (You will certainly want to mention it, for instance, if your archive does not permit photocopying.)

A few examples, to give you the flavor of the archival reference:

9] Concordia Parish Courthouse, Vidalia, Louisiana.
   General mortgage books: Delinquent taxpayers.
   Volume HH, page 459. Mortgagees, 13 May 1870.

18] Richard Blackmere to Sir Andrew Maurice, undated,
    probably 15 or 16 September 1885.
    North Riding County Archive, Yorkshire, England.
    Maurice family codex, 1884–1888 gathering, number
    139.

69] James Lucas: "My mother give me to know . . . "
    Longhand transcription of a slave narrative, apparently
    done for the Leeder study [16] but never collected.
    Dated 15 January 1939.
    File RL, item 12 (4 pages).

The first and second examples are self-contained. The third is part of a special section and depends on the explanatory preface of that section in order to make sense.

What to say in the preface depends on the state of the materials you have used. If you have the good fortune to use only cataloged material, a heading may suffice:

Archivo general de Indios
Seville, Spain

If a published catalog is available, be sure to mention it to your reader:

Archives Municipales
Chartres, France

There is a summary catalog through 1901 in Langlois [67], pages 399–415.

If your notation is likely to seem odd to your reader, explain:

Braseman Family Archive
Warwick, Rhode Island

The archive contains about three thousand items relating to the Braseman family in the eighteenth and nineteenth centuries. Much of the material up to 1750 has been cataloged; whenever possible, I have used the archive's identification numbers (for example, series 9, item 22). For the uncataloged materials, the name of the donor is the best identification (for example, Rebecca).

In writing an archival reference, you're on your own about breaking the information up and punctuating and capitalizing it. Use blocks and divisions within blocks to group related information and feed it to your reader in easy bites. Use one block or two or three or four, whatever you need to make your reference readable. Shun abbreviations. Punctuate no more heavily than you have to. Remember that uppers-and-lowers is harder to read than sentence capitalization and that italicized or underlined material is harder to read than plain roman. Spend a little time testing different formats before you settle on one.

Things Nobody Ever Tells You: If you've done research in an archive that doesn't charge you for the privilege and that's not supported by your taxes (even if it is by someone else's), you may quite properly offer a small donation for the upkeep of the archive as you're leaving. The offer may be refused, but it will be appreciated.


# Author Equals Publisher

Infrequently with books but very frequently with pamphlets, a corporate author publishes its own work. Furthermore, the title of such a pamphlet often incorporates the author's name yet again. Any attempt to use the three-block format produces laughable results:

> ▷  51] The Interseminarian Benevolent Association.
>           Annual report of the Interseminarian Benevolent Association.
>           The Interseminarian Benevolent Association, 1979.

Tidy all this up into two blocks with no repetition:

>     51] The Interseminarian Benevolent Association.
>           Annual report, 1979.

The address of an obscure author-publisher goes with its name:

>     30] The Nash Circle, Bath, England.
>           A report on the repair and restoration of the Haymarket Theatre, 1984.

If two references to an obscure author-publisher come together on your reference list, give the address only in the first:

>     7] The Association of Professional Historians of Music, Pennfield, Massachusetts 03277.
>           A brief life of Marianna Bulgarelli, 1981.

---

Bad examples are marked with an arrowhead (▷).

8] The Association of Professional Historians of Music.
Metastasio in Vienna, 1979.

## Conference Proceedings

Occasionally conferences result in the publication of perfectly normal volumes:

39] Ruth E. Hartley, editor.
*Understanding Children: Proceedings of the 16th Annual Convention of Child Psychiatrists and Psychotherapists.*
Academic Press, 1979.

But mostly what you get is a program committee and private publication. The attempt to fit this information to the usual three-block format is not successful:

▷ 41] Jane A. Krout, chairman; B. L. Forbush, Martha C. Reinert, and Peter Zeber, program committee.
*Proceedings of the 2nd Annual AIID Meeting.*
Association for the Investigation of Iatrogenic Diseases, 1926 Commonwealth Avenue, Boston, Massachusetts 02176. 1982.

The solution is to forget about the program committee and treat the organization as both author and publisher:

41] Association for the Investigation of Iatrogenic Diseases, 1926 Commonwealth Avenue, Boston, Massachusetts 02176.
*Proceedings of the 2nd Annual Meeting, 1982.*

Suppress needless repetition:

▷ 91] The Society for International Law, Geneva, Switzerland.
*218th Meeting of the Society for International Law,* 1983.

91] The Society for International Law, Geneva, Switzerland.
*218th Meeting, 1983.*

Suppress needless repetition of dates too, but be aware that the conference date and the publication date may differ. When they do, use the word "published" with the publication date to keep your reference from stuttering. Here the conference date and the publication date are the same:

▷    1] American Lexicographical Associates.
*19th Biennial Conference and Symposium Proceedings,
1975, 1975.*

1] American Lexicographical Associates.
*19th Biennial Conference and Symposium Proceedings,
1975.*

Here they're different:

▷   14] The Franco-English Translators' League, Bristol, England.
*Proceedings of the Annual Convention, 1972, 1974.*

14] The Franco-English Translators' League, Bristol, England.
*Proceedings of the Annual Convention, 1972,* published
1974.

I used to think that the conference site was of no concern, but I've since learned that people often refer to conferences by site. "Didn't she present that result at Málaga?" If the proceedings indicate a site, pass the information on to your reader:

▷ *Seventh Annual Symposium on Agricultural Pesticides,
1978.*

*Seventh Annual Symposium on Agricultural Pesticides, San
Francisco, California, 1978.*

As usual, you must tell your reader where an organization has its headquarters except when you're sure that she already knows it:

▷ The National Association of Toxicologists.

The National Association of Toxicologists, School of Agriculture, University of Oregon.

When two or more references to an organization fall together, only the first needs the address:

> 31] The Scots Gaelic Society, Aberdeen, Scotland. 22nd Meeting, 1949.
>
> 32] The Scots Gaelic Society. 24th Meeting, 1951.

Organizations have a maddening way of changing the style of their proceedings titles from one time to another. Follow the style of each original, but arrange two or more proceedings in chronological order.

> 18] Friends of Asian Literature. Minutes of the 3rd Annual Meeting, 1979.
>
> 19] Friends of Asian Literature. Eighth Annual Meeting: Proceedings, 1984.

Ignore alphabetical order (Eighth, Minutes) and pursue chronological order (1979, 1984).

# Correspondence

What your reader wants to know about a letter is who wrote to whom on what date and where she can find the letter. A simple reference to a published letter looks like this:

> 28] Edward Tinsley to Michael Sclafani, 6 March 1862. In Rebecca Waters, editor, *The Professional Publisher*, pages 313–315. Faber & Faber, 1978.

A compound reference to published letters from one person to several people looks like this:

Sarah Bernhardt.
In M. L. Evans, editor, *Selected Correspondence.*
   Pinnacle Books, 1971.
   [4] To Walter Treach, 8 May 1921, page 308.
   [5] To Alma Becker, 9 July 1922, page 340.

Choose chronological order (1921, 1922), page order (308, 340), or alphabetical order (Becker, Treach), whichever seems most useful to you.

A compound reference to published letters from one person to only one other person looks like this:

Herman Melville to Charles Trapp.
In P. L. Quincy, editor, *The Moby Dick Letters.*
   University of South Carolina Press, 1951.
   [39] 2 May 1850, pages 122–124.
   [40] 14 August 1850, pages 156–161.

Chronological order (May, August) and page order (122, 156) usually coincide; when they don't, choose the one that seems more useful to you.

Finally, there's the reference to a published interchange. Do not put all the letters that *A* wrote to *B* in one reference and all the ones that *B* wrote to *A* in another. Which name should go first? Choose the one that you're more interested in, or flip a coin; be sure to include a cross-reference at the other author's name:

   6] Fred Hoffmann, see Power and Hoffman [18].

      . . .

   18] Frederick Belding Power and Fred Hoffmann.
      In A. M. Maysles, editor, *The Correspondence of Frederick Belding Power: Scientist and Humanitarian.* Plenum, 1949.
      [51] FBP to FH, 13 August 1917, page 304.
      [52] FBP to FH, 19 November 1917, page 322.
      [53] FH to FBP, 2 December 1917, page 329.
      [54] FBP to FH, 4 January 1918, page 340.

Chronological order is usually the best one in this circumstance.

Play it by ear in dealing with unpublished correspondence. The different formats for published correspondence can serve as a rough guide, but you will also need to include archival information, which tends to be longer and less straightforward than information about publication.

## Court Cases

If you are writing a legal paper, you shouldn't be following the system of citation and reference set out in this book. The Harvard Law Review Association publishes a guide called *A Uniform System of Citation* designed especially for the uses that lawyers make of court cases. Every lawyer should know it and follow it.

Now. If all the lawyers have left the room, we can speak frankly. The forms described in *A Uniform System* are slick, sophisticated, clean as a whistle—and utterly unsuited to lay use. I can attest (having tried it) that walking into a law library and asking for an English translation of "30 Ala. 49 (1847)" or "9 Mo. 690 (1846)" is a rattling experience. One might almost entertain the uncharitable thought that lawyers don't want other people to look at court cases.

But the courts belong to us all, and the records of court cases are a rich source in social history, for instance, or in situation ethics or historical linguistics. So it behooves the rest of us to work out our own way of writing references to court cases, a way that will permit us to march boldly up to the desk in a law library and look the librarian in the eye.

Start a reference to a court case by giving its short name. The court reports usually suggest a short name by using full caps amidst ordinary uppers and lowers: "Arthur L. SMITHY v. Melissa MANDERS." That becomes:

Smithy v. Manders.

You needn't construct your short name only from what's capitalized; it is an informal designation. The capitalization in one report, for instance, would have yielded the short name "United States v. Florida," when "United States v. Richard Florida" seems a more revealing name. Regardless of the style of the original, do not underline or italicize the expressions "ex parte," "in re," and "ex rel."; lawyers sometimes italicize these expressions and sometimes do not, so we might as well do it the easier way uniformly.

Then give the name of the court and the date:

> Supreme Court of Arkansas, 18 September 1982.

> Colorado Court of Appeals, Division I, 29 August 1980.

Then write the reference to the report:

> Volume 484 South Western Reporter (second series), page 517.

> Volume 252 Federal Supplement, page 806.

Some reports have two names, one for the jurisdiction, one for the reporter. Give both names, with the reporter in parentheses:

> Volume 211 Tennessee Reports (McCanless), page 599.

Here are a few examples:

> 6] Green v. Arkansas.
> Supreme Court of Arkansas, 18 September 1982.
> Volume 484 South Western Reporter (second series), page 517.

> 111] Muller v. Daws.
> Supreme Court of the United States, October 1876.
> Volume 94 United States Reports, page 444.

> 38] Sedalia Land Company v. Robinson Brick and Tile.
> Colorado Court of Appeals, Division I, 29 September 1980.
> Volume 475 Pacific Reporter (second series), page 351.

> 12] Ex parte Hartman.
> Circuit Court of Appeals, Fifth Circuit, 11 April 1911.
> Volume 186 Federal Reporter, page 434.

81] United States v. Mudge et al.
United States District Court, 10 December 1975.
Volume 252 Federal Supplement, page 806.

37] Mid-State Baptist Hospital v. City of Nashville.
Supreme Court of Tennessee, April 1973.
Volume 211 Tennessee Reports (McCanless), page 599.

78] State v. Fouts.
Court of Appeals of Ohio, 25 January 1947.
Volume 79 Ohio Appellate Reports (Henney), page 255.

## Government Documents

Sometimes in doing research you may suddenly find yourself in a strange world where none of your ordinary patterns of thinking apply any more. Government documents represent such a world; in every country and at every level, governments publish their papers in ways that bear no relation to ordinary publishing practices.

To write a first-rate reference to a government document, you would have to understand the whole system of publication behind it. Appendix 2, for instance, spells out the main features of one such system, United States federal documents. As you can see from glancing at this appendix, a great deal of background information is necessary. If you deal extensively with the documents of a government, you will have to master its publication system. But it would be madness to expect such mastery if all you have is one or two references to write. Do the best you can. Ask yourself, as you would with any source, "How did I find this? What would I need to know to find it again? How do I help someone else find it?"

Start by identifying what government you're talking about:

Illinois.

West Riding, Yorkshire, England.

Brandenburg, Germany.

Portugal.

Call foreign countries and cities by their conventional English names—Mexico, not los Estados Unidos de Mexico; Moscow, not Moskva.

Next name the governmental body (if you can) and give a date. Then copy out every piece of identification you can from the document. Some of what you copy may be significant and some may be completely useless, but since you have no way of knowing you should not let embarrassment stand in your way.

Finally, tell the reader where your copy is. In other words, treat it as archival even though it is a publication. That way, if all else fails, your reader can get a photocopy or an interlibrary loan.

References written under these constraints look horrible. Don't feel shy; everyone else's will look just as bad as yours.

> 18] Montana. The Governor's Commission on Alternative
>       Uses for State Lands, 22–29, March 1978.
>       Hearings on JL1 14, known as Barton's Park. C-1 14.
>       MPC 1,841. 99138-R. #541, series F.
>       There is a copy at the Widener Library of Harvard Uni-
>       versity cataloged M 13994.381, 3966.278.

See? Horrible, but it has a chance of serving its purpose, which is to help your reader get a copy.

If it's at all feasible, consider the possibility of reproducing the document in question as an appendix to your work.


# Microfilm and Microfiche

### Microphotographic Archives

Some archival material exists only in microfilm or microfiche; some archival material is so fragile that scholars must use micro-photographic copies rather than the originals, which may be sitting no more than six feet away in glass cases or evacuated containers. Don't let the technology spook you—there's nothing special about references to microphotographed archives. Like all other references, their job is to answer the question "How do I put my hands on these sources?" Like all other archival references, they are likely to give the question idiosyncratic answers:

8] Carey County Records Office, Freestone, Kansas.
Register of title, Northeast quadrant.
Reel RT-69/6: Mary Blandish, widow of K. Blandish,
30 June 1869.

71] C. to Dear father. (Charles Blice to his father, Rudolph
Blice, or Plice.) 18 February; probably 1914.
Alton Group, reel 13.

The first example could stand on its own in a reference list; the second would have to appear as part of a special section with a preface explaining how the archive is organized.

## Microphotographic Reprints

It's usually a matter of complete indifference to your reader whether you happen to be working with the paper original of a publication or a microphotographed copy. Take this as an example:

47] Martin Traub.
The guest word: Reanimated corpses.
*The New York Times Book Review*, page 39. 13 June
1986.

Your reader has no reason to care whether you're sitting with the *Book Review* spread out across your lap or squinting into the fishy light of a microfilm reader. Make mention of the mode of reproduction only to help your reader get hold of elusive sources:

16] Simon Ankers.
*A History of the Ankers Family in North Carolina.*
Privately printed, 1948.
Available on microfilm from the Family History Project,
University of North Carolina.

Here again it makes no difference to your reader whether you're working with the original or a copy, but she does want to know how to get a copy for herself.

## Microphotographic Publications

Publication directly in microfilm or microfiche is still rare, but it may become more common. I started to say alas, but I suppose a medieval monk would have said alas at the distortions and deformities of early printing, and that worked out well enough. Microphotographed publications may present other difficulties, but there's nothing hard about writing references to them:

> 12] Joan Wells.
> Hypertension in confined adult male primates.
> University of Washington Medical School Report
> 11R3219 (microfiche), 1986.

# Newspapers

## Unsigned Items

References to unsigned articles and editorials in newspapers fall into two blocks:

> 7] *The New Haven Register* 164(80):1, 21 March 1986.
> All-state hoop squads.

> 44] *The World* (Newcastle-on-Tyne, England) CXII(128):
> 26, 19 September 1939.
> Remonetisation crisis.

Volume, number, and page are given in the same way as they are for journals:

When it's not clear from context where a paper is published, put the information in parentheses after the name of the paper. Do not interpolate into the name.

▷ *The Chelmsford [Massachusetts] Tribune* 26(17):39, 18 February 1958.

*The Chelmsford Tribune* (Chelmsford, Massachusetts) 26(17):39, 18 February 1958.

Show broken pagination with the plus sign (+):

▷ *The Wyler News* XXXII(3):14,16,17–19,22, 8 March 1981.

*The Wyler News* XXXII(3):14+, 8 March 1981.

Always give a fully extended date for a newspaper reference; the date is your reader's best hope of finding the original.

▷ *The Trumpet* XLVI(8):27, 1978.
▷ *The Trumpet* XLVI(8):27, December 1978.

*The Trumpet* XLVI(8):27, 23 December 1978.

You may if you like leave off the volume-number information, since the fully extended date is sufficient to specify an issue.

*The Daily News* 26(7):13–14, 30 April 1971.

or

*The Daily News*, pages 13–14, 30 April 1971.

You may want to indicate which edition of a newspaper you're referring to. Sometimes a story appears in full only in one edition and is subsequently cut to make room for other news. Some newspapers have colorful designations for their editions, and it's up to you whether to repeat them or to translate them into ordinary language.

*The Star* 76(22):33+, sundowner edition 5 May 1958.

or

*The Star* 76(22):33+, evening edition 5 May 1958.

Use the headline of an article as the title:

48] *The Sun* 31(2):16–18, 7 July 1934.
Panel find abuses in deferral of pay rises.

Suppress subheads unless they clarify obscure headlines. But stick
with headlines, even the very long ones, through to the bitter end.

2] *The Advocate* CCXIV(17):15+, 17 December 1982.
South Vietnam, after 30 years of war, is land of wide-
spread disease, U.N. group says.

You may sometimes want to indicate the place of origin of a story,
called (confusingly) the dateline:

84] *The Tribune* LV(344):1+, 14 October 1933.
Rice crisis continues: Thousands swarm Delhi ministry.
Dateline London, England.

And you may sometimes want to mark off an item as an editorial
rather than a news story:

15] *The Crier-Dispatch* 42(76):18, 15 July 1922.
A fig for progress (editorial).

Signed items: The reference to an item with a byline starts with the
name of the author, not the newspaper:

▷ 37] *The Reporter* XLIII(26):16+, 21 August 1974.
State legislature flip-flops, by Martha Hamlin.

8] Martha Hamlin.
State legislature flip-flops.
*The Reporter* XLIII(26):16+, 21 August 1974.

Consider the wire services corporate authors:

▷ 64] *The Post-Times* XXXI(86):17+, 15 July 1944.
Iaban Atoll falls (UPI).

99] United Press International.
Iaban Atoll falls.
*The Post-Times* XXXI(86):17+, 15 July 1944.

# Reference Works

References to reference works (that sounds like something from Gilbert and Sullivan) fall into a two-block format much like the one for unsigned newspaper articles. The first block gives all of the publication information; the second gives the title, or catchword, of the item.

> 8] *The Concise Oxford Dictionary of Current English.*
>    Oxford University Press, fifth edition 1964.
>    Maffick.

> 23] *The Encyclopaedia Britannica.* 11th edition 1910.
>    Aberration.

If the work is arranged alphabetically and you're referring to a main entry, no more information is necessary. Otherwise, give enough information with the catchword so that your reader can find it easily. No universal format is possible; use your knowledge of the work to supply your reader with clues.

> 4] *The Encyclopedia Americana.* Americana Corporation,
>    1949.
>    Texas:population. Volume 17, page 382.

> 56] *Roget's International Thesaurus.* T. Y. Crowell, third
>    edition 1962.
>    Nonobservance. Item 767.

Signed articles in reference works fit the standard three-block format.

> ▷ 14] *The Encyclopedia of Psychology.* Prentice-Hall, 1984.
>    Memory, by Joanna Gutas.

> 19] Joanna Gutas.
>    Memory.
>    In *The Encyclopedia of Psychology.* Prentice-Hall,
>    1984.

Speaking of signatures, many modern reference works acknowledge editors and compilers who would have remained anonymous fifty or a hundred years ago. The tradition of the scholarly mole, scraping away at underground passages, invisible and silent, ill suits today's temperament. We like to see our names in print. For the scholar at work on a reference list, this trend poses a problem. She has no wish to slight honest toil, but the authority of many a reference work rests on the entire enterprise rather than on the collection of people around the current edition. What weight should you give these considerations?

If only one person's name appears on the title page of a reference work, you need have no hesitation about fitting the reference to the familiar three-block format:

76] Eric Partridge.
   *Origins: A Short Etymological Dictionary of Modern English.*
   Macmillan, second edition 1959.

At the other extreme, if the names of half a dozen people appear, each with her own job title, you're safe in using the standard reference-work format:

▷ 16] M. G. Heany, editor-in-chief. R. Collins Broom, general editor, with the assistance of Helen Ailesworth, E. L. Chioffi, and Randall Means. F. X. Malcolm and Sheila M. Jones, associate editors.
   *The Dictionary of Saints.* Mary the Egyptian.
   Little, Brown, 1972.

   *The Dictionary of Saints.* Little, Brown, 1972.
   Mary the Egyptian.

Short of either extreme, you may have to flip a coin.

A word of caution: Some reference works stand at one remove from scholarship. This is no disparagement—what would the general reader do without them?—but it does mean that the young scholar must eye them suspiciously as references. To give a far-fetched example, the agronomist who finds herself referring to *The Oxford Book of Food Plants* has probably gone awry; but the work is perfectly suitable for explaining a pastoral image in a poem or a play. Getting to know what constitutes an authority is one of the most important parts of learning the ropes of scholarship. When in doubt, ask an old hand in your field for advice.

## Shoes and Ships and Sealing Wax

Besides the written word, scholars also deal with music, paintings, buildings, and artifacts of all kinds—nothing squeaks by the analytic mind. Often the explanation and description you give in your text obviates any need for a reference to such a work. But if you should ever need them, here are a few hints.

### Architecture

A minimal description of a building contains the name of the architect, the name of the building or a brief description, the date, and the location. Frequently you will mention all of these naturally in your text and have no need to write a reference. If, for instance, your text says, "The construction of Durham Cathedral [8] proceeded at a remarkable pace from 1093 to its completion in 1133," you add nothing to your reader's knowledge by writing a reference that says:

▷ Anonymous.
   Durham Cathedral, 1093–1133.
   Durham, England.

If she doesn't already know that Durham is in England, there's something wrong with your text. Similarly, the anonymity of medieval architects should not be news to her. Don't clutter up your reference list with self-evident information.

On the other hand, street addresses for all buildings short of the monumental are a blessing to the reader. Addresses generally do not fit easily into your text, so references are a good idea:

38] Dwight H. Perkins.
   Grover Cleveland Elementary School, 1910.
   3850 North Albany, Chicago, Illinois.

Expand the format when you have more information to share by adding a double-indented paragraph:

38] Dwight H. Perkins.
     Grover Cleveland Elementary School, 1910.
     3850 North Albany, Chicago, Illinois.
     The left wing was damaged by fire in the 1940s and the reconstruction (by an unknown contractor) does not match the rest. A gymnasium (1954) now abuts the right wing.

Refer to buildings you haven't seen yourself by using a variation on the format for secondary references.

## Art Works

The name of the artist, the name and date of the work, and the current location constitute a minimal description of a work of art. When they don't fit naturally into your text, write a reference:

19] Pietro Lorenzetti.
     The birth of the Virgin, 1342.
     Cathedral Museum, Siena.

For purposes of punctuation, the names of works of art are non-books; use sentence capitalization and don't underline them.
     References to ancient works will usually require brief descriptions in place of the name of the artist and the name of the work:

13] Anonymous Susa artisan.
     Painted beaker, approximately 4500 B.C.
     The Louvre, item #371009.

All works of art are archival; that is to say, they all require descriptions of location. For major works, the name of the repository is sufficient:

41] Henri Rousseau.
     The dream, 1910.
     The Museum of Modern Art, New York.

Minor works require more explanation:

> 56] Paul Klee.
>> Drawing, 1922.
>> The Art Institute of Chicago, Prints and Drawings Collection, catalog #6/21.133.

Many works of art are in private hands:

> 20] Anonymous Choctaw artisan.
>> Mortar and pestle, approximately 1800.
>> Collection of Sylvia Choate, 2619 Parker Lane, Philadelphia, Pennsylvania 16069.

Some collectors prefer to remain anonymous, to the detriment of scholarship. Never broach the subject; discuss anonymity only if the collector brings it up, and then do your best to dissuade her. If you must, write the reference like this:

> 48] Robert Motherwell.
>> Homage to the fathers, 1968.
>> Private collection.

You can expect letters from readers asking for more information and decide what to do then on the basis of your conscience and your relationship with the collector.

These references contain only the bare necessities and should usually be enlarged on. Start with the minimum reference and then double-indent a paragraph of explanation.

> 48] Robert Motherwell.
>> Homage to the fathers, 1968.
>> Private collection.
>> Acrylic on canvas, 5'8" × 13'. Sold by the Sabarsky Gallery, 1969; the gallery has black-and-white photographs of the painting.

Refer to works of art you haven't seen yourself by using a variation on the format for secondary references.

## CD-ROMs

Where the data and the accessing software come from two different sources, you should try to make the distinction clear. For instance, you would write a reference to the first *OED*, CD-ROM that was issued like this:

> 29] *The Oxford English Dictionary on Compact Disc.*
>     Text, Oxford University Press, 1884–1933.
>     Software, TriStar Publishing, 475 Virginia Drive, Fort
>     Washington, Pennsylvania 19034–9930.

Otherwise, treat CD-ROM publication like any other (and remember to give addresses for obscure publishers).

## Electronic Mail and Electronic Bulletin Boards

So far there are no reliable repositories for electronic communication. If you want to refer to an electronic message, you have to provide your own archive. Make a paper copy and put it in your files. Now write your reference with full confidence that you can respond to your readers' requests for help:

> 27]  Martin Minow
>      Re: Electronic house arrest units.
>      RISKS-FORUM Digest (risks@csl.sri.com), 10(26), 29
>      August 1990.

A piece of electronic mail sent only to you or to a limited distribution list is a private communication:

> 88]  Jorge Stolfi.
>      Private communication, 28 September 1990.

## Movies

A minimal description of a movie contains the name of the director, the name of the movie, the name of the production company or the distributor or the country of origin (whichever best establishes the provenance of the film), and the release date. Often the information fits smoothly into your text: "Douglas Sirk's *The First Legion* (United Artists, 1951) took Boyer out of his usual pretty-boy role." No entry on your reference list is necessary unless you need to say more. But sometimes you do need to say more.

You need to say more, for instance, if you need to write a secondary reference. The disgraceful practice of talking about movies that they have never seen makes most film buffs' pretensions to scholarship a farce. If you want to write for a fan magazine in this style, fine. But if you want to do film scholarship, you have to play by the scholarly rules. If I sound like a Dutch uncle, it's because there are now a number of wholly imaginary film titles floating around. So if you haven't seen a movie, reveal the source that leads you to believe it exists:

41] Douglas Sirk.
*The First Legion.*
United Artists, 1951. Described in R. A. Blackmer, Sirk's middle years. Films in Transition XII(3):41–56, 1979.

If you've read about a movie in several places, give the secondary reference that your reader will find most useful or give more than one secondary reference:

41] Douglas Sirk.
*The First Legion.*
United Artists, 1951. Described in R. A. Blackmer, Sirk's middle years. *Films in Transition* XII(3):41–56, 1979. Also in Chalmers Coop, *The Director's Eye.* New American Library, 1971.

If you work mostly with plot and theme, exact running times will not be important to you. If you work mostly with the visual side of movies, with camera work and editing, go out and buy a stopwatch. You will want to add to your reference the running time you've clocked yourself:

21] Jean Segal.
*Predictable Complications,* 86 minutes.
Orion, 1989.

Never accept the distributor's word; never, never go by something you've read about the film. It is better to give no running time than to give one you didn't clock yourself. Only your own measure can give your reader some indication of what version you've seen. A literary scholar would recoil in horror at the thought of referring to the Classic Comic of *Great Expectations* or the *Reader's Digest* condensed version of *Too Late the Phalarope*. But film scholars have to do the equivalent every day; they have no choice. They are at the mercy of producers and distributors who feel free to hack away at movies, their lackwittedness held in check only by their venality. Giving the running time doesn't solve the problem, but it does advance the cause of serious film scholarship by specifying what the dimensions of the problem are.

Do not tack on endless lists of credits to your film references. If you're interested in the screenplay, list the scriptwriter; if you're interested in the editing, list the editor; and so on. All such information should, of course, be taken from the print of the movie itself. If you know about it from some other source, use a variation on the format for secondary reference.

If you set off a section of your reference list for references to films, a good title for the section is "Films." "Movies" is a good title; "Cinema" is not so good, but acceptable. "Filmography" is a grotesque mutant and will undermine your reader's confidence in your good taste and common sense.

## Music

Start a reference to a piece of music by giving the composer. Then give the title. For purposes of punctuation, operas and cantatas and albums and masses are books, arias and songs and cuts and kyries are not.

So far, so good. Now, for a published piece of music you proceed as you would for any other publication:

83] Flor Peeters.
   *Missa in Honorem Sanctae Lutgardis* (opus 15).
   McLaughlin & Reilly, 1950.

36] Robert Schumann.
   Faschingsschwank aus Wien (Viennese carnival, opus

26), 1838.
Edited by Harold Bauer. G. Schirmer, 1946.

19]  Wolfgang Amadeus Mozart.
Ah! fuggi il traditor!
In *Don Giovanni* (1787), page 69. C. F. Peters, 1965.

A reference to a recorded performance should include the per-
former's name and the recording company's identification number:

13]  Johann Sebastian Bach.
Von Himmel hoch, da komm' ich her (BWV 769, 1738).
Played by Helmut Walcha. Archive ARC 3030, 14553
APM. Approximately 1960.

The date of the recording is frequently impossible to discover; use
your knowledge of the source to make the best guess you can.

In most cases, jazz musicians should be treated as the "com-
posers" of pieces of music they use for improvisation, even though
the basic melodies are someone else's.

53]  Sonny Rollins Quartet, featuring Thelonious Monk.
The way you look tonight.
On *Work*, Prestige 7169, 25 October 1954.

These are minimal references. Frequently you will want to add a
good deal more information. A good format for this is to start with
the minimal reference and then double-indent a paragraph of explanation.

53]  Sonny Rollins Quartet, featuring Thelonious Monk.
The way you look tonight.
On *Work*, Prestige 7169, 25 October 1954. Sonny
Rollins, tenor sax; Thelonious Monk, piano; Tommy
Potter, bass; Arthur Taylor, drums. Recording by Van
Gelder, supervised by Bob Weinstock. Re-recording
by Matt Baines. Compare this version to Rollins [58].

References to music in manuscript or in noncommercial recordings must be treated as archival; you must tell your reader how she
can see it or hear it for herself.

## Radio and Television Programs

Begin your reference by giving the call letters of the station or the abbreviated name of the network; say whether it's radio or TV you're talking about; and for local stations give the location:

> WAVZ radio, New Haven, Connecticut.
>
> WTTW-TV, Hartford, Connecticut.
>
> KXXX-FM radio, San Francisco, California.
>
> NBC-TV.

Then give the name of the show and the air date. It's usually but not always necessary to add a brief description.

> *Nova:* The language of genes, 28 March 1986.
>
> *Face the Nation,* 15 August 1960. Interview with Richard Goodwin.
>
> *Twin Peaks,* 30 September 1990. Start of the second season.
>
> *Morning Pro Musica,* 12 February 1968. Interview with Al-fred Deller.
>
> *Eyewitness News,* 9 July 1969. Hurricane Connie.

Series are books (uppers-and-lowers, underlined); episodes are not (sentence capitalization, no underline).

For network shows since roughly 1960, this is sufficient. For local shows and for older footage and recordings, it is a joke. Writing a reference implies that the reader can get her hands on the source unless you tell her otherwise. Since many local stations destroy or tape over their footage within forty-eight hours of broadcasting it, you'd better investigate your material before you send your reader off on a wild-goose chase. Very often, your reference will have to read:

> 59]  KXLM radio, Kansas City, Missouri.
>
>     *Fiddling Around,* 10 April 1981. Interview with Blind Joe Crockett.
>
>     The station has no copy.

In other words, all your reader has to go by is your word for it. On the other hand, if there is a copy, give her whatever additional information you've found that will help her trace it:

> 17] WRYE-TV, Macon, Georgia.
>    11 *O'Clock News,* 30 May 1981. George Wallace on the food-stamp program.
>    Dope #328.

The responsibility for doing this investigation is yours, not your reader's. If your source is not the original broadcasting station, let her know:

> 36] KXXM radio, Fargo, North Dakota.
>    *The Ready Ear,* 26 April 1944. Leo Haines reading Dickens.
>    Audio-Visual Workshop, University of North Dakota.

It's not uncommon for a radio station to change its call-sign. If you refer to something that was broadcast on KPQR in 1950 and that station still exists but is now K-103, mention K-103 in block V.

## Software

First you need to distinguish whether you're talking about a description of the program or the program itself. Treat the description of the program like any other written work. Write a reference in the format for a pamphlet, a journal article, an item in a conference proceedings, or whatever it happens to be. If you're writing a reference to the documentation for the program, the author will probably be corporate.

For the program itself, either the source or the runnable code, give the name of the program, the version number, the platform on which you have run it, and where to get it:

> 61] Tru-Champ 3.4 for the Macintosh.
>    Electronic Equipment Corporation, 1483 Meller Road, Cambridge, Massachusetts 02138.

7]  CLINGER for VAX VMS.
    Computer Science Department, University of Texas at
    Austin.

29]  Proxima 12.0 for the PC.
    Computer Accessories Corporation, 6610 Nancy Ridge
    Drive, San Diego, California 92121.

On those rare occasions when you know the author of a piece of
software, give her credit:

26]  Richard Stallman.
    GNU emacs 13 for Unix.
    Free Software Foundation, 675 Massachusetts Avenue,
    Cambridge, Massachusetts 02139.

## Unpublished Interviews and Studies

Sometimes in the course of your research you may conduct an interview or a study that is too slight to merit independent publication
but can be incorporated into a larger work.

The reference to an interview should give the name of the person
you talked to, a description of her if that's necessary, the date of the
interview, and any other relevant information:

28]  Robert Lowell.
    15–19 June 1956, interviews during the Alton Grove
    Writers' Conference.

12]  Ida Barrett, District 69 member.
    29 October 1955, interview after the resolution of the
    May Company warehouse strike.

Be prepared to respond to requests for your notes or tapes.

The reference to a study should at the barest minimum indicate
the date, the population, the sample, and the procedure or the tool.
No one format will suit all cases:

61]  Merchants' and Mechanics' Bank, Haverhill, Massachu-
    setts.
    Interviews with 25 of the Bank's 34,000 depositors,
    May–July 1975.

36] MMPI and TAT on all 36 children with hearing dys-
function in the Alice Lovett School, San Diego,
California. 12 January 1986.

Be prepared to respond to requests for your data. Or better yet,
forestall requests by forgetting about the reference and working
your material up into an appendix.

References to unpublished interviews and studies by other people
follow the usual format for works not yet published.

# THE
# REFERENCE LIST

It's hard to think of your reference list as a communication. Young scholars sometimes call it, with more disrespect than affection, the grocery list and throw the items together no more thoughtfully than they would "two lbs. boiling potatoes, 1 fish, what kind?, for Saturday, six lemons if not disgusting, 1h gal. skim milk."

But if you've worked hard, as I hope you have, at making each of your individual references useful and helpful for your reader, this is not the time to abandon her. If you're using a computer system that assembles your reference list for you, don't be so enthralled by its convenience that you neglect to hold it to the standards you've maintained elsewhere.

Yes, it's true that your reader can make her own way through whatever you provide her, but why discard the chance to help her one last time? Wouldn't a cross-reference from item [14] to item [46] show her a connection she might not otherwise make? Wouldn't collapsing that compound reference into a simple one reflect more accurately the use you want her to make of the source? Wouldn't a special section, arranged chronologically, help her to follow the historical background of your subject? You've gone the first mile with her, and the second; don't leave her to finish the journey alone.

# Reference List versus Bibliography

Reference lists are sometimes called bibliographies, but a useful distinction can be made. A reference list need be neither exhaustive nor formative; a bibliography should be either one or the other. If you have put together a list of all the works of such-and-such a description, all of Woodrow Wilson's published papers, for instance, or all the books and articles on color vision in human neonates, then you may call that a bibliography. If you have put together a list of works you recommend, the best English grammars in each of the several schools, for instance, or the most useful analyses of East Coast immigrant patterns, call that a bibliography. But if your list contains nothing more than the sources you've used in working on a piece of research, call that a reference list. Most research produces a reference list, not a bibliography. A bibliography is usually a project in its own right.

Dissertations are the major exception to this rule. By and large, the dissertation writer is expected to produce a genuine bibliography, a list of all the works that have some direct bearing on her topic. The requirement is an outgrowth of the requirement that a dissertation be an original piece of research, not just a mosaic of previous results. Some dissertation bibliographies are nothing but a polite acknowledgment of the tradition; others make a real contribution by identifying obscure sources or organizing and classifying sources or both.

Some of the items on a bibliography may lack citations in the text. Does this present a problem? Not a bit of it—simply number the items that have matching citations in the text and leave the others unnumbered:

81] Margaret Tobin.
Wordsworth and the image of the daemonic.
*19th Century Studies* CIV(ii):38–69, 1981.

Herman Toole.
*A Life at Odds: Wordsworth in the Lake District.*
University of Illinois Press, 1955.
Pages 30–55.
Pages 155–168.

82] F. G. Tynan.
Mystery and brightness in Wordsworth.

In William D. Church, editor, *Visions of Light: The English Romantics,* pages 213–265. Harvard University Press, 1979.

C. M. Upham
Wordsworth's last decade, pages 308–314.
*Poetry Review* XIII(1):288–340, 1959.

This dissertation is not, of course, about Wordsworth—that bibliography would run to several volumes—but about Wordsworth's light imagery, or religious sentiment in Wordsworth, or some other manageable topic.

# Compound References

If you haven't already constructed compound references in your draft, this is the time to do it. If you have, this is the time to check them over and improve them.

Suppose, for instance, that you have three references:

▷ 36] Charles Miner.
*A Chronicle of the Provincial American Theater,* page 414.
University of Oklahoma Press, 1981.

37] Charles Miner.
*A Chronicle of the Provincial American Theater,* pages 167–172.
University of Oklahoma Press, 1981.

38] Charles Miner.
*A Chronicle of the Provincial American Theater,* pages 232–238.
University of Oklahoma Press, 1981.

These get combined into one big reference, with the points of reference arranged in order, the heading unnumbered, and the points of reference numbered:

---

Bad examples are marked with an arrowhead (▷).

Charles Miner.
A Chronicle of the Provincial American Theater.
University of Oklahoma Press, 1981.
 [36] Pages 167–172.
 [37] Pages 232–238.
 [38] Page 414.

Sometimes, on the other hand, you may find that your draft uses a compound reference where a simple one would be better. Suppose that you have the two references:

▷  56] Bridget Riley.
     *Atomic Thermometry*, pages 212–215.
     Crane, Russak, 1985.

   57] Bridget Riley.
     *Atomic Thermometry*, pages 216–224.
     Crane, Russak, 1985.

Do not blindly combine these into a compound reference:

▷  Bridget Riley.
   *Atomic Thermometry*.
   Crane, Russak, 1985.
   [56] Pages 212–215.
   [57] Pages 216–224.

Now, it is possible that a compound reference might be the right thing here, if for instance there's a chapter break at page 216 in the source. But probably what you want your reader to do is read the passage through from one end to the other; probably your reference should read:

   56] Bridget Riley.
     *Atomic Thermometry*, pages 212–224.
     Crane, Russak, 1985.

Both citations in the text get the bracketed number [56].
   Compound references to sources like articles and pamphlets are seldom justified. Keep a sharp eye out for needless compound references:

▷ Robert Wagenknecht.
   The empty sea.
   *American Geophysical Journal* XXII(3), 1971.
     [126] Page 130.        [129] Pages 136–139.
     [127] Pages 132–135.    [130] Pages 138–141.
     [128] Page 136.

This is a hangover from the worst of the old footnote style; it is almost inconceivable that the author really intends for her reader to use the source as she has indicated. The whole mess should be collapsed into one simple reference:

126] Robert Wagenknecht.
   The empty sea.
   *American Geophysical Journal* XXII(3):130–141,
   1971.

All the citations in the text get the plain bracketed number [126]. Excessive pinpointing is characteristic of pseudoscholarship. All those nitty little page numbers look impressive to the uninformed. When a real scholar wants her reader to make use of a whole article, she refers to it whole, not in bits and pieces.

As you have probably already noticed, you may run your points of reference in double or triple columns:

J. D. Fiore.
*Music at the Court of Frederick the Great.*
University of Missouri Press, 1937.
  [9] Pages 38–41.      [12] Page 343.
  [10] Page 115.       [13] Pages 412–414.
  [11] Pages 166–168.

Choose a format, whether single, double, or triple columns, and stick to it through any one reference list.

The points of reference are usually page numbers, but they might just as easily be other kinds.

If your points of reference are of several different kinds, don't jumble them all together:

▷ Gaylord Fite.
   Fissure and jointure in hyperplanes.

In Wanda Farnham, editor, *A Symposium on Hyperplane Geometry*, pages 303–379. Plenum Press, 1982.

[28] Page 318.        [31] Page 366.
[29] Theorem 2.5.     [32] Theorem 5.7.
[30] Theorem 3.1.

Give all of one kind first, then all of the next:

Gaylord Fite.
Fissure and jointure in hyperplanes.
In Wanda Farnham, editor, *A Symposium on Hyperplane Geometry*, pages 303–379. Plenum Press, 1982.

[28] Page 318.        [30] Theorem 2.5.
[29] Page 366.        [31] Theorem 3.1.
                      [32] Theorem 5.7.

Some kinds of research produce massive compound references. You may sometimes need to carry a compound reference over a page break. Repeat just enough of the heading to remind your reader of what's going on:

Steinman, continued.

[95] Page 315.        [99] Page 531.
[96] Pages 344–346.   [100] Pages 560–564.
[97] Page 412.        [101] Page 654.
[98] Pages 441–450.   [102] Pages 730–735.

# Special Sections

The next step is to decide on the over-all organization of your reference list. Most lists will simply run from beginning to end in alphabetical order by author, but you should keep in mind the possibility of setting aside special sections for special sources.

For example, a study of Orson Welles might have a special section set aside for films; a study of working conditions in the Pennsylvania mines might have a special section set aside for the legislative history; a study of the efforts to canonize John of Kanti might have two special sections for archival references, one for the archive in

Poland, the other for the archive in the Vatican. A study of local charities in Grenoble from 1500 to 1800 might have a very long reference list divided into the following sections:

> The 16th Century
> > Primary Sources
> > Secondary Sources
>
> The 17th Century
> > Primary Sources
> > Secondary Sources
>
> The 18th Century
> > Primary Sources
> > Secondary Sources

You must use your knowledge of your sources and your topic to decide whether special sections are appropriate for your reference list. Never set aside a special section with fewer than, say, half a dozen references.

The heading of a special section may make it possible for you to shorten the references that fall under it. For instance, all the references under the heading "Works by E. M. Forster" can omit block I. All the references under the heading "United States Government Documents" can omit the words "United States" from block I.

Center your section headings or lay them out flush left, so that they stand out from the references; you may also want to underline or italicize them.

> 26] Valerie Zetman.
> > The printing trades in Brussels.
> > *Modern European Letters* 26(3):122–203, 1982.

> *Antwerp*

> 27] M. H. R. Carruthers.
> > *The House of Plantin.*
> > University of Michigan Press, 1978.

> 28] R. V. Dantzig.
> > The French "colony" in Antwerp, 1535–1585.
> > *Journal of the Netherlands Historical Association*
> > CIX(2):13–55, 1979.

# Cross-reference

Already in working on your draft you have probably used some cross-references from one reference to another. This is the time to polish them up and add any others your reader may find useful. Cross-references can fall in any of the blocks except, I think, block II. They can also stand alone, in which case they are not numbered. The following example is constructed to illustrate all the different placements; on any real reference list, it's most unlikely for cross-references to come so thick and fast.

7] Charlotte Baile (later Charlotte Baile Wyatt [56–59]).
*The Fragile Compact.*
Matthews & Sommerville, New York, 1893.
I suspect that this book is plagiarized from Norcross [35].

8] Henry Baile.
The gothic heroine as feminist.
*Short Fiction Studies* IX(4):39–123, 1984.
Also in Vennit [54], pages 412–490.

9] J. C. Ballard.
*The Stranger Within.*
Volume II in Plachette [42], 1979.
Roselyn Bamette (pseudonym of T. Rodeheffer [32–35])

10] A. M. Barnard (pseudonym of Louisa May Alcott [2–4]).
*Twice Again, or The Revenge of the Egyptian.*
Gasset & Mayes Brothers, 1868.

11] A. M. Barnard.
*The Vampire Beau.*
Gassett & Mayes Brothers, 1866.
Badly abridged in Roth [48].

Be sure in doing cross-references never to write:

▷ See [12].

The bracketed reference numbers are not words. You must always write:

See Coleman [12].

Whenever you can, say why you want the reader to look at the other reference:

Coleman [12] gives more elegant proofs for several of the central lemmas.

## Alphabetical Order

Believe it or not, alphabetizing is a controversial topic. I mention this because you may at some time in your life have occasion to work with an editor who follows a different alphabetizing scheme from the one recommended here. If you work with a computer system that alphabetizes your reference list for you, it is most unlikely to understand all the subtleties of the problem. You must decide for yourself whether the matter is worth struggling over.

My rule for alphabetizing is "Nothing before something."

Think of the alphabet as starting space—$A$—$B$—$C$ rather than $A$—$B$—$C$. Some people skip over spaces in alphabetizing:

▷ Dogged.

Dog star.

Instead, you should treat a space as though it came first in the alphabet:

Dog star.

Dogged.

Begin alphabetizing by the authors' family names:

Nider.

Nissen.

Nye.

Overton.

Ignore internal punctuation except for hyphens:

▷ O'Hara.

Oberly.

Oberly.

O'Hara.

Treat hyphens as you do spaces; remember that your alphabet starts space—*A—B—C*:

▷ Bateson.

Bates-Simpson.

Bates-Simpson.

Bateson.

If you have two or more authors with the same family name, alphabetize them by given name:

A. Vitale.

R. L. Vitale.

T. Vitale.

Again, nothing goes before something:

W. R. Bernstein.

William Bernstein.

William Bernstein, editor.

Following the rule nothing before something yet again, sole authorship precedes first authorship:

M. R. Kain.

M. R. Kain, G. Downes, and E. Riefstahl.

For joint authors, alphabetize first by the first author, then by the second, and then if necessary by the third and so on:

P. Linders, C. R. Matthew, and L. Carey.

P. Linders, C. R. Matthew, and B. F. Taine.

P. Linders and A. H. Seton.


If you have two or more items with the same author or the same joint authors, alphabetize them by title. Ignore the words "a," "an," and "the" and their foreign equivalents. Book and non-book titles are alphabetized together.

S. J. Ezell.
*The Conquest of the Plains.*

S. J. Ezell.
Southerners forever: A chronicle of the Georgia settlers in Oklahoma.

S. J. Ezell.
States' rights as reflected in the Nebraska Constitution.


When a person's name appears in a title, it's alphabetized first name first, not family name first—in the example below it's Maria, Methods, not Methods, Montessori:

L. H. Wren.
Maria Montessori and the tactile sense.

L. H. Wren.
Methods and procedures in encouraging group play.


Alphabetize numerals and symbols as if they were spelled out:

B. I. Singeman.
Backsearch routines.

B. I. Singeman.
The $B^2$ searching algorithm: A reconsideration.

B. I. Singeman.
Blanket search in dense data bases.

B. I. Singeman.
□ □ queries in quick searching.

The symbolic expressions are alphabetized as if they were spelled out "beta squared" and "block-block." Sometimes there's more than one way to spell out an expression. Many people would spell out Stanley Kubrick's *2001* as "two thousand and one"; some would do it "twenty ought one." In a reference list, where the entries are grouped first by author, it makes no particular difference. If you were doing an index, you might want a cross-reference from one version to the other.

## Hard Names

You will sometimes see the advice to alphabetize family names by the rules of their mother tongues, French names by French rules, Italian names by Italian rules, and so on. The trouble with this advice is that scholarship is a gloriously mongrel calling, and even the simplest reference list is likely to include names from a dozen backgrounds. If you find the mother-tongue rule attractive, test yourself on the following list:

C. O. Gofter.

Helmut af Tunderhatz.

Michele Del Rio.

Antoine Ste. Fauvelle.

Raymond V. Scandolo.

H. L. von Bülow.

Erin M'Naughton.

Michael X. MacPatton.

A. K. da Tandera.

Sheila McOrdry.

M-J. de La Fontaine.

Alfred Goltel.

Ready? Here's the list in order by the mother-tongue rule:

H. L. von Bülow.

Michele Del Rio.

Alfred Goltel.

C. O. Gofter.

M-J. de La Fontaine.

Erin M'Naughton.

Sheila McOrdry.

Michael K. MacPatton.

Antoine Ste. Fauvelle.

Raymond V. Scandolo.

A. K. da Tandera.

Helmut af Tunderhatz.

Only if you scored one hundred percent should you even consider alphabetizing by mother tongue. Even then, you should ask yourself whether you want to be the sort of person who parades small knowledge. And be warned that you must go on making perfect scores forever; there's nothing funnier than a failed finick.

The safer and seemlier way is to forget about language of origin and alphabetize with bald literalism:

Helmut af Tunderhatz.

A. K. da Tandera.

M-J. de La Fontaine.

Michele Del Rio.

C. O. Gofter.

Alfred Goltel.

Michael MacPatton.

Sheila McOrdry.

Erin M'Naughton.

Raymond V. Scandolo.

Antoine Ste. Fauvelle.

H. L. von Bülow.

With some names, the naive reader has no way of telling whether the middle section represents a given name or the first part of an unhyphenated family name. If your list has thirty or more items, use a cross-reference to give your reader a hand. Suppose, for instance, that you alphabetize Arthur Wicklowe Townes under *W* on a long list; a cross-reference under *T* will do a service to your reader without compromising your erudition.

The same reasoning applies to names where the family name comes first and the given name after. By all means alphabetize Lee Chin under *L*, but on a long list you should also have a cross-reference under *C*.

Some people are known by only one name; use that for alphabetizing and remember the rule "Nothing before something":

> H. V. Batton.
>
> Bede.
>
> Alicia Bede.
>
> R. L. Bedford.

Count honorifics and designations only in ordering two or more people who use single names; ignore them otherwise:

> Gregory of Nazianzus.
>
> Gregory of Tours.
>
> Michael Gregorylich.

Monarchs and popes and such have alphanumeric designations; order two or more of them with the same name numerically, not alphabetically:

> ▷ Charles Fourth.
>
> Charles Third.
>
> Charles Third.
>
> Charles Fourth.

## Tidying

Some authors simply cannot decide what to call themselves. And, in all fairness, it must also be said that some authors have to work with high-handed editors who impose a house style on every name they get into their clutches. So you may from time to time be faced with alphabetizing two or more different versions of the same name. Use bracketed information to bring all the versions into conformity and then alphabetize by title:

J[udith] R[illington] Farme.
The Arab minorities in Israel.

Judith Rillington Farme.
Israeli policy in Galilee.

Judith R[illington] Farme.
Separatist Palestinian nationalism: Its origins and its future.

Unfortunately, the longest version always wins, regardless of the author's preference, but at least your reader knows that all three items are by the same person. You must, of course, be absolutely certain that they really are by the same person. If there's the slightest doubt in your mind, add no extra information and alphabetize by the usual rules:

J. R. Farme.
The Arab minorities in Israel.

Judith R. Farme.
Separatist Palestinian nationalism: Its origins and its future.

Judith Rillington Farme.
Israeli policy in Galilee.

## Mixed Lists

Not all references have authors by which to alphabetize. Alphabetize ones without authors' names right along with the authored ones, first word first, ignoring "a," "an," and "the," and their foreign equivalents:

Edith Nance.
*The New York Times.*
Morris Newton.

The Noncooperation League.

L. G. O'Keefe.

When the name of a person is part of the name of an organization or a group, alphabetize it first name first, not family name first. The Robert Browning Society, for example, goes under *R*, not *B*. But on a long list a cross-reference under *B* certainly can't hurt anything:

5] M. R. Bascombe.
Uplift and enlightenment in the workers' study circle. *19th Century Studies* XXXII(1):28–74, 1981.

The Robert Browning Society [71].

6] Rebecca Byrman.
*A History of the Popular Lecture in England and America.*
University of Louisiana Press, 1978.

## Breaks in Alpha Order

There are a few cases where strict alphabetical order is relaxed in order to make your reference list more readable. Regardless of what the alphabetical order would be, the books of a multivolume work by one author are listed in volume order, the proceedings of conferences of an organization are listed in chronological order, and popes or monarchs of the same name are listed in numerical order.

# Chronological Order

Although there's seldom any reason for arranging a whole reference list in chronological order, some special sections lend themselves to this organization, and it's a happy way around the alphabetical chaos of some sources. Feel free to use chronological order wherever it seems suitable to you; just be sure to let your reader know what you're doing:

123] Laura Shires Wooten.
Themes of change in Ozark Mountain stories after the
Great War.
*Studies in American Ethnology* VII(6):41–60, 1981.

124] C. H. Ying.
*Tellers of Tall Tales,* pages 235–246.
Princeton University Press, 1958.

The Ozark Mountain Archive
St. Louis University
(in chronological order)

125] Harry Weeks. ("Blind Harry.")
One day six bear rose up . . . (twenty-six stanzas, ap-
parently fragmentary.)
Gathering LL-134, 1850.

126] "Little Zeb."
Fishing-bear story.
Gathering RO-916, postdated 1855.

127] Anonymous Missouri tale-teller.
Honey-bear story.
Gathering RO-901, 1868.

# Order of Mention

Sometimes the best way to arrange your references is by the order in which you mentioned them in your text. Suppose that the first citation in your text comes on page 3:

Johnson and Boone [1], however, argue against using lithotripsy to crush calculi so that they can be passed.

You explain Johnson and Boone's point of view, continue your own exposition, and reach the second and third citations on page 5:

In 1981, Abramsen [2] and Mellors et al. [3] almost simulta-neously discovered the possibility of inducing autotripsy by chemical means.

The matching references read:

1] R. E. Johnson and C. F. Boone.
Cystorrhexic incidents following lithotripsy.
*The Journal of Renopathic Medicine* XXII(1):144–198,
1976.

2] N. W. Abramsen.
Inducing autotripsy and ectasis by chemotherapy.
*The Journal of Renopathic Medicine* XXVII(3):12–47,
1981.

3] T. A. Mellors, G. N. Marsh, P. I. Donati, and T. L. Champion.
The dread stone: A quassia-picrotoxin technique for the
inducement of autotripsis.
*Asclepius* XXXIX(7):602–647, 1981.

When is this method preferable to alphabetical order or
chronological order? It depends on the style of exposition characteristic of your own work and of work in your discipline. In medicine, for instance, as you may have guessed from the example, the
tendency is for each source to be introduced, sucked dry, and set
aside. There is none of the complicated interweaving of sources that
you find in, say, literary criticism or historiography.

The advantage to arranging your reference list by order of mention is that it permits your reader to go backwards, list to text, as
well as forwards, text to list. Suppose, for instance, that your reader
has very little interest in crushing kidney stones but a great deal of
interest in picrotoxin therapies. If in skimming through your reference list her eye lights on item [3], it is very handy for her to be able
to go back to your text and find the citation after [2] and before [4].
If your list were in alphabetical or chronological order, she might
have to leaf through your whole article looking for Mellors et al.

If you choose this arrangement for your reference list, you should
have very few compound references, and the citations for them
should all come together:

P. L. Corbett.
Hepatic transposition in drill operators.

In F. V. Ormans, editor, *Occupational Hazards*, pages 220–
271. University of Idaho Press, 1983.
[19] Pages 255–262.
[20] Pages 230–238.

Notice that in this method the points of reference as well as the main
entries come in order of mention—pages 255–262 first because
they were mentioned first.

Every now and then you may return to a source that you cited
before. Do not abandon your over-all scheme:

▷ Barnes [38], Abramsen [2], and Stametz [39] all report cases
of caudal aerocelism.

Number the late citation in order:

Barnes [38], Abramsen [39], and Stametz [40] all report
cases of caudal aerocelism.

On your reference list, use cross-reference both at the main entry
and at the late entry:

2] N. W. Abramsen (also reference [39]).
Inducing autotripsy and ectasis by chemotherapy.
*The Journal of Renopathic Medicine* XXVII(3):12–47,
1981.

. . .

39] Abramsen [2], page 44.

These late mentions should be rare; if you have many of them,
you've chosen the wrong arrangement for your reference list.

## Last-minute Changes

It does sometimes happen that you need to change your reference
list at the last minute, and it isn't necessarily your fault. Some

blasted graduate student has just written a dissertation that supports one of your shakier conclusions; you've got to refer to her. Or some infernal colleague has written months after you asked her to read your manuscript, telling you that your use of a source is in error; you've got to pull the reference. The article is already in page proofs and the journal's been on the phone to you twice asking where they are. And of course, the change is always in the worst possible position—if you're using alphabetical order, the author's name is Aademsen; if you're using order of mention, the topic is the very first thing you discuss; and if you're using chronological order, the date is practically prehistoric. These are the times when the computer systems that maintain your citation and reference numbers for you automatically really earn their keep. But what if you're not using one?

Contain yourself. Form is never more important than sense. If you must add a reference at the last minute, tack it onto the end of your list:

83] C. R. Zeisman.
    *Lee's Tactics.*
    Dutton, 1981.

84] Violet Aademsen.
    *Popular Views of Robert E. Lee: 1870–1885.*
    PhD thesis, Marquette University, 1988.

If you must delete a reference at the last minute, mention the gap in your list so that your reader won't be confused:

3] Chalmers V. Asmond.
    The case for Panamanian sovereignty.
    *Time and Tide* 39(15):43–48, 1985.

    No reference [4].

5] Ricardo Barrio.
    Torrijos at the crossroads.
    *Latin American Studies* XX(2):103–124, 1986.

These eleventh-hour changes are distressingly unbeautiful, but beauty is a secondary consideration. Informing your reader comes first.

Now be honest. Weren't you really working a bit close to the wire?


# Compression

Almost all of the examples in this book use the open reference format:

15] A. R. Montley.
    The preparation of malachite green by petroleum substitution.
    *The Journal of the Royal Chemical Association* XVIII(3):14–21, 1938.

16] Sharon Perl.
    Benzine ring formation and modification in the production of malachite green.
    *Proceedings of the 9th Annual Meeting of the United Petrochemical Association*, pages 231–236. 1941.

But another possibility exists. Exactly the same information in exactly the same order can be given in the compressed format:

15] A. R. Montley. The preparation of malachite green by petroleum substitution. *The Journal of the Royal Chemical Association* XVIII(3):14–21, 1938.

16] Sharon Perl. Benzine ring formation and modification in the production of malachite green. *Proceedings of the 9th Annual Meeting of the United Petrochemical Association*, pages 231–236. 1941.


The sole advantage of the compressed format is that it saves space, but that can be a prime consideration. If, for instance, you find yourself editing a professional journal, you can be sure that your budget will be as tight as a steel corset. You will be in no position to overlook any opportunity for holding down your paper costs, and over many articles in many issues in many copies the savings that result from using the compressed format will mount up.

Even when you're not worried about cutting costs, you should still give a thought to saving paper, and the trees that must be felled to make it. If your reference list is simple and straightforward, with few annotations and comments, consider using the compressed format.

Just remember that mistakes are much harder to catch in the compressed format than in the open one. The typographical errors most likely to occur and most difficult to see are in the numerical information—volume number, issue number, page number, and date. Even a minor error is an irritation to the conscientious reader, and a major one may render the whole reference useless. Don't trust your eyes. If you must do your checking alone, check numbers by reading them aloud. It's better to read aloud from your original notes while a friend checks the final version.

## The Finishing Touch

If you're doing your reference list by hand, all that remains is to number your reference list and go back through your text inserting the reference numbers into the brackets that wait for them. The task seems so mechanical that you might almost be tempted to ask a friendly six-year-old to do it for you. But don't.

If you're using a computer system to maintain the correspondence between your citation and reference numbers, you might be tempted to let it rip without going back to check the results. But again, don't.

Any chance to look at your text in a fresh light is precious. There are a thousand tricks for fooling yourself into seeing with fresh eyes. Read the carbon; photocopy the text onto yellow paper; read it backwards (page by page, not word by word); read it aloud; have a friend read it to you; diagram every tenth sentence; make a list of your most common faults and search for them; get the text typed on a strange typewriter; search every sentence for two words you can delete; circle all conjunctions and prepositions and relative pronouns; take at least one word on every page and look it up in the dictionary—in other words, use any device, however silly it feels, to wrench the reality of expression away from the context of intention. Improving what you've said is not the hardest part; it's seeing what needs improvement. All of us read in our own words not what we've said but what we meant to say, what we hoped to say. Any gimmick that checks this tendency is a godsend to the careful writer.

So, as you enter or check the bracketed numbers in your text, let your eye stray over the page, taking advantage of the queer context in which you can now see what you've written. Is that word really spelled with an *e?* Haven't you used that turn of phrase elsewhere? Is that transition as fluent as it might be? What's that flab doing there in the middle of the paragraph? Have you done the best you can?

# Special Schemes

You will by now have realized that the form in which you do your documentation is considerably less important than the content. Complete and thoughtful instruction on how to get hold of your sources—that's what your reader needs, and as long as she gets it almost any vehicle will do. Given a bent for innovation in small things, you may decide to invent your own format, some unique combination of sidenotes, footnotes, endnotes, and interpolation. Well, it's a minor vice, but there are better uses for your ingenuity.

With that warning in mind, I have some hesitation about presenting the two special schemes in this chapter. They are not meant as an invitation to proliferate new systems of documentation. They should, in fact, be ignored in ninety-nine cases out of a hundred and eyed, even in the hundredth, with suspicion.

## White Copy

This is the most beautiful of all the systems of documentation. The text is completely unmarred with the apparatus of scholarship; there are no bells and whistles, just smooth, unbroken copy. Between the text and the reference list comes a section of notes keyed backwards to the text by means of page and line numbers and forward to the reference list by means of short names. The notes section can't be done until the text is finished and paginated; that means you have to do a demanding, picky task at the last minute, under pressure. A white-copy system would be an ideal computer application, but I don't know of anyone who's attempted it.

Here's how white copy works. The beginning of page 56 in the text reads:

> their origins. These children are fearful about any small alteration in their routine. If juice appears at break for four days and soup for the fifth, the change will trouble them. Rage and tantrum among the outspoken ones may be difficult to deal with, but even more upsetting is the nausea the quiet child experiences, the wary, shamed expression you notice in the one who stays

The corresponding section of the notes reads:

> Page 56, lines 1–2. Wykoff, pages 366–401; Zeeman, pages 38–67.
> Page 56, line 4, tantrum. Seefer, Reaction Formation, pages 22–35; Zeeman, page 47.

And the corresponding sections of the reference list read:

> Maria Seefer.
> Reaction formation among child schizophrenics.
> *The Journal of Abnormal Child Psychology* XI(3):20–46, 1981.
>
> . . .
>
> H. L. Wykoff.
> *The Mark of Cain: Child Schizophrenics and Their Families.*
> Basic Books, 1982.
>
> . . .
>
> Martin O. Zeeman.
> Schizophrenic children in pseudo-classroom situations.
> *The Journal of Abnormal Child Psychology* XII(2):38–80, 1982.

Why would anyone go to all this trouble? For the scholarly reader there's no advantage to this system; on the contrary, she may find the absence of visible documentation in the text an irritation. But for the lay reader it's a blessing. The layman is likely to classify any work studded with notes and numbers and the paraphernalia of scholarship as heavy stuff and set it aside till she has more time. In other words, she never reads it. So the white-copy method is worth considering when you hope to reach both a scholarly and a popular audience. Reserve it for times when there is real hope—when your topic is broadly attractive, when you're being published for general distribution, and when you've tried twice as hard as usual to make your writing open, clear, and graceful.

## Super-quick

Of course, you should never do anything at the last minute. No one should ever run behind schedule, approach or pass a deadline, no one should ever be late. Of course. But somehow, mysteriously, all of us have found ourselves at seven-fifteen working on page 6 of a twenty-page paper due at nine o'clock. Turn in such an emergency to this method; the little time you have should be spent on composition, not on technical details of bibliographic style.

The lightning method of doing documentation simply encloses short names in parentheses and drops them directly into the text:

> under the influence of his advisors (Kappel, page 541). He was reluctant to call out the army, as he indicated in his diary (pages 322–329), but Manders, Fulsome, and Lord Barley convinced him that he had no choice (Raymond, The Little War, pages 211–215). By the beginning of

The reference list has no numbers for the items and no pinpointing, but otherwise it looks just like a standard reference list.

As you can see, for elegance and grace this system is strictly Rube Goldberg, but it works. It is suitable only for informal presentations, for student papers, say, or manuscripts to be circulated in draft. I hope you'll never have to use it.

## Short Names

Both of these require that you assign short names to your sources. The simplest short names are the last names of authors. Suppose, for instance, that your reference list includes A. J. Weston's *The Evolution of English Syntax,* that she's the only Weston on your list, and that this book is the only work of hers that you use. Then you may call it simply:

Weston.

If your reference list includes two or more authors with the same last name, use their initials or their given names to differentiate them. Suppose that you list both A. J. Weston's *The Evolution of English Syntax* and Susan Weston's "Notes on the Pluperfect" but no other works by either author. Then the short names for the two works are:

A. J. Weston.

Susan Weston.

If you have two or more works by the same author, use abbreviated titles along with her name. Suppose that you list one work for A. J. Weston, *The Evolution of English Syntax,* and two for Susan Weston, "Notes on the Pluperfect" and *Tense and Mode in Middle English.* Then the short names for the three works are:

A. J. Weston.

Susan Weston, Pluperfect.

Susan Weston, Tense and Mode.

There's a knack to doing these abbreviated titles. Try to suck the pith out of the full title. Take, for instance, Simon Chaney's "An Interpretation of Vandalism as the Expression of Loss of Ego":

▷ Chaney, Interpretation.

Chaney, Vandalism.

Good abbreviated titles depend on context. In an article on com-

---

Bad examples are marked with an arrowhead (▷).

putation, the best short title for Stephanie Maysles's "Fast Algorithms for Floating-Point Numbers" might be:

Maysles, Floating-Point.

In an article on floating-point numbers, the best short name for the same work might be:

Maysles, Fast Algorithms.

Using initials for abbreviated titles seldom works well. Take for instance Krishnan Alkamir's *An Account of the Development of the Wool Trade in the Early Period of the Republic:*

▷ Alkamir, ADWTEPR.
　Alkamir, Wool.

Don't go overboard in abbreviating titles, especially when you're dealing with well-known works:

▷ James, Portrait.
　James, Portrait of a Lady.

There are no underlines, italics, or quotation marks in short names, even for titles like the one in the example above, which has not been abbreviated. No distinction is made between books and non-books.
　Editors and compilers are treated just like authors when you're assigning short names:

▷ Mayhew (ed.), Energy.
　Mayhew, Energy.

Give the names of both authors when there are two, but only the first of three or more. H. M. Kronenberger and B. G. Katz's *Immaterial Expectations* becomes:

Kronenberger and Katz.

T. L. Sale, V. Brazier, and G. Colter's "An Etiology of the Falling Sickness" becomes:

> Sale et al.

Notice that "et al." can make different sets of joint authors look the same. Sale, Brazier, and Colter and Sale, Harkness, and O'Hare both collapse to "Sale et al." Restore the names of the second and following authors or use abbreviated titles to make the distinction.

> Sale, Brazier, and Colter.
>
> Sale, Harkness, and O'Hare.

or

> Sale et al., Etiology.
>
> Sale et al., Symptomatology and Spread.

In some contexts, a title or an abbreviated title may be enough of a short name without the author:

> Shaw, The Devil's Disciple.

or

> The Devil's Disciple.

Sources without authors use titles or abbreviated titles alone as short names:

> NY Times.
>
> Commerce Handbook.
>
> Panjika.

For both the white-copy and the super-quick systems, short names are used to tie the text and the reference list together; the reference list therefore needs no numbers. Pinpointing accompanies the short names; the reference list therefore needs no pinpointing, and there are no compound references. Otherwise, the reference list is just like the one in the standard system. Short names never appear on reference lists.

# MANUSCRIPT PREPARATION

Words, phrases, clauses; the balanced weight of an argument set out and then refuted; the savor of an adumbrating introduction; the bell-like tones of a perfectly cast allusion—these are the heights of scholarly writing. From them we must descend into the abyss of line widths, widows, smudges, and spent cartridges. Late at night, wrestling with a recalcitrant page break, who among us hasn't wished that we could somehow beam our words directly into our readers' heads without the intervention of print and paper?

## The Medium of Composition

In order to have a manuscript to prepare, you have to compose it, and to compose it you have to get it down. Even Edward Gibbon, who was legendary for his ability to compose long passages in his head, did eventually need to commit them to paper. The story goes that he would pace for an hour or so every morning, then sit down abruptly and write out a thousand or two thousand words without pause or emendation, as if copying from some angelic source. (I can do that too, though for me it's usually only two or three words that result from the hour of pacing.)

Most of us have four media of composition available to us: handwriting, typewriters, audiotape, and computers. By far the most popular of these is the computer, by which I mean everything from a PC running a smart-typewriter program to a time-sharing machine formating in batch to a workstation doing interactive page layout. What they all have in common is the ease of revision they offer. Over and over, users exclaim about how liberating it is to compose on a computer.

If you had ever seen these people's handwritten or typewritten drafts, you would know what they are exclaiming about. Here's what makes a handwritten or typed draft hard to revise:

Here's what makes it easy to revise:

If you don't have a computer available to you, you can provide yourself with nearly all its benefits for composition—not for manuscript preparation, but for composition—simply by leaving yourself enormous margins on all four sides of your paper. Only if your handwriting is so vile or your typing so incompetent that you yourself cannot read it do you really need a computer for composition.

If you do choose to use a computer, beware the temptation it offers to let manuscript preparation displace composition. They are two separate activities, best done separately. Hyphenation and exposition are at war with one another. Pagination vies with content. The mind busy fretting over point size has no time left over to consider clarity. If you need a break from the ardors of composition, try the time-honored ones like poking the fire or baking bread. They smell good, and thy don't give you any illusion that your paper is making progress while you indulge in them.

The other difficulty that people often have in using a computer for composition is an excess of the very quality they most prize. The ease with which they can revise imposes no limit on revision. The young ornithologist writes:

**The white spots on the tail are normally concealed.**

"Normally"? Perhaps not the best word.

**The white spots on the tail are usually concealed.**

Or how about this instead?

**Usually, the white spots on the tail are concealed.**

Or maybe this would be better:

**Often, the white spots on the tail are concealed.**

But maybe it was better the other way:

**The white spots . . .**

If she had been writing and rewriting the sentence by hand, or typing and retyping it, common sense would have intervened at some point. But on a computer system she can continue all afternoon.

A useful feature for the computer systems of the future would be color-coded revisions. At the first change, the sentence becomes pearl-colored; at the second change, pink; then blush, then rose, then lipstick. When the whole sentence glows cherry red, the writer will know it is time to let it be for a while and go on to other things.

If you use a computer for either composition or manuscript preparation or both, do not trust the only current copy of your manuscript to the machine. You should always have two current copies: one on paper, one on the machine; one on floppy, one on hard disk; one on each of two machines—whatever arrangement suits you best, but always two current copies.

# Fair Copy

Fair copy is intended for someone else to read, but a small audience. It's what you give your colleagues when you ask them to read your paper in draft; it's what you submit to a publisher; it's what you give to a typist or a printer who's going to prepare photo-ready copy for you; it's what you hand in for classroom assignments.

One criterion for fair copy is that a stranger find it immediately, easily readable. It doesn't have to be free of corrections; it doesn't have to be beautiful; it just has to be accessible, accessible without hesitation. No puzzling, no pondering; no late-night telephone calls to ask what that word is in the upper left-hand corner of page 178.

The other criterion for fair copy is that it should invite your reader to revise it or mark it up. The openness of the layout should bespeak humility: big margins and lots of space between the lines. Somebody recently asked me to look at a manuscript printed two columns to the page with no space between the lines and only a quarter of an inch for margins and between the columns. It was hard for me to believe that this person wanted help; the message that his manuscript sent loud and clear was that he thought himself above assistance. The page was so crowded that I could hardly even read it, let alone comment—maybe I was supposed to press it up against my forehead to see how it felt.

## Typing Fair Copy

Here is a reduced copy of a page of $8\frac{1}{2} \times 11''$ fair copy done on a typewriter:

a symbolic, formalistic way. Since symbols can be written and moved about with negligible expenditure of energy, it is tempting to leap to the conclusion that anything is possible in the symbolic realm.* But it is no more possible to construct symbolic structures without using energy than it is to construct material structures for free. If symbols and material objects are to be identified in t̶h̶e̶ this way, then we should perhaps pay special attention to the way material artifacts are engineered. We might expect the same limitations to apply to symbolic artifacts.

Engineers are adept at creating reliable structures despite two human failings: People cannot create perfect mechanisms and tend to plunge into activities before they understand them. This reconciliation is accomplished by means of the same social mechanisms that work to convert mathematical intuitions into mathematical proofs.† First, in mature engineering disciplines,

---

* This is the feeling behind computability theory — solvable versus unsolvable problems — and also behind complexity theory — solvable problems versus feasibly solvable problems.

† "One of the chief duties of the mathematician in acting as an adviser to scientists . . . is to discourage them from expecting too much of mathematics." — Norbert Weiner

## Cut, Tape, and Photocopy

The best way to make corrections on typed fair copy is with a scissors, paper, a roll of cellophane tape, and a photocopying machine (or with scissors, cover-up tape, and a photocopying machine). Say that in checking over a page you find the line:

```
had learned that teh Moscow Embassy was
```

You take a piece of paper big enough so that it won't wobble around in your carriage (this is an excellent use for the margins of discarded pages), or you peel the cover-up tape (so it won't wobble) and put it in your typewriter, and you type:

```
learned that the
```

You cut it out with your scissors, trimming it close; if you're using cover-up tape, choose the size that corresponds to the size of your typing. If you're using paper, lay it against a piece of tape a little longer than the scrap; if you're using cover-up tape, it's already sticky on one side. Position the cellophane tape or the cover-up tape above the errors, and flatten it out. You can use your thumbs if you're using cellophane tape; with cover-up tape, you have to flatten it delicately around the edges with your fingernails. Presto, you now have:

```
had learned that the Moscow Embassy was
```

Continue down the page, cutting and taping over any errors you find. Now the copying machine comes into play. As long as the tape is clean and the scrap is pressed down so that it can't throw a shadow, a photocopy of the page looks fine.

For larger mistakes or revisions—and this method works for changes of every size—position the correct copy on top of the incorrect copy first. Anchor it with four little bits of cellophane tape, one at each corner. Then tape down the top and the bottom edge with ten-inch pieces of tape, folding the tape over onto the back of the page. Again, remember that tape does not copy if it's clean; shadows do.

But now for the real beauty of the system: Suppose that, in looking back over the line that you corrected, you decide it's still not exactly right. "Learned" is a little too strong; what you really want to say is "thought." So you type on another piece of paper the word:

```
thought
```

You cut it out, lay it against a piece of tape, press the tape down in place, and you have:

```
had thought that the Moscow Embassy was
```

There may be an upper limit on this process, where there are so many layers of tape that they start to obscure the original typing, but I have photocopied pages that were five or six layers thick in some spots and the results still looked good.

For fair copy, the error and the correction needn't be exactly the same length. You could, for instance, substitute "heard" for "learned" in the example above, centering it so that it would look like this:

```
had heard that the Moscow Embassy was
```

The correction needn't be perfectly aligned. It shouldn't be cockeyed, but a degree or two off the true horizon will do no harm. Remember, the object is legibility, not beauty.

## White Out

Use correction fluid to white out extra characters. Suppose you have the line:

```
larger programs or routines in the library
```

If you decide to change from the plural to the singular, whiting out produces a line that's still easily readable:

```
larger program  or routine  in the library
```

Whiting out more than an extra character or two makes your copy difficult to read. Suppose that you decide to say just "routine" in the line above. Do not white out the extra words:

```
▷ larger              routine  in the library
```

---

Bad examples are marked with an arrowhead (▷). In this chapter, "bad" often means not lines with mistakes in them, but lines in which the mistakes have been badly corrected.

Cut and tape the correct version:

```
larger routine in the library
```

Don't worry about the shortness of the line; you have no obligation to maintain exact margins in fair copy.

## White Out and Type Over

Be patient and wait till the correction fluid is dry; otherwise the fresh typing appears to be sunk into little canyons. Perfect alignment is not necessary in fair copy.

## Correction Tape

Correction tape is very useful for making fair copy. For the amateur typist, however, correction tape works only on mistakes caught while the page is still in the carriage. Once it's out, it will never go back in the same way again.

## Ex Out

Ex out no more than, say, a dozen characters. For more than that, cut and tape.

Ex out with one string of lower-case letters; the object is just to indicate omission, not to blast your errors off the face of the earth.

```
▷ proposal he XXXXXXXXXX soon wished he had

  proposal he xxxxxxxxx soon wished he had
```

Punctuation should not be left at the end of the exing out:

```
▷ for future research xxxxxxxxx. The
```

Ex out the punctuation too, backspace, and put it in where it now belongs:

```
  for future research. xxxxxxxxx The
```

## Ex Out and Type Above

Do not ex out a character and type another above it:

```
                  e
▷ no consistxnt approach to the epiphenomenal
```

Ex out the whole word and type above it:

```
      consistent
no xxxxxxxxxx approach to the epiphenomenal
```

Better yet, cut and tape the correct version.

## Strikeovers

Never correct an error by backspacing and typing the correct version on top of it, even if you think your reader can guess what you intend:

```
▷ sounds that the patient feels are related
```

Strikeovers are even worse on unfamiliar words or, worst of all, on proper names:

```
▷ some home truths that Feeldman doesn't want
```

Ex out the whole word and type above, or cut and tape the correction.

## Cross Out

Hand corrections should always be done in non-smearing black ink. Not in pencil; not in colored ink, not even blue, let alone red or green or violet; not in the beady, syrupy ink of cheap ballpoints. A black felt-tip pen is a good choice so long as the felt is not worn down; a high-quality ballpoint is even better. A fountain pen with a narrow nib is good, but a broad-nibbed pen is not.

Taking your pen in hand, you should cross out no more than roughly a dozen characters; for more than that, cut and tape. Cross out with one or two neat horizontal lines. Do not leave punctuation at the end of your crossing out; cross it out as well as put it in by hand, neatly, where it now belongs.

## Cross Out and Print Above

Never, never, never enter corrections on fair copy in handwriting. Print. Print with ordinary sentence capitalization, not all in caps. Form your letters scrupulously, as if you were a diligent and unusually dextrous first-grader.

Do not cross out a character and print above it; cross out the whole word and print the whole word correctly above.

## Insertions

Insert punctuation if there's space for it; if there's not, cut and tape.

Do not insert a single character; cross out the whole word and print the whole word correctly above.

It is acceptable to insert two or three words above the line, with a caret to show where. The words may be printed:

> larger than any tank they had ever seen

*(handwritten insertion: "other" above a caret between "any" and "tank")*

If the words are typed, show the placement with a caret, not a slash:

> ▷ much/if not more than earlier models.

*(typed insertion "as" above "much")*

> much if not more than earlier models.

*(typed insertion "as" above "much", with caret)*

Do not attempt to make an insertion between a word and a mark of punctuation:

> ▷ subsequently contradicted, others are

*(typed insertion "or disallowed" above, with caret after "contradicted")*

White out the mark and put it where it now belongs, at the end of the insertion:

> subsequently contradicted others are

*(typed insertion "or disallowed," above, with caret before "others")*

For insertions longer than two or three words, cut and tape. Slice the original page apart at the spot where the insertion should go. Type the insertion out in full. Mortise the two together with tape against backing sheets. If what used to be one page has now expanded to two or more, number the new pages with the number of the original one and a letter. For instance, if because of insertions what used to be page 126 is now three pages long, number the three pages 126a, 126b, and 126c.

## Cumulate and Retype

Corrections made by cutting and taping, by whiting out, and by using correction tape don't detract from legibility. You may have as many as you need on a page. But corrections made by exing out or crossing out and by printing or typing above the line do add up. Set yourself a limit of, say, four to a page. If you have more than that, either retype the page or cut and tape over corrections that were first made by some other method.

## Spacing

In general, everything in fair copy should be double-spaced. Footnotes should be double-spaced. Displayed quotations should be double-spaced. Your reference list should be double-spaced. The spacing invites corrections and improvements.

The only exception is for diagrams and tables. It would be crazy to double-space a binary tree, for instance:

What you are doing here is not really typing but drawing with your typewriter; space whatever way makes the drawing come out right:

Make corrections in diagrams and tables only by cutting and taping.

## Numbering Citations

When the final draft of your reference list is done, go back to your text, fill the bracketed numbers in neatly by hand, and white out whatever marginal notes you made to yourself about what belongs there:

    on the dark side of the moon [6, 18]. Here

## Syllabication

The only purpose for syllabicating a word at the end of a line is to maintain your right-hand margin. Since you have no obligation to maintain right-hand margins in fair copy, do not syllabicate any words.

  ▷  annual contributions continued to grow pro-
     portionately but accomplished no more.
     annual contributions continued to grow
     proportionately but accomplished no more.

It's especially important not to break hyphenated words at the ends of lines:

  ▷  the role that the conspirators, heart-
     stricken at the results of their actions,

If you give fair copy with a break like that one to a typist or a printer, you're likely to get back "heartstricken," and it's your own fault. Do it the safe way:

```
the role that the conspirators,
heart-stricken at the results of their
```

# Computerized Fair Copy

Here is a reduced copy of a page of $8\frac{1}{2} \times 11''$ fair copy done with a computerized typesetting system:

a symbolic, formalistic way. Since symbols can be written and moved about with negligible expenditure of energy, it is tempting to leap to the conclusion that anything is possible in the symbolic realm.* But it is no more possible to construct symbolic structures without using energy than it is to construct material structures for free. If symbols and material objects are to be identified in this way, then we should perhaps pay special attention to the way material artifacts are engineered. We might in principle expect that the same limitations apply to symbolic artifacts.

Engineers have been remarkably adept at reconciling the creation of reliable structures with two human failings: People cannot create perfect mechanisms, and people tend to plunge into activities before they understand them perfectly. This reconciliation is accomplished by means of the same social mechanisms that work to convert mathematical intuitions into mathematical proofs.† First, in mature engineering disciplines,

---

* This is the feeling behind computability theory—solvable versus unsolvable problems—and also behind complexity theory—solvable problems versus feasibly solvable problems.

† "One of the chief duties of the mathematician in acting as an adviser to scientists . . . is to discourage them from expecting too much of mathematics."—Norbert Weiner

## Spacing and Margins

Ideally you would like to have the lines in fair copy spaced out far enough to invite interlinear corrections from your readers. In some systems, however, such spacing may be impractical—it might take more futzing around with the internals of the system than you should undertake. But you must be able to provide spacious margins. Test the system out before you start to use it, and reject it if you cannot use it to produce fair copy with huge side margins ready to accept your readers' comments, questions, and corrections.

## Flexibility

If you are also going to make photo-ready copy, you may be hard put to find software that will switch back and forth from the very open fair-copy layout to a more compressed, printerly-looking version. This kind of flexibility is well worth paying for.

## Bookkeeping

Another worthwhile feature is automatic handling of some of the small details of producing fair copy. For instance, some systems will number your reference list for you and then drop the right numbers into your text. Anyone who's ever added a new reference to a paper at the last minute will bless this ability. Instead of searching through the text laboriously for all occurrences of citation 15 to change them to 16, all 16 to 17, etc., you add the new reference, turn the crank, and all the new numbers get generated automatically.

Be sure, however, that you aren't asked to pay too high a price for bookkeeping. Some systems have a very narrow, rigid view of reference format, which might prevent you from conveying all the information about a reference that your reader would find useful. Be sure that the reference format will accommodate your needs or ignore the automatic bookkeeping features and lay out your references yourself. Even if you end up arranging and numbering your references for yourself, you can use computerized search-and-replace to do renumbering more conveniently than you could on paper.

## Footnotes or Endnotes

If your system can lay out footnotes for you at the bottom of the page, fine. If it can't, switch to endnotes. Do not attempt to get your knee on its throat and force it to do footnotes against its will—your time would be better spent writing a dozen additional papers.

## Syllabication

The purpose of syllabicating words at the ends of lines is to maintain a perfect right margin. But the margins in fair copy don't matter—they aren't the ones you're going to end up with anyway. And syllabicated words are (a little) harder to read than whole ones. If your system does automatic syllabication, turn it off for doing fair copy; if it can produce ragged-right margins, so much the better.

## On-line Fair Copy

The ultimate in circulating fair copy is presentation on-line. (Be sure to provide your reader with a copy, not with the original.) You and your reader can work out a convention for differentiating her words from yours; she could for instance shove yours over to the right and put hers at the left-hand edge, or enclose her words in double brackets.

For teachers, reading fair copy on-line is so superior to paper that I believe it will come to be the norm. One of the best things about on-line presentation is that it gives the teacher no excuse for taking cheap shots. There's seldom room to scribble more than "Confusing" in the margin of a paper, or "Awkward," or "Wordy." The on-line version invites revision, not just labeling, and students learn more by seeing their own words transformed than they ever can from textbook examples. Reading student papers becomes harder, but more effective.

# Hiring Fair Copy Done

Fair copy needn't be beautifully laid out. It can contain visible corrections, exings out, and insertions. So why should you hire somebody else to do it for you? Maybe you really can't type at all. Or maybe you plan to have the same person produce both fair copy and photo-ready copy. It's conceivable that you might not have a computer system; it's not conceivable that a professional typist won't. If all that's wanted is fair copy, a word-processing system will do; if you want photo-ready copy, then you want your typist to have a typesetting system.

Explain what you're after. Carry this book along with you and go over the characteristics of fair copy with the typist. It's very important, for instance, that she understand what kinds of corrections she can make. She needs to know about double-spacing everything. If your handwriting is, like most people's, illegible in spots, tell her to leave space for words she can't read so that you can fill them in later. Be sure to mention that she should not syllabicate words at the ends of lines; most typists do it by second nature.

I no longer have any sense of what good typists charge because no one I know uses typists any more. Inquire around, and be suspicious of too low a rate; you may end up with another rough draft.

The typist is of course responsible for correcting her own mistakes without charge. But since fifty of the mistakes are likely to be yours for every one of hers, it would be mean-spirited and unbecoming to haggle over typographical errors. Correct hers neatly by hand, along with your own mistakes. If you make so many mistakes on a page that it needs to be done over, pay with good grace whatever she asks. If she makes so many mistakes that a page needs to be done over, get another typist.

Never give the only copy of your manuscript to anyone. Make a copy of your draft before you let it out of your hands.

# Photo-ready Copy

Photo-ready copy is what you send out to the world to read. Its purpose is publication. It no longer has the intimacy and openness that your fair copy had, when you were soliciting advice and comment from your readers. Now you take your stand. The layout of the page says: This is my best. As of today, this is where I am and what I think.

If you are preparing your own photo-ready copy, wait till your words are done. Wait till they are indeed your best. Then change hats, turn yourself into a typographer, and treat what you have written as respectfully as you would expect a stranger to. If a typist rewrote your sentence to make it fit on the page, you'd be outraged. Don't commit the outrage on yourself.

People keep telling me horrific stories about alterations they've worked on their prose in the name of typography, often wholly misguided notions of typography. One fellow—you will think I made this up, but I didn't—one fellow noticed that chapters in published books typically begin on odd-numbered, right-hand pages. He failed to notice that the facing page in a typical book might be blank. So he cut or padded every chapter in his dissertation to make it end on an even-numbered page, thereby permitting the next chapter to begin in what he felt was the correct, the *professional* position.

Real typographers and book designers produce structures that are both legible and beautiful. The best that the rest of us can hope for, in situations where we're forced to do our own typography, is legibility. In judging an effect, do not ask yourself how it looks. Ask yourself how it reads.

# Fixed-pitch Photo-ready Copy

If you have a choice, here is how you should lay out fixed-pitch photo-ready copy.

> 10-pitch (pica) type
> > 1″ margins left, top, and right
> > 1.5″ bottom margins
> > double-spaced or single-spaced with double spacing between paragraphs and above and below displays
> > 5-character paragraph indentation
> > 8-character display indentation, with a 2-character indentation for paragraphs within displays
>
> 12-pitch (elite) type
> > 1.5″ margins left, top, and right
> > 2″ bottom margins
> > double-spaced or single-spaced with double spacing between paragraphs and above and below displays
> > 6-character paragraph indentation
> > 9-character display indentation, with a 3-character indentation for paragraphs within displays

You may single-space displays, footnotes, and your reference list even if the rest of your text is double-spaced.

## Corrections

My assumption is that you're going to be producing this copy with some kind of word-processing system—it's really not sensible any more to try to do photo-ready copy on an ordinary typewriter. But just because you're using word processing doesn't mean you should become its prisoner. You should always stay alert to the possibility of making corrections on paper rather than trying to coerce a rebellious word processer to do your bidding. Do not permit a word-processing system to hold you in bondage. You may have as many corrections as you like on photo-ready as long as they are invisible to the camera.

## Right Margin

Do not use right-justification with a fixed-width font:

> ▷ ` can argue, of course, that whereas one does `
> ` not hear so-called basilectal creole items, `
> ` one does often hear the intermediate, so- `
> ` called mesolectal patterns in Georgetown. `
> ` But the question of the linguistic source of `
> ` these intermediate forms is by no means `
> ` settled. Are these so-called intermediate `
> ` forms mutated basilectal forms on the march `
> ` to the acrolect, or urban creole forms `

> ` can argue, of course, that whereas one does `
> ` not hear so-called basilectal creole items, `
> ` one does often hear the intermediate, `
> ` so-called mesolectal patterns in Georgetown. `
> ` But the question of the linguistic source of `
> ` these intermediate forms is by no means `
> ` settled. Are these so-called intermediate `
> ` forms mutated basilectal forms on the march `
> ` to the acrolect, or urban creole forms `

With a ragged-right margin, which is the kind you should be using, you have the problem of buck teeth. A buck tooth is a line that ends with a word dangling out over the line below it:

> ▷ ` ways in the secret documents that Moulton and `
> ` his assistant had prepared. There could `

If the autowrap on your word-processing system is correctly implemented, it will not produce buck teeth. If it does give you buck teeth, override the autowrap by hitting the carriage return yourself. Draw an invisible line seven characters to the left of the margin. At the end of the first word that ends as or after you touch the invisible line, hit the carriage return instead of the space bar. If you always hit the carriage return at the first opportunity, the dangling word gets moved down:

```
ways in the secret documents that Moulton
and his assistant had prepared. There could
```

Don't try to jam as many words on the line as you can.

So far so good. But what if you have a word that starts before the invisible line and ends after the right margin?

If the word contains only one syllable, you can't syllabicate it. Type it on the next line.

If the word is already hyphenated, you can syllabicate it only on its own hyphens. "Self-gen-" "erating" is not a legal syllabication.

If you can syllabicate the word so that the end-of-line hyphen falls under characters in the line above or above characters in the line below and if neither the line above nor the line below ends with a hyphen, syllabicate it. Otherwise type it on the next line.

Sometimes a particularly perverse paragraph may take several passes before it can be made to conform to these rules.

## Typeset Photo-ready Copy

In the 1950s, an experimental psychologist named Miles Tinker did a series of studies on page layout and reported his results in:

> Miles A. Tinker.
> *Legibility of Print.*
> Iowa State University Press, 1963.

He found that for legibility a line should not exceed 72 or 73 characters. Above that length the eye cannot find the beginning of the next line accurately, and the reader experiences fatigue, irritation, and loss of comprehension.

Now, that makes an 8.5 × 11″ page ideal for copy typed on a 10-pitch typewriter. With an inch margin to the left and right, the lines come out no longer than 65 characters, the reader's eye can track from one line to the next effortlessly, and nothing distracts from what you've written.

Unfortunately, the same 8.5 × 11″ piece of paper is very far from ideal for a 10-point typeface. With inch margins, the lines would average 120 characters long or longer, depending on how compressed the face is. You would be foolish to ask your reader to stumble over 120-character lines. Till the standard page size changes, you have two choices: exaggerated margins or two columns.

Here is a reduced copy of an 8.5 × 11″ page of photo-ready copy prepared with a computerized typesetting system:

a symbolic, formalistic way. Since symbols can be written and moved about with negligible expenditure of energy, it is tempting to leap to the conclusion that anything is possible in the symbolic realm.* But it is no more possible to construct symbolic structures without using energy than it is to construct material structures for free. If symbols and material objects are to be identified in this way, then we should perhaps pay special attention to the way material artifacts are engineered. We might in principle expect that the same limitations apply to symbolic artifacts.

Engineers have been remarkable adept at reconciling the creation of reliable structures with two human failings: People cannot create perfect mechanisms, and people tend to plunge into activities before they understand them perfectly. This reconciliation is accomplished by means of the same social mechanisms that work to convert mathematical intuitions into mathematical proofs.† First, in mature engineering disciplines,

## Mixed Fonts and Sizes

In newspaper circles, they tell the story of the young assistant editor who got left in charge of the paper when the managing editor had to

---

* This is the feeling behind computability theory—solvable versus unsolvable problems—and also behind complexity theory—solvable problems versus feasibly solvable problems.

† "One of the chief duties of the mathematician in acting as an adviser to scientists . . . is to discourage them from expecting too much of mathematics."—Norbert Weiner

leave town for three days. On her return, the managing editor called the young assistant into her office.

"Big story you had here on the front page on Monday," she said. "Big headline."

"Well yes," said the assistant. " 'Chickens Escape James Poultry Farm.' That was a big story."

"Big headline," said the editor. "See you used the 42-point type."

"Yes," said the assistant.

"Even bigger story on Tuesday, I see," said the editor.

"Yes, it was," said the assistant. " 'Council Rejects Sewer Tax Hike.' That was a big one. I covered it myself."

"See you used the 48-point type on that one," said the editor.

"Well, yes, I did," said the assistant. "I hope I didn't give it too much prominence, seeing it was my own story and all, but I thought it was really more—of more general impact than Monday's story, so I wanted to, you know—"

"Yup," said the grizzled editor. "Biggest story of all on Wednesday. 'Fire in Smith Bakery.' 65-point type for that one. We never used that type before."

"Oh really? Is that so? I thought a fire was so much more important than either the chickens or the sewer tax, so I thought I would try to emphasize it. I hope that was OK?"

"Well," sighed the editor. "Yes. Yes, I guess it was OK. I have to admit to you, though, that I am a little bit disappointed. I had kind of been saving that type to use for the Second Coming."

The people who sell computerized typesetting systems know what their public wants: It wants fonts. What could be more fun than Helvetica, Courier, Times Roman, Palatino—all on the same page! And all those sizes! The resultant pages have a certain kind of charm, but you have to ask yourself whether you want your reader to think of you as touchingly goofy. If you don't, cultivate a modest severity, an almost Shaker sensibility. Less is less. You won't get to show off all your fancy fonts, but you also won't look like a chucklehead.

But what about encoding information in fonts? Surely that's a responsible, mature way of exploiting available technology and not mere hedonism? Well, OK. Up to you. Fools rush in, and so on. The smaller the units you want to encode, the more dramatic the contrast has to be; don't ask your reader to distinguish, say, a *T* in Garamond from one in Baskerville. Choose a contrast either in style or in weight but not both. And be sure to leave something on tap for the Second Coming.

## Syllabication

If your typesetting system does syllabication by Don Knuth's TeX rules, which are available for anyone to copy, it syllabicates more consistently and accurately than you can yourself. (A system other than TeX itself that uses the TeX rules should advertise the fact.) If it does syllabication by some other method, you must watch it like a hawk. Syllabications like "r-" "ed" and "th-" "ing" are all too common. You are responsible for the confusion your reader will suffer if your typesetting system inflicts "mole-" "ster" or "archipe-" "lago" or "mishy-" "phenation" on her.

# Communicating with Typists and Typographers

In these days of home-brew publishing, it is a blessed luxury to have a professional typist or typographer deal with your work. Conduct yourself so as to be worthy of the honor. If your work is being published, you may also have the joy of working with a professional editor. You must provide your typist or typographer and your editor with fair copy from which to work; it needs to be instantly, effortlessly readable. The fair copy should be perfect in everything but the typing. No sentence, no word, no comma should be anything but your very best. Once you have passed the stage of fair copy, corrections are expensive, irritating, and dangerous to make. Do not rush to thrust your work into their hands. Linger a little; read it again; mull it over. This is your last chance to make corrections without causing yourself and other people a good deal of grief; grasp the opportunity.

## Instructions

As much as you can, try to show on your fair copy rather than just tell. When you must give instructions, print them neatly in full caps:

```
convicted of behavior unbecoming to an of-
ficer.
```

            The 57th Regiment
               of Foot

```
The 57th Regiment were the original
```

That's acceptable, but it's not in your best interests. A few minutes more, a snip of the scissors, a dab of tape, and you have a much safer version:

```
convicted of behavior unbecoming to an of-
ficer.
```

            The 57th Regiment
               of Foot

```
The 57th Regiment were the original
```

## Proofreading

Photo-ready copy (or galleys or page proofs leading to photo-ready copy) should not just be checked over; it should be proofed. Get a friend or a colleague or hire someone if you must to go over it with you. You, the copyholder, read from your fair copy aloud, word for word, with all the tricky punctuation too. For instance, you would read the first sentence of this paragraph, "Photo-hyphen-ready copy, paren, or galleys or page proofs leading to photo-ready copy, close-paren, should not just be checked over, semi, it should be proofed." Show the capital letter at the beginning of a sentence and the period at the end by letting your voice rise and fall naturally, but don't rely on vocal cues to communicate other marks of punctuation; give their names aloud. Your friend, the proofreader, reads silently through the photo-ready copy, noting on a separate piece of paper any errors that she finds; later you will transcribe her corrections onto the photo-ready copy yourself.

Mark photo-ready copy with a #2 pencil, neatly. Learn to use the

simplest of the proofreader's marks—delete, close up space, open
up space, insert.

| delete | with the ~~the~~ same kind of | |
| close up space | medalion of the‿same kind | |
| open up space | send a message to⟍the source | |
| insert | in a⟍time when we can see | *future* |
| insert comma | pushing the button⟍each | |
| insert apostrophe | certain peoples irritation | |

(Notice that there's always a mark both in the text and in the
margin. If a paragraph contains more than one mark, connect each
mark to its corresponding entry in the margin.)

If there's something wrong and you don't know how to mark it,
don't guess; explain in words in the margin or on a gummed press-
on note what's troubling you. Don't mark the copy till your mind is
made up.

Mark each error with an assignment of blame: "ae" for author's
error, "te" for typist's, "pe" for printer's. Just in case there's any
doubt in your mind, the faithful transcription of a typographical
error in fair copy is an author's error, not a typist's error. If your fair
copy reads "study teh question" and your typist or typographer
renders it "study teh question," that's your mistake, not hers. You
pay (or your publisher does) for correcting your errors, the typist or
printer pays for correcting hers.


Proofreading is not, repeat not, an invitation to revise. Your task is
to check for typographical errors. Inevitably you will find mistakes
of your own as well; be firm with yourself. An error of spelling or
punctuation must be set right; an outright error of fact must also be

corrected, at whatever cost is necessary. But the time for improving your style has passed. It's too late now. Unless you learn to accept that fact, you will never do your utmost beforehand, and every typist or typographer who deals with you will hold your name in infamy.

## Deadlines

Many deadlines are indications, guesses, orders of magnitude. Press deadlines are deadlines. Don't try the old abducted-by-a-band-of-gypsies, escaped-only-with-your-life excuse; your editor has already heard it. Be on time.

# The End

I wish that I could end this book with the section at the end of the chapter on the reference list: "Have you done your best?" That would be good rhetoric, but bad sense. The time to ask the question is past. Once you get to photo-ready copy, all you can do by tinkering with your prose is injure and infuriate the people you have to work with.

That's a bitter pill to swallow if you have really tried. The harder you work at your writing, the more aware you become of its failings, its weaknesses, places where you're not quite up to the mark. There's a sadness about seeing your words when it's too late to change them. Good; sometimes very good; but not good enough. Store up the lessons you learn as you read your photo-ready copy. Next time you can remember to beef up your examples, to spend a little longer on your opening paragraphs, to eliminate wordiness, to put what you have to say more directly, to conquer hard transitions instead of finessing them. Next time, next time, you can do better.

# Appendix 1
## The Vita

The idea of a vita is perfectly straightforward—it presents your qualifications for a post. There are three names current for this document, "vita," "curriculum vitae," and "résumé." (It requires no acute psychological insight to observe that we set job-hunting off in its nomenclature as something foreign.) Of the three names, "vita" is the least common, but it has the most to recommend it; it's short, it forms an acceptable Englished plural, and it needs no accents. So vita is what we'll call it.

Many manuals have been published about writing vitas for jobs in business and industry, but this information is no help with academic vitas. The academic vita is much more highly stylized than its counterpart in the outside world, much narrower, and therefore much easier to prepare. A thousand minute, delicate decisions that face the writer of a business vita have already been settled for you by the rigid format of the academic vita.

This rigidity can cause great discomfort in young scholars putting together their first vitas. They feel themselves reduced to the level of name–rank–and–serial–number. Where in these bland and faceless phrases is the writer's essence, her person, her spirit? The answer is: Nowhere. You might (while chafing) think about what the restrictions of the vita format represent. Not only in pious theory but also frequently in fact, academic posts are awarded solely on qualifications. If the academic vita reflects a little game with rules and points and goals, the game is at least acknowledged, the rules are set out clearly. Academy has its own peculiar definition of merit, but at least it spells that definition out, and often sticks by it. Small consolation if you're a brilliant weirdo, a square peg in a round hole; but compared to the rest of the world, where the shapes of the holes are often kept secret, some consolation nonetheless. Here are the rules of the game. (These forms apply for most academic positions in the United States. If you are applying for a position in another country, seek out an academic whose career has been spent there and find out from her what that country's conventions are for vitas.)

# Heading

There is no need to use a heading on a vita—vitas look like nothing else in the world and proclaim themselves instantly.

# Name, Post, Address, and Telephone Number

Begin by giving the name you commonly use for your signature. Give your current academic post, address, and telephone number below and your home address and telephone number at the right:

```
Dwayne L. Marchant                 home:
Assistant Professor of             1315 Ridge Road
    Music Theory                   Woodly, Maine 06519
University of Maine                203-477-9431
    Music School
Storrs, Maine 06112
203-983-1166
```

If you're still in graduate school, you'll need to check whether your department will accept mail and telephone calls for you. If so, give both your academic and your home address (your own residence, not your parents'):

```
Adele Vionnet                      home:
Department of Near Eastern         RFD Route 7
    Languages                      Bindale, Iowa 77189
Iowa State University              851-229-8437
Missoula, Iowa 77188
851-234-1550 x366
```

Otherwise, give only your home address:

> Martin Wyler
> 2297 Flora Avenue
> St. Louis, Missouri 51674
> 510-484-9075

If you're currently working in a non-academic job, probably you'll list only your home address and telephone number. To do otherwise would require that your job be academically prestigious, that your employer know about your job search, and that she be willing for you to conduct it on company time—an unlikely combination of circumstances.

Simple though this section looks, there are several pitfalls to avoid. Do not, for instance, attach to your name any titles or designations of degrees; they make you look very small-time:

▷ Philip Itisaki, MA, MFAT, PhD

 Philip Itisaki

Pare down your academic address to the minimum that will permit mail to reach you:

▷ Weak Force Group, Physics Department
 University of Wisconsin—Milwaukee Campus
 Sherrill Memorial Hall, Room 39
 1536 Maple Avenue
 Milwaukee, Wisconsin 65998

 Physics Department
 University of Wisconsin
 Milwaukee, Wisconsin 65998

If you have no phone, say so:

 home:
 3314 East 57th Street
 Chicago, Illinois 60615
 no phone

---

Bad examples are marked with an arrowhead (▷).

# Degrees

Under this heading, list your degrees with dates and granting institutions:

> BA 1981, Antioch College
> MA 1983, PhD 1988, State University of New
> York at Rochester

Abbreviate the names of your degrees unless they will be unfamiliar to your reader:

▷ Doctorate of Philosophy 1965, Brown
>  University

> PhD 1965, Brown University

▷ LTS 1974, Uppsala University

> Licentiate in Sacred Theology 1974, Uppsala
> University

Two styles of abbreviations are current, one with periods, one without. The one with the periods looks statelier, the one without, snappier. Use either as long as you're consistent.

> B.A., B.S., M.A., M.A.T., LL.D., Ph.D.

or

> BA, BS, MA, MAT, LLD, PhD

List commencement honors with your degrees:

> BS magna cum laude with departmental honors
> 1979, Webster College

To indicate the breadth of your background, you may want to append informal designations to your degrees:

> BS (microbiology) 1977, Coe College
> MS (microbiology and biophysics) 1979,
> Arizona State University

```
PhD (history of science) 1984, Harvard
    University
```

There is no point, however, in adding such designations if your career has followed an undeviating path:

```
▷ BA (history) 1971, University of Michigan
  MA (history) 1974, PhD (history) 1976, Yale
```

Nor are you obliged to volunteer the information that one or more of your earlier degrees is in a field inappropriate to the post that you're applying for:

```
▷ BA (political science) 1972, Rosary College
  PhD (history of art) 1977, Ohio State
```

The presumption is that your highest degree is appropriate; if it's not, explain in your cover letter why you think you're qualified anyway. For a post in the history of art, this candidate should write:

```
BA 1972, Rosary College
PhD 1977, Ohio State
```

In using these designations, remember that they are informal; you need not adopt any awkward or misleading nomenclature your particular school happens to use. Suppose, for instance, that you do work in ethics at a school that calls the field moral philosophy for historical reasons:

```
▷ PhD (moral philosophy) 1971, Hapwood
    Divinity School
  PhD (ethics) 1971, Hapwood Divinity School
```

Don't be excessively specific:

```
▷ PhD (analysis of small-business failures)
    1984, McGill University
  PhD (microeconomics) 1984, McGill University
```

The title of your dissertation, which appears later in the vita, will reveal your precise area of specialization.

If you are right on the verge of receiving a degree, you may list it:

```
PhD 1992 (expected), Vanderbilt University
```

All the old saws about counting chickens before they're hatched apply here. Nothing chills a prospective employer faster than learning that a degree a candidate lists as expected is, according to her department, more accurately classed as an aspiration.

Some schools need place designations:

```
▷ BA 1965, Trinity College
  BA 1965, Trinity College, Burlington,
        Vermont
```

Some do not:

```
▷ PhD 1981, The Johns Hopkins University,
        Baltimore, Maryland
  PhD 1981, The Johns Hopkins University
```

For schools with several campuses, indicate succinctly which one you attended:

```
BA 1979, University of California at Irvine
```

## Additional Education

This is an optional section even early in your career, and later it will tend to disappear altogether. The object is to describe schooling that did not lead to a degree but that is relevant to the post you're seeking. A lesser goal, but one that crops up occasionally, is to explain what would otherwise appear as large gaps in your history. Probably the best way to discuss these possibilities is to invent several examples.

Case *A*, for instance, is a young historian of the Edwardian period in England who does a special program on methods for social history. She enters the information on her vita thus:

```
The Family and Community History Summer
    Training Institute, Newberry Library,
    1986
```

Both because the Institute is very prestigious and because it has a formative influence on her work, this same item will continue to appear on her vita till the day she dies.

Case *B* is a small-group sociologist who does an immersion course in German so as to be able to read the many important materials in that language. Early in her career she lists this training:

```
Marquette University Summer Language Program
    (German), 1977
```

Later on, by the time that she's an associate professor, it no longer seems so significant to her that she's able to slog her way through a German text with the aid of a dictionary, and the item disappears from her vita.

Case *C* is a psychologist who has participated in countless numbers of training sessions and workshops. Rather than list them all, she weeds them out severely and mentions only five, the four best ones and the one most recent. Five is a large enough number to indicate that she has a lively interest in this kind of activity, but not so many as to give her vita a frantic, excessive appearance.

Case *D* is a botanist who planned originally to go into math. After two years of graduate school, she changed her mind and switched fields. Although the mathematics has no direct bearing on her present work, she feels that it gives her a greater sophistication than some of her colleagues have, and the change of fields explains why she didn't get her PhD until nine years after her BS. So she enters the information on her vita:

```
University of Indiana, graduate work in
    mathematics, 1971–73
```

Once she's done some research that makes use of her mathematical background and published several articles that demonstrate it, she will no longer feel the need to mention the false start she made years ago.

Case *E* is a late bloomer. As an undergraduate, she did a major in English and a minor in chemistry. She started doing graduate work in American literature, changed schools, dropped out, started in again in political science, dropped out again, and took several years off, working as a carpenter and taking night courses in philosophy, anthropology, and linguistics. Eventually she decided that what she wanted to do was linguistics, entered graduate school once again, and settled down very nicely. Despite the extensive additional education Case *E* has, she lists none of it on her vita; it's too tangled a trail to ask anyone else to follow.

Taken together, these cases illustrate three important points about the vita: It's a summary, not a recapitulation; stick to the high points. It's a construction, not a cumulation; updating requires the elimination of old material as well as the addition of new. And it's a presentation, not a confession; don't burden your reader with confidences.

# Experience

Every part of your vita requires steady reexamination and reevaluation as your career progresses, but none more than this section. In looking for your first post, you will list rafts of information that disappear as soon as you have been hired. From then on, no single transformation will be so great, but you should strive constantly to compress this information, to paint in bold strokes.

### Experience for Your First Job

At this point you should drag out whatever relevant experience you can—any teaching you've done and any work that bears some relationship to your field. Some items that might typically appear are teaching assistantships (with topics, not titles, for courses):

▷ Carnegie–Mellon University. Teaching
      assistant in Engineering 101, 1981–82;
      in Engineering 226, 1984.

Carnegie–Mellon University. Teaching
assistant in introductory engineering,
1981–82; in materials and stress
analysis, 1984.

Research assistantships:

Ohio Wesleyan University. Research assistant
in human physiology, 1981–84.

Teaching below the university level:

Francis Scott Key Consolidated School,
Amundsen, Minnesota. High–school math
and English, 1978–80.

Tutoring (notice that volunteer work appears here along with paid
employment):

The Strick Street Project, East Orange, New
Jersey. Tutoring in remedial reading and
business English, summers 1982–85.

Relevant employment in business and industry, whether full-time or
part-time—but be sure that it is relevant to the post you're seeking:

IBM Watson Research Center, Yorktown Heights,
New York. Systems programming, summer
1985.

Gather all the items you can think of, arrange them in chronological order (by opening date), and then check over the list to see
whether it needs consolidation and trimming. The following list, for
instance, is too long and spotty to let stand:

▷ Blackstone Public Library, Chicago,
Illinois. Part–time library aide,
summers 1976–77.
First Baptist Church of Hyde Park Book Fair,
Chicago, Illinois. Volunteer, 1976–79;
chairman, 1980.

Stephen Slaman Publishers, Madison,
  Wisconsin. Proofreader and copyholder,
  evenings 1977–80.
The Beeman Press, Chicago, Illinois.
  Proofreader and copyholder, summers
  1978–80.
University of Wisconsin. Senior grader in
  English, 1979–80.
United Methodist Bookmobile, Urbana,
  Illinois. Volunteer, 1980.
Henry Regnery Company, Chicago, Illinois.
  Proofreader, summers 1981–82; copy
  editor, summers 1982–86.
University of Illinois. Teaching assistant
  in freshman composition, fall 1981,
  spring 1983, spring 1984; in various
  English literature courses, 1983–86
  (four semesters).
Chalmers House Outreach, Urbana, Illinois.
  Hospital reading program supervisor,
  1982–84; youth group leader, 1985.

The point is not that any one of these items is bad. It's just that
lumped together they're too difficult for the reader to sort out. The
author's task is now to look over the whole list with a cold eye and
produce a better version:

University of Wisconsin. Senior grader in
  English, 1979–80.
Henry Regnery Company, Chicago, Illinois.
  Proofreader and copy editor, summers
  1981–86.
University of Illinois. Teaching assistant
  in freshman composition, 1981–84; in
  Victorian literature, 1983–85; in the
  modern American novel, 1985; in the short
  story, 1986.

Notice the alterations in the University of Illinois item—specifics
about the courses are significant; specifics about the semesters
aren't.

You may be aware that on business vitas experience is listed in reverse chronological order; that's because the business applicant is expected to account for every waking moment from birth onward. On an academic vita, where you give only the highlights of your experience, plain chronological order, unreversed, is better.

Don't expect to be able to put a good vita together in an afternoon. What you're doing is presenting yourself in a highly artificial capsule form, and you shouldn't be surprised that it takes a good deal of discipline and humility. It's hard to get help with a vita because you're the only person in possession of all the necessary information. But you might ask a teacher or an older colleague to look over your best effort and then tell you what it says. Her unconscious omissions are likely to suggest items you can profitably cut. If she forgets an item you consider crucial, perhaps you've buried it among too many other things.

Remember that your reader is going to have to sort you out from many other applicants, perhaps hundreds. You want to be memorable as "Oh yes, the one from Illinois who's done so much TA-ing," not as "Oh yes, the one with all those thousands of little jobs."

## Experience Thereafter

You got the job. It probably won't be your first thought, but you may immediately revise your vita, so that the "Experience" section begins with your first full-time faculty post and forget about everything that came before. There are some few exceptions to this amnesiac rule; if, for instance, your first appointment is solely in research, as a postdoc or a research associate, you might want to continue to list previous teaching experience.

Give the closing as well as the opening date for a term appointment:

```
MIT. Assistant Professor of Comparative
     Linguistics, 1986–89.
```

Use the magic word "since" in dating a tenured or open-ended appointment that you hold currently:

```
▷ Kent State University. Professor of
     Sinology, 1978–
```

▷ Kent State University. Professor of
     Sinology, 1978–now.

Kent State University. Professor of
     Sinology, since 1978.

A tenured appointment that you've left obviously gets a closing
date:

Harvard Divinity School. Professor of
     Christian Ethics, 1971–78.

Cluster appointments at the same school:

Duke University. Assistant Professor of
     Economics, 1969–71. Associate Professor
     of Economics, 1971–75. Professor of
     Economics, since 1975. Reginald Heald
     Professor of Economics, since 1981.

Don't break open an item with a sabbatical appointment; drop it
below:

▷ Gonzaga University. Associate Professor of
     History, 1981–82.
Catholic University of America. Visiting
     Associate Professor of History, 1982.
Gonzaga University. Associate Professor of
     History, 1983–85.

Gonzaga University. Associate Professor of
     History, 1981–85.
Catholic University of America. Visiting
     Associate Professor of History, 1982.

Unless you're applying for an administrative post, ignore all administrative and committee assignments below the level of department chairman:

▷ University of Arizona. Assistant Professor
     of Romance Languages, 1982–85. Member,
     Committee on Joint Degrees, 1984.

Departmental chairs, deanships, and such do get mentioned—as a rule of thumb, list any administrative appointment that carries with it a reduction in teaching load:

> Princeton University. Associate Professor of
>     Physics, 1961–65. Professor of Physics,
>     since 1965. Chairman of the Physics
>     Department, 1968–71; 1977–78. Dean of the
>     Faculty of Arts and Sciences, since 1981.

Moonlighting, even in the exalted form known as consultantship, gets listed on an academic vita only when it's very prestigious:

> W. H. Freeman Company. Consulting editor,
>     biology series, since 1981.

Being the editor of a journal or a member of the editorial board is always listed:

> Bulletin of the American Anthropological
>     Association. Member, review board, since
>     1979; editor, 1984–76.

It's possible to have so many editorships and reviewerships that you will want to set aside another section of your vita, headed "Journals," and group this information there.

## Applications from Outside

Not everyone is transformed immediately from a graduate student to a faculty member, and not everyone goes directly from one faculty to another. There are some special problems about applying for an academic job from outside. For instance, there's no uniform system of nomenclature in the business world. An assistant professor is an assistant professor—your reader knows what that means. But what's an assistant line supervisor? Try to describe what you've done rather than give a vacuous formal title:

> ▷ Encyclopaedia Britannica, Inc. Section
>     manager, since 1981.

```
Encyclopaedia Britannica, Inc. Supervised
     six social-science editors, since 1981.
```

Don't, on the other hand, go into the sort of long description typical of business vitas; you'd better face the fact that no one in academy is going to take your outside experience very seriously unless it's both highly prestigious and highly relevant to your academic field.

If you've been doing a completely unserious job, driving a taxi or cooking in a hash house or panning for gold, forget about it on your vita. You might want to mention it in your cover letter if you can find a way to seem colorful but not flippant.

# Honors

This section is likely to appear on your first vita, disappear for a long time, and return only toward the end of your career.

When you're just getting out of graduate school, you should list all your scholarships and fellowships from college on:

```
University of Rhode Island. College
     scholarship, 1979-82. Laura May Fellowes
     Memorial Scholarship, 1982-83.
University of Connecticut. University
     fellowship, 1983-86.
```

Many schools blur the distinctions between fellowships, teaching assistantships, and research assistantships. If you must choose one or the other, it's better to list an appointment under "Experience"; but often you can justify a listing both here and there without the appearance of padding. Mention all your prizes, awards, and distinctions here as long as they're both academic and reasonably relevant. Undergraduate essay awards for applicants in English or history, yes; for applicants in biology or physics, maybe. Scout badges and ROTC awards, no. Honors societies get listed here, with explanations for all but the most famous of them:

```
Phi Beta Kappa, 1981.
Alpha Beta Tau (history honors society),
     1981.
```

Some groups straddle the line between honors societies and professional societies; give a listing here or under "Memberships," but not both. There's no reason to prefer one place or the other. Flip a coin.

Just as with your work experience, once you've gotten your first full-time faculty position you can drink the water of forgetfulness and stop listing all but the highest honors of your former life. There may be a long period when this section disappears from your vita altogether. Late in life, you can use it for honorary doctorates and National Book Awards and such.

## Grants

Under this heading you should list all your grants, contracts, faculty fellowships, and similar awards with opening and closing dates:

```
Office of Naval Research grant GJ-
    331479-0-96 for the investigation of
    numerical methods, 1974-76.
```

If a grant that you now hold is renewable, mention it:

```
National Institutes of Mental Health grant
    39956-V-CDOC-1228 for investigating
    speech acquisition patterns in the
    children of the deaf, 1987-89
    (renewable).
```

If you held a renewable grant that wasn't renewed, mention only the grant.

If it's the custom in your field, list the amount—but be sure that it is the custom; it will look tasteless otherwise. In general, people who work in areas that require heavy laboratory and equipment expenses disclose the amounts of their grants freely. Any technicalities about transfer from one school to another can be worked out when you're a serious candidate for a job; don't jump the gun by mentioning the matter on your vita or in your covering letter.

# Memberships

This section is optional, and you should check to see whether it's customary in your field. If so, list only professional memberships relevant to the post you're seeking, not the Kiwanis or the Knights of Columbus. Give no dates except for offices. List only current memberships.

```
National Association of Art Historians.
The Ford Madox Brown Society; chairman, 1981–
    83.
```

# Personal Information

It's no longer necessary or even desirable to list any personal information whatsoever on your vita. Your date of birth and your marital status and so on are irrelevant to your qualifications. During the course of the application procedure you may be asked for some personal information, and if you get hired you may be asked for some more, but it's better not to volunteer anything.

# References

Never give anyone's name as a reference without asking her permission first. Your dissertation director has already agreed by implication to write letters of recommendation for you, but that's not true of anyone else. Two or three references are usual, certainly no more than four. Give the names and addresses just as they would appear on envelopes:

```
Professor Andrea J. Popoff
Department of Sociology
University of Montreal
Montreal, Quebec
```

Don't be afraid to repeat; it looks tacky to say something like "Same address for all." Don't explain your relationships with these people—it's up to them to do so in their letters.

If your school has a placement office that will hold blanket letters of recommendation on file and send copies out to prospective employers, by all means make use of the service in looking for your first job. (Recommendations for later jobs should be individually written.) Give the address of the office and, just for safety's sake, mention what letters should be there:

```
Letters of recommendation from A. E. Keyman,
Raymond S. van Dyne, and Harriet Bowman are
available from:
     Office of Student Placement
     Stanford University
     Drawer D, University Station
     Stanford, California 94305
```

A placement service may offer you the opportunity to look at your letters of recommendation. Don't do it; the service will then have to annotate them with the fact that you've seen them. This is not to say that you won't know what's in your letters. You wouldn't ask for a recommendation that you knew was going to be rotten. And one of your reference writers might herself offer to show you her letter; whether you should then look or not depends entirely on your relationship with her. You just want to avoid getting yourself down on public record as someone who's so insecure that you had to peek.

## Publications

Everywhere else on your vita you may, within the limits of honesty, expand or contract information, trim it down or plump it up, but your publications list must be complete and uncensored. Not one publication from your professional career may be omitted—not even if you've changed your interpretation of the material, not even if your exposition now seems juvenile and vacant, not even if your results have been proved false. (Think about that before you rush into print with an ill-considered piece.)

Only what you've written outside your academic field should be ignored. If you write mysteries or cookbooks in the evening, leave them off your list and use the heading "Professional Publications" to account for the omission. An academic vita is no place to reveal your secret life as Agatha Christie or Julia Child.

The format for listing a publication on your vita is a little different from the one used on reference lists and bibliographies. If you wrote an item by yourself, there's no need to mention authorship:

> The guru and enlightenment in the novels of
>    Ruth Prawer Jhabvala. Carolina Quarterly
>    LVI(2):37–91, 1985.

If you have co-authors, their names go after the title:

> L–differentiates of the "coagulating" sets,
>    with H. N. Avrakian and D. Monsart.
>    American Association of Applied
>    Mathematicians Newsletter VII(5):64–65,
>    1981.

People who work in fields where first authorship is a big deal will notice that this format knocks precedence into a cocked hat—no one can tell whether you were first author or last. If you insist, use "by" instead of "with" and insert your name in its proper order:

> L–differentiates of the "coagulating" sets,
>    by H. N. Avrakian, C. L. Thomas, and D.
>    Monsart. American Association of Applied
>    Mathematicians Newsletter VII(5):64–65,
>    1981.

I think of my Aunt Mary's three children, who always used to shove and push each other and pull each other's hair in order to be first. Finally one day Aunt Mary said, "You know, children, being last is not only last, it's also third." I would like to report that the children profited from this insight, but of course they only began to shove and push each other for the privilege of being third.

For works you've edited, the format is:

> Pattern Recognition (editor). Oxford
>     University Press, 1975.

It's assumed that editing will include writing some front matter, which merits no special mention. If you edit a compilation that includes one of your own articles, use the format:

> Pattern Recognition (editor). Heuristic
>     search techniques that learn, pages
>     69–74. Oxford University Press, 1975.

Co-editorship follows the same pattern as co-authorship:

> Wilson Follett: The Correspondence (editor,
>     with Simon Teale). Crowell, 1978.

Never list the same item more than once:

> ▷ Nesting and territory among the warblers.
>     Scientific American CXIV(9):71–93, 1959.
>   Nesting and territory among the warblers. In
>     G. V. Simms and A. Trachtenberg, editors,
>     Notes Toward a North American
>     Ornithology, pages 240–259. Seamans
>     Press, 1970.
>
>   Nesting and territory among the warblers.
>     Scientific American CXIV(9):71–93, 1969.
>     Reprinted in G. V. Simms and A.
>     Trachtenberg, editors, Notes Toward a
>     North American Ornithology, pages 240–
>     259. Seamans Press, 1970.

The rule against double-listing carries through a change of title if the work is essentially the same:

> An Analysis of Masculine Stereotypes in
>     American Detective Fiction 1920–1950.
>   PhD thesis, University of New Hampshire,

> 1982. Published as <u>Tough Guys.</u> Harvard
> University Press, 1983.

But if you carve your thesis up into several chops and joints and publish them separately or publish a series of articles and essays later collected as a book, each gets a separate listing.

Notice that items on your publications list are always in the compressed format, not in the open format:

▷ Distribution and frequency of the double
    genitive in American speech.
  <u>Lingua</u> 8(1):37–64, 1978.

  Distribution and frequency of the double
    genitive in American speech. <u>Lingua</u> 8(1)
    37–64, 1978.

Do not number the items on your publications list.

Otherwise, these items are pretty much like references, and the chapters on references can help you if you're in difficulty.

The list is arranged in chronological order by year of first publication, and then alphabetically by title within each year. It is a good idea to close the list by indicating what you're working on now:

  The idea of the natural knowledge of good in
    the Lutheran Symbolical Books. In
    preparation.

If you don't yet have a title, choose something sensible and descriptive; you're not under oath to stick by it. You may list two or three works in preparation, but never more than that, lest you look like a great dreamer. If you're really working on eight things at once, choose the three best.

## Mechanics

It's no longer true that the only acceptable way to prepare your vita is on a typewriter, but be on your guard against flashy typesetting, lest you look like a professional job applicant. The effect to aim for is sobriety, even severity, and extreme understatement.

Do not update simply by adding on; rethink and revise the material each time you have an addition to make.

If your vita is more than one page long, put your staple diagonally through the upper left corner; do not staple the cover letter to the vita.

The sample vitas that follow are to give you a reasonable pattern for the layout, not a rigid formula. What you're after is the maximum compression compatible with clarity. Again, don't expect to be able to lay your vita out in one pass. Play around with different arrangements till you get one that pleases your eye. Don't feel that you have to stick to that format next time around; as the information changes, the way you choose to present it may also change.

```
Arthur Siddons                     home:
Department of Engineering and      7236 Rowley Boulevard
    Applied Science                Tucson, Arizona 76001
University of Arizona              690-459-8667
Tucson, Arizona 76045
690-594-7785


Degrees:   BS 1986, Illinois Institute of Technology
           PhD 1991 (expected), University of Arizona


Experience:  University of Arizona. Teaching assistant in
                introductory calculus, 1986; in engineering
                for humanities majors, 1987; in physical
                oceanography, 1987-90.
             Stratton Brothers, Inc., Tampa, Florida. Diver
                and mechanic, summer 1979; assistant
                engineer, summers 1980-85.


Honors:  National Merit Scholarship, 1977-71.
         University of Arizona, departmental fellowship,
         1986-87.
         Sigma Xi (national science honors society), 1982.


References:
Professor Simone Lashky             Assistant Professor
Department of Engineering              Charles Welch
   and Applied Science             Department of Engineering
University of Arizona                  and Applied Science
Tucson, Arizona 76045              University of Arizona
                                   Tucson, Arizona 76045
```

Publications:
Lesser Saline Distributions in the Florida Keys. PhD thesis,
    University of Arizona. In preparation.

Lynn Marcus                          home:
Assistant Professor of               8862 Oak Ridge Terrace
    Modern European History          New Brunswick, New Jersey
Rutgers University                       06615
New Brunswick, New Jersey            413-388-1293
    06620
413-976-4459

Degrees:  BA (economics) 1976, Harvard College
          MA 1980, PhD 1984, Brown University
Additional education:  London School of Economics summer
                       course in quantitative history, 1979.
Experience  Rutgers University. Assistant Professor of
            Modern European History, 1984–88.

References:
Professor Townsend J. Warner         Professor A. N. McGillis
History Department                   Department of History
Rutgers University                   Brown University
New Brunswick, New Jersey            Providence, Rhode Island
    06620                                14459

Publications:
The cotton manufacturers of the Ruhr Valley, 1848–1860.
    Bulletin of the Economic History Association XII(4):311–
    369, 1982.
Hendke's pamphlets and the labor theory of value. Minutes of
    the Third Annual Meeting of the Caucus for Modern Economic
    History, pages 141–167. Association of American
    Historians, 1983.
The Effects of Wage and Price Controls on German Manufacture.
    1848–1860. PhD thesis, Brown University, 1984.
Bismarck's economic advisors. Modern European Notes
    VIII(2):31–56, 1985.
The Koesterwerke: A case study in wage and price controls
    Modern European Notes VIII(1):122–146, 1985.
The Iron Chancellor and the thirst for steel. Bulletin of the
    Association of American Historians 41(3) 48–81, 1986.
An inquiry into the use of child labor in German cotton
    manufacture. In preparation.
The impact of technological innovation on labor practices in
    German cotton manufacture. In preparation.

# The Cover Letter

For all the good your cover letter will do you, you might as well not write one. It would in fact be more rational just to mail your vita off by itself, but for some reason that's not done. There's no such thing as a good cover letter, only one that avoids being bad. Here are a few things to avoid:

Don't be too long about it. Take a hundred words as your outside limit and try to stay well within it. Nothing you can say will balance off your reader's irritation at your saying too much.

Don't apologize. "Although my background appears not to suit me for this position . . . " "I realize that I may not seem . . . " "While my formal course work does not . . . " "I wish that it were possible for me to say . . . " Your reader will have no trouble noting your defects without any assistance from you.

Don't be cute. "If there's anything a weary chairperson needs less than another applicant, it's one who . . . " "Rising from my bed this morning, I was struck by the thought . . . " Don't be breezy, don't be slick, don't try to sound like an advertising brochure.

Don't be hyperspecific. "I could teach an advanced seminar on recent findings in the treatment of postnatal depression . . . " Wait to dicker about your assignment till someone's offered to hire you.

Don't be self-centered. That includes the phrase "I would be interested . . . " Your reader has at this point no reason to care what interests you; the only issue is what interests her.

Don't grovel. "Almost any sort of opening . . . " "I realize that you may be in no position . . . " "I would be willing . . . " Don't invite your reader to sell you short.

Don't mention money.

What's left. Very little. Tell what position you're applying for; if no post has been advertised, tell what you're looking for. Say when you'll be available. If you have outstanding qualifications to bring to the job, mention them briefly, but remember that you needn't repeat anything covered in your vita. Sincerely yours, the end. Save your warm, expansive nature, your wit and whimsy, for somewhere else; in this context they would be as out of place as ruby-heeled tap shoes on a funeral director. Let your vita, over which you've labored long and hard, speak for itself.

# Appendix 2

## Federal Documents
## of the United States

In every other section of this book, I've taken advantage of doing a new edition to correct errors, bring things up to date, and polish. But I haven't the strength to touch this appendix. I closed the door on the Government Documents Room in Sterling Library at Yale some time late in 1976 or early in 1977 and walked quietly away. Perhaps everything has changed since then. Perhaps everything has gotten organized. The words that follow were my best shot at describing things as they were then.

## Congressional Documents

This book is about how to write references to sources, not about the sources, but you need a little background information on Congressional publication in order to write a good reference to a Congressional document. Congress publishes four major series:

(a) The *Congressional Record*.
(b) House and Senate Reports and Documents.
(c) Bills, resolutions, acts, statutes, laws.
(d) Hearings and Committee Prints.

Here is how these series reflect Congressional activity:

(a) The proceedings of the two houses in plenary session appear in the *Congressional Record*. That is to say, the House in plenary session and the Senate in plenary session—they don't meet together. The *Record* is like the minutes of the houses. A member of Congress may read into the *Record* almost anything she likes, including prayers, poems, newspaper articles, letters from her constituents, what have you. Bills are introduced, labeled, numbered, named, and debated in plenary session, and all this is recorded in the *Record;* but the full texts of bills appear elsewhere (c). The *Record* appears in a daily version and then, eventually, in a bound version.

(b) Each house publishes a Reports and Documents series. Again, almost anything can appear in these series; for instance, Congress usually publishes the annual reports of the Boy Scouts and the Girl Scouts and the Daughters of the American Revolution in the Reports and Documents series. The various commissions such as Securities and Exchange and the Federal Communications Commission provide Congress with reports that appear in the Reports and Documents series. The houses may commission or adopt treatises, articles, studies, and disquisitions of all kinds and publish them as Reports and Documents. Items in these series appear first in slip form (that means as pamphlets) and then bound together.

(c) The complete text of every draft of every bill and resolution appears in slip form. Even depository libraries receive only the first draft, and intermediate drafts are printed in so few copies that they are quite rare—not rare and valuable, just hard to come by. At enactment, a law appears first in slip form, and then later it's bound into *U.S. Statutes at Large.*

(d) The Congressional committees have their own series of publications, the Hearings and Committee Prints series. Hearings— that's what they're called, not "Recorded Hearings" or "Minutes of Hearings"—are just what you would expect, the recorded testimony of witnesses called before the committees; a committee may hold a hearing on a specific bill or a group of bills or on any topic that might lead to legislation. Every hearing results in a "Hearing," the publication of its minutes. Committee Prints are anything else the committees want to publish—monographs, canvasses, reports, or chronicles, their own or others'.

Now we can go through each of these series.

## (a) *The Congressional Record*

Most references will be to the bound version of the *Record;* if you have a choice, that should be your preference. Begin by specifying the Congress, the session, and the date:

United States, 94th Congress, second session, 2 June 1976.

Then give the reference to the Record:

$$\text{volume} \quad \text{page}$$
$$\downarrow \qquad \downarrow$$

*Congressional Record* 114(17):22455.

$$\uparrow$$
part

If you must refer to the daily version, be aware that your reader is more likely by far to be using the bound version; most libraries throw out the daily when the bound arrives. The date of the material you're referring to will be the same, but a great deal happens in Congress on any one day, so the page reference is crucial. And—wouldn't you know it?—the two versions are paged differently, with no automatic correspondence between them and no index from one version to the other. Pages in the daily have letter prefixes, while pages in the bound do not, but it's a little stiff to expect your reader to notice such a fine distinction. Spell it out for her:

▷ *Congressional Record* 122(83):H 5193.

*Congressional Record* (daily) 122(83):H 5193.

Finding the page in the bound copy that corresponds to H 5193 is no easy task, but at least you've warned your reader what lies before her.

Fine points: The number within the parentheses refers to the part in the bound version, to the issue in the daily; once your reader has the materials before her, she should have no trouble making this out. Sometimes beneath the date of an issue of the *Record* there appears the legend "Legislative day of . . . " with a different date; ignore this legend and give only the large date in your reference.

Now give a brief description of what it is that you're referring to. Sometimes there will be a handy subhead you can copy:

97] United States, 94th Congress, second session, 2 June 1976.
    *Congressional Record* (daily) 122(83):H 5193.
    Laws applicable to the outer continental shelf.

---

Bad examples are marked with an arrowhead (▷).

Sometimes you will want to quote the first few words of a speech:

76] United States, 90th Congress, second session, 20 July
   1968.
   *Congressional Record* 114(7) 22455.
   Mr. Holland of Florida: "We have felt, since hearings . . . "

(As you can see, a disadvantage to this method is that the first few
words of a speech often make no particular sense.) Usually you will
want to describe the speaker and the topic:

29] United States, 91st Congress, first session, 22 May
   1969.
   *Congressional Record* 115(10):13528–13529.

58] United States, 89th Congress, second session, 27 May
   1966.
   *Congressional Record* 112(9):11710.
   Mr. Reuss of Wisconsin on the Selective Service System.

## (b) Reports and Documents

Most references will be to the bound versions. Start by specifying
the Congress, the session, and the date; the year is usually sufficient.

United States, 85th Congress, second session, 1957.

Then give the name of the house (call the House of Representatives
"House"), the name of the item (Report or Document), the number,
the serial set number, and the title:

house    item    number    serial set    title
 ↓        ↓        ↓          ↓           ↓
House Document 85-384 (serial 12106): 2nd annual report
   on trade agreements program.

Notice that the item number repeats the number of the Congress—
85-384 was published by the 85th Congress. The serial set is sometimes called the Congressional set or the sheep set, for its once
splendid binding; it is tempting to think of writing the reference to

"(sheep 12106)." Notice that a report, the 2nd annual report, can be a Document, House Document 85-384. It's also possible for a document to be a Report.

Now here is a very nice point: If the version you're working with is in slip form, it won't have a serial set number. In the past, for reasons that no one can comprehend, some guides on government documents recommended against giving the serial set number in a reference to a bound Document or Report. Bound and slip forms looked just alike:

▷ House Document 85-384: 2nd annual report on trade agreements program.

▷ Senate Report 94-803: The Antitrust Improvements Act of 1976.

Since most libraries throw out the slip forms when the bound copies arrive and then catalog and shelve the bound copies by serial set number, documents librarians were puzzled and infuriated by the recommendation. So, if the version that you're working with has not yet been bound, use the word "slip" in parentheses in place of the serial set number:

Senate Report 94-803 (slip): The Antitrust Improvements Act of 1976.

There is an index that links Reports and Documents numbers to serial set numbers, and the librarian will have to look it up. But your saying "slip" will let her know that you did not suppress the information, and she will feel cheered up.

Many publications in the Reports and Documents series have acknowledged authors, but they're almost never cataloged by author, so there's no point in leading your reader astray:

▷ Allen J. Ellender.
　Senate Document 85-78 (serial 12088): A review of United States foreign policy and operations.
　United States, 85th Congress, second session, 1957.

　United States, 85th Congress, second session, 1957.
　Senate Document 85-78 (serial 12088): A review of United States foreign policy and operations, by Allen J. Ellender.

Many items in the Reports and Documents series mention the congressional committees in their titles. Again, most libraries catalog and keep this material by Congress, not by committee; putting your reader on the right track here is especially important because of the possibility of confusion with Committee Prints:

▷ United States, House Special Committee to Investigate Campaign Expenditures.
House Report 83-2685 (serial 11750): Report of the Committee.
United States, 83rd Congress, second session, 1955.

United States, 83rd Congress, second session, 1955.
House Report 83-2685 (serial 11750): Report of the Special Committee to Investigate Campaign Expenditures.

Usually an item in the Reports and Documents series has a handy slip title at the top of its title page, above the formal title; if you have a choice, the slip title is always the one to use. If you're dealing with an item that has only a formal title, you may want to invent an informal title:

House Report 81-2263 (serial 11381): Report of the Committee on the Judiciary on HR-6709, for the relief of Ed Howard Russell.

or

House Report 81-2263 (serial 11381): On the relief of Ed Howard Russell.

## (c) Bills and Statutes

For a bill, start by specifying the Congress, the session, and the extended date (day-month-year).

United States, 89th Congress, second session, 27 May 1966.

Then give the bill's label, its number, and its name. Bills are labeled S or HR, not plain H as the pages of the daily Record are.

S-644: Consumer Product Safety Commission Improvements Act of 1976.

Most bills specify their own short names. Use the short name, not the formal one:

> ▷ An Act to Amend the Consumer Product Safety Act, to Improve the Consumer Product Safety Commission, to Authorize New Appropriations, and for Other Purposes.
>
> Consumer Product Safety Commission Improvements Act of 1976.

If necessary, invent a short name:

> ▷ An Act to Clarify the Application of Section 507 of the Classification Act of 1949 with respect to the Preservation of the Rates of Basic Compensation of Certain Officers or Employees in Cases Involving Downgrading Actions.
>
> Amendment to the Classification Act of 1949.

Notice that bills and statutes have proper names but not titles; in other words, they're capitalized but not italicized or underlined.

If your research requires working with bills, you already know how elusive and ephemeral they are. Don't suddenly forget about that when you start to write a reference. Whenever you can, provide documentation from the more readily available sources like the *Congressional Record,* where the interesting points in a bill may be subjected to debate.

Few bills are ever enacted into law. In the 93rd Congress, for example, 17,688 bills were introduced in the House, 4,260 in the Senate. Only 649 became laws. But once a bill becomes a law, you can refer to it with confidence. If you come across it in slip form, your reference will look like this:

> 87] United States, 94th Congress, second session, 11 May 1976.
> Public Law 94-284: Consumer Product Safety Commission Improvements Act of 1976.

The public law number incorporates the number of the Congress— 94-284 was enacted by the 94th Congress. Your reader will have no trouble finding this law when it's bound into *Statutes at Large.* If you're using the bound version yourself, you should, of course, give your reader all the information you have, even though she can easily find it elsewhere:

> 51]  United States, 85th Congress, second session, 23 August 1958.
> U.S. *Statutes at Large* 72(1):767.
> Public Law 85-726: Federal Aviation Act of 1958.

The reference to the *Statutes* means:

$$\text{volume} \quad \text{page}$$
$$\downarrow \qquad \downarrow$$

U.S. *Statutes at Large* 72(1):767.

$$\uparrow$$
$$\text{part}$$

If a bill or a law has a nickname, be sure to give it:

> 121]  United States, 76th Congress, first session, 15 April 1947.
> U.S. *Statutes at Large* 61(1):156.
> Public Law 76-43: Labor Management Relations Act.
> (The Taft-Hartley Act.)

References to private acts and resolutions look just like references to public laws:

> 47]  United States, 57th Congress, first session, 27 June 1902.
> U.S. *Statutes at Large* 32(2):1487.
> Private Act 57-1113: An Act Granting a Pension to Fannie Reardon.

Another source of information about legislation is the *United States Code,* which organizes the laws in force by subject. A reference to the Code looks like this:

> 36]  *United States Code,* 1970 edition.
> Title 16: Conservation. Section 512: Segregation of land for homestead entry.

125] *United States Code,* 1970 edition, supplement IV.
Title 42: The public health and welfare. Section 4913:
Research, technical assistance, and public informa-
tion.

### (d) Hearings and Committee Prints

A reference to an item in this series, unlike all other references to
congressional publications, starts with the name of the committee:

United States, House Committee on Interstate and Foreign
Commerce.

United States, Senate Committee on the Judiciary.

The name of the subcommittee is irrelevant to finding the source;
include it only if it has some bearing on your work:

United States, House Committee on Appropriations, Subcommittee on the Departments of Labor; Health and Human Services; and Education.

or

United States, House Committee on Appropriations.

It's all too easy to confuse this series with the Reports and Documents series, especially because the titles of many Committee Prints
include the word "report." Therefore start the second line of your
reference with "Hearing" or "Hearings" or "Committee Print":

Hearings on Department of Labor and Health and Human
Services appropriations for 1977.

Committee Print: Cumulative bibliography on water pollu-
tion.

If a Committee Print or a Hearing has a slip title at the top of its
title page as well as a formal title in the center, the slip title is always
the one to use:

▷ Committee Print: A compilation of information relating to

agriculture made by direction of the Committee on Agriculture of the House of Representatives.

Committee Print: Food costs—farm prices.

Do not let yourself be lured into using the formal title because it looks, superficially, more informative. It's not. Items in this series are cataloged by slip title, not by formal title. If you like, you may use a combination of the two, but the slip title is the essential piece of information:

▷ Hearings on matters pursuant to H-155 and H-156.

Hearings on milk labeling.

or

Hearings on H-155 and H-156: Milk labeling.

Some Committee Prints have acknowledged authors, who get their credits buried in the references, not displayed at the top:

▷ Elwin Hill.
Committee Print: Projected effects of damming the upper Snake.

United States, Senate Committee on Public Works.
Committee Print: Projected effects of damming the upper Snake, by Elwin Hill.

Close the reference by specifying the Congress, the session, and the year:

88] United States, House Committee on Interstate and Foreign Commerce.
Hearings on cigarette labeling and advertising.
89th Congress, first session, 1965.

39] United States, Senate Committee on the Judiciary.
Hearings on psychological tests and constitutional rights.
89th Congress, first session, 1965.

113] United States, House Committee on Interior and Insular Affairs.

Committee Print: Accomplishments of the Committee
during the 89th Congress.
89th Congress, second session, 1966.

# Judicial Documents

Federal court reports are exactly like regional and state reports, and
references to federal cases are covered in the section on court cases.
You will be delighted to hear that, other than cases, the judiciary
publishes nothing.

# Executive Documents

### Federal Regulations

The sole glimmer of organization among the executive documents
comes from the federal regulations, which are set out by subject
from their first appearance in the *Federal Register:*

67] *Federal Register* 41(114):23685, 11 June 1976.
Title 7: Agriculture. Part 70: Grading and inspection of
poultry and edible products. Section 36: Withdrawal
of application.

They are then bound together, still by subject, in the *Code of
Federal Regulations:*

77] *Code of Federal Regulations,* 1 October 1975.
Title 47: Telecommunications. Part 18: Industrial, sci-
entific, and medical equipment. Section 21: When
license is required.

81] *Code of Federal Regulations,* 1 January 1976.
Title 7: Agriculture. Part 48: Regulations of the Secre-
tary of Agriculture for the enforcement of the Produce
Agency Act. Section 4: Destroying or dumping.

49] *Code of Federal Regulations,* 1 April 1975.
Title 25: Indians. Part 42: Enrollment appeals. Section
5: Supporting evidence.

It's a simple, attractive system, with only one minor point to notice: Many of the titles are divided into chapters as well as parts: ignore the chapter divisions in writing references.

## Departmental Documents

Now the fog begins. There is no uniformity among the documents that the executive departments put out. Many of them don't even have decent title pages; you must search the front cover, the back cover, the spine, the introduction, the text, and the last page to come up with a reference. There seems always to be too little information or too much. Series abound, with no pattern from one to the next. The documents arrive already cataloged at depository libraries; even trained specialists in government documents sometimes have trouble figuring out whether a peculiar catalog number is an insight or an error. Size and shape vary wildly, to encourage shelving mistakes. So what's a poor scholar to do? Hold on to her sense of humor, and proceed as best she can.

Try to start every reference to a document of the executive by telling what body it comes from. The major agencies are much too large to suffice for identification; the lowest subdivisions are much too small. When in doubt, give all the information you have, listing the units from the largest to the smallest:

▷ United States Department of Health and Human Services

▷ United States Division of Local Statistics.

United States Department of Health and Human Services; Office of Education; Division of Local Statistics.

▷ United States Department of Agriculture.

▷ United States Plains States Section.

United States Department of Agriculture; Farm Security Administration; Plains States Section.

Next give the title. Give the author's name if there seems to be a genuine author acknowledged, but don't mention the secretaries and bureaucrats who strew their names and messages through the first few pages of so many of these documents.

▷ Triticale yields in six sites.

Triticale yields in six sites, by D. Unger.

▷ Technical assistance and related programs, prepared under
the direction of Undersecretary Boynton M. Boynton, Jr.

Technical assistance and related programs.

Begin the next line of your reference by giving whatever identification numbers your source bears. Don't be embarrassed by od-
dities; remember that your reader's interests are better served by
scraggly completeness than by orderly sterility. Close with the
printer and the date. Most but not all of these documents are
printed by the Government Printing Office.

The following examples hint at the range of possibilities:

54] United States Department of Health, Education, and
Welfare; Office of Education.
Psychology and the handicapped child.
DHEW publication number (OE) 73-05000. Govern-
ment Printing Office, 1974.

83] United States, National Science Foundation.
Grants and awards for fiscal year 1968.
NSF 69-2. Government Printing Office, 1968.

32] United States Department of Housing and Urban Development; Office of the Assistant Secretary for Policy Development and Research.
Residential energy consumption: Multifamily housing.
Final report.
Stock number 2300-00282. Government Printing Office, 1974.

131] United States National Aeronautics and Space Admin-
istration; Lyndon B. Johnson Space Center.
Skylab earth resources data catalog.
JSC 09016. Stock number 3300-00586. Government
Printing Office, 1974.

75] United States Department of the Interior; National
Park Service.
The giant sequoia of the Sierra Nevada.
0-596-106 Government Printing Office, 1976.

44] United States Watergate Special Prosecution Force. Report.
Serial number 027-000-00335-4. Government Printing Office, October 1975.

143] United States Department of the Interior; Census Office.
10th Census of the United States (1880). *The U.S. Mining Laws and Regulations Thereunder.*
Government Printing Office, 1885.

82] United States Department of Labor; Bureau of Labor Statistics.
Industry wage survey: Men's and boys' shirts (except work shirts) and nightwear, October 1968.
Bulletin 1659. Government Printing Office, 1970.

## Presidential Documents

Presidential documents are published in a weekly compilation and then bound together, a year at a time. A reference to the bound version looks like this:

95] United States President: Richard M. Nixon, 1 July 1973.
195. Statement on signing the Second Supplemental and Continuing Appropriations bills.

56] United States President: Harry S. Truman, 2 May 1950.
99. Special message to the Senate transmitting treaty with Canada concerning uses of the water of the Niagara River.

All the documents in the bound version are numbered and titled.
If you have occasion to refer to the weekly compilation, your reference should look like this:

133] United States President: Gerald R. Ford, 4 June 1976 (week ending 5 June 1976).
Meeting with delegation of British parliamentarians.

Documents in the weekly version are titled but not numbered.

References to presidential documents that appear in the *Congressional Record* look like all other references to the *Record*:

> 87]  United States, 89th Congress, second session, 28 May
>        1966.
>        *Congressional Record* 112(9):11798.
>        Special message from the President.

References to publications of presidential commissions and such look like all other references to documents of the executive departments:

> 71]  United States Executive Office of the President; Special
>        Commission on Immigration.
>        The role of immigration in meeting skilled-labor needs,
>        by F. M. Wassily.
>        Stock number 1993-00381. Government Printing Of-
>        fice, 1958.

You may by now have the feeling that presidential documents are not so hard as you expected. But most presidential papers (to say nothing of tapes) are not official government publications; official documents make up perhaps only one percent of the total. A few are available in other published sources and treated like ordinary publications. Most are archival.

## The Constitution

While nothing could be harder than most references to government documents, nothing could be easier than references to the Constitution:

> 87]  United States Constitution, Article I, section 4.

> 23]  United States Constitution, 16th Amendment, section 2.

I can't help feeling that there's something significant about the contrast.

# Where to Go for Help

Only the major kinds of current government publications have been touched on here. If you are going to work extensively with government documents, it would be a good idea to read:

> Laurence F. Schmeckebier and Roy B. Eastin.
> *Government Publications and Their Use.*
> The Brookings Institution, Washington DC, second edition 1969.

Any librarian who specializes in government documents can help you write a good reference to an obscure document you've come across. Most librarians are delighted to give this kind of help. They're the ones who have to cope with bad references; a bad reference can cost a librarian hours and days of dreary, thankless work. Too many people think of going to a librarian for help only in reading a bad reference, not in writing a good one.

# Index